Reforming Higher Education

Higher Education Policy Series

Edited by Maurice Kogan

Higher education is now the subject of far reaching and rapid policy change. This series will be of value to those who have to manage that change, as well as to consumers and evaluators of higher education in the UK and elsewhere. It offers information and analysis of new developments in a concise and usable form. It also provides reflective accounts of the impacts of higher education policy. Higher education administrators, governors and policy makers will use it, as well as students and specialists in education policy.

Maurice Kogan is Professor of Government and Social Administration at Brunel University and Joint Director of the Centre for the Evaluation of Public Policy and Practice.

Policy and Practice in Higher Education:
Reforming Norwegian Universities
Ivar Bleiklie, Roar Hostaker, Agnete Vabo
Higher Education Policy 49
ISBN 1 85302 705 7

Transforming Universities
Changing Patterns of Governance, Structure
and Learning in Swedish Higher Education
Marianne Bauer, Susan Marton, Berit Askling and Ference Marton
Higher Education Policy 48
ISBN 1 85302 675 1

Academic Identities and Policy Change in Higher Education
Mary Henkel
Higher Education Policy 46
ISBN 1 85302 662 X

Changing Relationships between Higher Education
and the State
Edited by Mary Henkel and Brenda Little
Higher Education Policy 45
ISBN 1 85302 645 X pb
ISBN 1 85302 644 1 hb

University and Society Essays on the Social Role
of Research and Higher Education
Edited by Martin A. Trow and Thorsten Nybom
Higher Education Policy 12
ISBN 1 85302 525 9

Higher Education Policy Series 50

Reforming Higher Education

Maurice Kogan and Stephen Hanney

Jessica Kingsley Publishers
London and Philadelphia

First published in the United Kingdom in 2000 by
Jessica Kingsley Publishers Ltd,
116 Pentonville Road, London
N1 9JB, England
and
325 Chestnut Street,
Philadelphia PA 19106,
USA.

www.jkp.com

© Copyright 2000 Maurice Kogan and Stephen Hanney

Library of Congress Cataloging in Publication Data
Kogan, Maurice,
Reforming higher education / Maurice Kogan and Stephen Hanney.
p.   cm. -- (Higher education policy : 50)
Includes bibliographical references (p.   ) and index.
ISBN 1 85302 715 4 (pb. : alk. paper)
1. Higher education and state--Great Britain. 2. Educational change--Great Britain. I. Hanney. Stephen. II. Title. III. Series: Higher education policy : 50.
LC178.G7K66   1999   99--39965
378.41--dc21   CIP

British Library Cataloguing in Publication Data
A CIP catalogue record for this book is available from the British Library

ISBN 1 85302 715 4 pb

Printed and Bound in Great Britain by
Athenaeum Press, Gateshead, Tyne and Wear

Contents

List of Tables

List of Figures

Preface

This book is one of the products of a major international study undertaken in conjunction with Swedish and Norwegian colleagues. Our first debt is to Marianne Bauer, Susan Marton, Berit Askling, Ference Marton, Ivar Bleiklie, Roar Høstaker and Agnete Vabø with whom the overarching scheme for the international study of which this book is part was formulated.

The project was directed by Mary Henkel, whose *Academic Identities and Policy Change in Higher Education* is the indispensable companion volume to this. Our debt to her for both leadership and scholarly critique is immense.

The work was made possible by the generous funding afforded to us by the Swedish Council for Higher Education Studies who financed both the Swedish and the English studies. However, its contribution went far beyond that of finance: Professor Thorsten Nybom, now of the University of Uppsala, was, throughout, an entirely supportive and skilled sponsor, combining flexibility in funding arrangements with a deep knowledge and sophisticated understanding of the research issues involved. Distinct aspects of the study were considerably advanced by the award of an Emeritus Fellowship to Maurice Kogan by the Leverhulme Trust and, earlier in our total project, by finance for a brief pilot study on the nature of academic elites awarded by the Spencer Foundation of Chicago. And at the end of the project we received help from the Tercentenary Fund of the Royal Bank of Sweden as a contribution towards our publication and dissemination costs. To all of these sources of funding we express our gratitude.

Our book relies to a large extent on the documentary evidence worked on by ourselves and by other authorities in the field, notably the work of Brian Salter and Ted Tapper and, in particular, *The State and Higher Education* (Woburn Press, 1994). But our main source, and this would be our claim of differentiation from the Salter and Tapper work, has been that of our 90 interviewees who patiently worked through key issues, in interviews that lasted between half an hour and three hours. Some of the most eminent of our interviewees even invited us to come back for a second interview. They were as follows: Sir Geoffrey Allen; Lord Baker; Ray Baker; Sir Christopher Ball; Bahram Bekradnia; the late Lord Beloff; David Bethel; William

Birch; Richard Bird; Roger Blows; Sir Tom Blundell; Clive Booth; Tim Boswell; Sir Rhodes Boyson; Peter Brooke; Tom Burgner; Anthony Chamier; Geoffrey Cockerill; Patrick Coldstream; Ivor Crewe; Bryan Davies; Sir Graeme Davies; Roger Dawe; Lord Ron Dearing; Sir Ken Edwards; Sir Brian Fender; Lord Flowers; Nigel Forman; David Forrester; Raoul Franklin; Sir Douglas Hague; Sir Peter Hall; Sir James Hamilton; Sir David Hancock; Norman Hardyman; Sir David Harrison; Peter Hennessy; Sir Geoffrey Holland; Alan Howarth; Robert Jackson; Sir Alex Jarratt; Stephen Jones; Sir John Kingman; Sir Tim Lankester; Neil McKendrick; Elizabeth Mills; David Neave; Howard Newby; Gordon Oakes; Patrick O'Brien; John O'Leary; Baroness (Pauline) Perry; the late Lord Phillips; Ben Pimlott; Christopher Price; Sir Robert Rhodes James; George Radda; Sir Mark Richmond; the late Sir Ray Rickett; Patrick Riley; Clive Saville; Peter Scott; David Shapiro; Michael Shattock; Sir Maurice Shock; John Sizer; Sir Albert Sloman; Auriol Stevens; Sir William Stubbs; Barry Supple; Sir Peter Swinnerton-Dyer; Brian Taylor; Sir William Taylor; Sir Keith Thomas; David Triesman; Lord William Waldegrave; Jim Walsh; Baroness Diana Warwick; Sir Toby Weaver; Tony Webb; Tim Whitaker; Gareth Williams; Peter Williams; Baroness (Shirley) Williams; Tony Woollard; Lord Young; John Ziman. We also acknowledge help given by some interviewees who did not wish to be listed by name.

Throughout our work we were able to rely on critical inputs from our Swedish and Norwegian friends, at meetings in London, Stockholm, Gothenburg, Bergen and Oslo. Our indebtness to them for intellectual stimulation and collegial support is immense. We also had a series of reporting meetings: our sponsors convened senior researchers and policy makers in Stockholm halfway through our project and we presented several interim reports at academic conferences throughout our project. And we have had the benefit of critical reading of our work by our Norwegian and Swedish colleagues.

Over a period of some four years we have depended on quite a deal of both research and secretarial assistance. We express our gratitude to Mary Brightwell, Melanie Foody, Matthew Hanney, Caroline Healy and Tom Kogan.

PART I

Themes, Methods and Theories

Chapter 1

Our Main Themes and Methods

The origins of this work

Perhaps no area of public policy has been subjected to such radical changes over the last 20 years as higher education. Whilst, however, a great deal has been written about the changes in policy (e.g. Salter and Tapper 1994; Scott 1995; Shattock 1994, 1996), analysis of their impacts has been to a large extent inferential rather than empirical. Nor has there been much academic research which relies on detailed interviews with key participants about the ways in which the policies emerged and the groups that were involved in their evolution. This book, which is part of a research project on the impact of higher education reforms on academic working and values in English universities, concentrates particularly on analysis of policies and their geneses at the national level. A companion volume[1] takes up our themes by analysing the impacts of the policies at the institutional and basic unit and individual levels.

Our work forms part of an international project conducted by a team from the Department of Government, Brunel University and colleagues from the Universities of Gothenburg, Sweden and Bergen, Norway. It began with informal discussions with senior members of the Swedish academic world. Our Swedish discussants, the Directors of the Swedish Council for Higher Education Studies, the Royal Bank of Sweden Tercentenary Fund, the Karolinska Institute and Uppsala University, expressed support for a bi-national project. Colleagues at the University of Bergen were working on similar themes in Norway and it was decided to make it a tri-country study.

---

1   Henkel, M. (forthcoming) *Academic Identities and Policy Change in Higher Education*. London: Jessica Kingsley Publishers.

Each country would produce its own account,[2] but then combine their results in a comparative study. To this end, the three groups took trouble to ensure that the research frames were compatible and capable of being read across. We noted then how major changes were occurring in both the Swedish and the British welfare states and in the concept of the state in general. It seemed obvious that the different kinds of change in different countries must affect the way in which higher education policy was being formulated and the ways in which policy changes would then have an impact on academic working and values. Similar concerns affect the Norwegian scene.

Methods

Our methods are more fully described in the appendix to this chapter. They included joint identification by the three teams of the substantive content of the national studies; study of policy documentation; and interviews with past and present key informants on changes in the policies and structures of central government in relation to higher education. The total number of those interviewed specifically for the study of policy formation was 90. In addition, we have drawn on the over 300 interviews carried out as part of our study of the implications of policy change for academic identities, values and modes of working. This part of the project comprised two case studies of quality assurance and the Enterprise in Higher Education Initiative (EHP), as well as a study of the impacts upon academics of the whole raft of reforms carried out in our period.

The salience of higher education policy

Whilst our study primarily concerns the policy changes that took place from 1975 until the return of the Labour government in 1997, they cannot be separated from the changes that were already in train before that time. For most of the post-1945 period, higher education

2   Bauer, M., Marton, S., Askling, B. and Marton, F. (1999) *Transforming Universities. Patterns of Governance, Structure and Learning in Swedish Higher Education at the Millennial Turn.* London: Jessica Kingsley Publishers. Bleiklie, I., Høstaker, R. and Vabø, A. (forthcoming) *Policy and Practice in Higher Education: Reforming Norwegian Universities.* London: Jessica Kingsley Publishers. Henkel, M. (forthcoming) *Academic Identities and Policy Change in Higher Education.* London: Jessica Kingsley Publishers. Kogan, M., Bauer, M., Bleiklie, I. and Henkel, M. (forthcoming) *Transforming Higher Education: A Comparative Study.* London: Jessica Kingsley Publishers.

in this country was taken for granted as an area of public activity in which quite major policy changes (for example the creation of the binary system) could emerge without arousing much political interest or concern. The system expanded from accepting only 3 per cent of the school-leaving population in 1945 to a diversified system accepting 15 per cent of school leavers for higher education courses by 1970. All of this was treated as if it were an inevitable development of policies accepted on a consensual basis. Kingsley Amis's 'more will mean worse' was an exceptional view, and expansion was quickly absorbed into the academic and public consciousness (Halsey and Trow 1971).

In the early 1980s, Premfors (1980) noted how low a 'salience' higher education policy occupied in general policy making in Sweden, France and the UK. By the middle of the 1980s that had changed, although higher education concerns still occupied hardly any of the Prime Minister's time and only a small amount of that of the Secretary of State (mac.206). In the UK as a whole, the Age Participation Rate (APR) (that is, the recruitment rate from each cohort of school leavers) stayed at about 15 per cent until 1985 and then exploded to reach 31 per cent in 1992. (The English rate was somewhat less than that because the Scots and Northern Irish had a rate of 45 per cent.) If mature students are included, the total expansion was even greater: the proportion of entrants over 21 years had grown from 14.5 per cent to 29 per cent between 1986 and 1995 (Robertson and Hillman 1997, Tables 1.3 and 1.9). Expenditure on higher education rose by around 45 per cent in real terms between 1976 and 1996–97, but fell by about 40 per cent for each student over the same period (Dearing Report 1997).

The importance of higher education to the economy had long been taken for granted, and was one of the key assumptions of, for example, the Robbins Report (1963). But more purposeful attempts to make higher education, research and teaching more relevant to expressed economic objectives began to emerge. Increasingly, this was accompanied by a different understanding of the ways in which different forms of knowledge might be the route to economic prosperity and survival in a global economy (mac.115). Pressures from the economy and society were confronted by, and combined with, the ideologies, beliefs and prejudices that constituted Thatcherism. These were not only internally inconsistent (Jenkins 1996; Young 1989) but also created particular tensions when applied to higher education.

The result of both the expansion and the economic considerations was that higher education became far more vulnerable to political interventions. Demands from government, in what has been described as a Faustian bargain (mac.25), for stronger measures of efficiency and accountability became irresistible. The power of hitherto largely autonomous universities was reduced by the creation of a body of higher education law, which created a prescriptive framework for both their funding and their operation. The ending of the binary system also meant that the previously autonomous universities had to respond to forms of central regulation which had applied to the polytechnics and other non-university institutions but not to them.

In this study we track changes in the nature of the state and surrounding ideologies, depict how they are reflected in higher education policies and institutional relationships, assess the nature of the groups involved in the changes and analyse the impacts of the changes on the government of universities. In doing so, we have primarily adopted a historical approach whilst also attempting to treat our findings within a political science framework. A companion volume, emanating from the same research project, shows how far these major secular changes have affected the inner life of the universities, the professional identities of the academics who work in them and the structures, cultures and epistemological frameworks within which those identities are conducted and sustained.

In doing so, we bear in mind two assumptions that are put up for test by recent policy changes. It has been assumed that the particular characteristics of higher education government and management, and particularly those associated with academic autonomy, derive from an essentialism, an abiding combination of value and function, which is unlikely to yield to exogenous demands and pressures. The second assumption is that of higher education's exceptionalism; that is, that higher education has in some way been treated differently from other public institutions because of the nature of the work that it does. We will return to critically examine these assumptions in various points of our narrative.

Outline of the book

In Chapter 2 we disclose the theoretical assumptions which underpin our study. In discussing the changes in the nature of the UK state, we note how higher education fits into a range of public institutions and how, perhaps exemplifying its exceptionalism in doing so, it has developed normative political theories of its own. The particular issue of university autonomy is taken up and assessed against the concept of Clark's triangle of co-ordination (Clark 1983). We then offer a range of possible typifications of changes in the way in which the state operates. We examine how far these moves can be analysed in terms of recently formulated concepts such as New Public Management (NPM) (Pollitt 1995) and the rise of the Evaluative State (Neave 1988). Further theoretical concerns include the extent to which policies are determined by economic, social and ideological contexts or by individual actors. The nature of higher education policy making is considered along with role of elites and interest groups.

The empirical material begins in Chapter 3 with a historical account of the contexts within which policy changed and, in particular, we describe the great expansion of higher education which constituted both a context and consequence of policy change.

From the immediate postwar period until the latter 1970s, universities – if not the rest of the higher education system – enjoyed state-subsidised independence. This shifted to ambiguous but increased dependence on, and deference to, state policies. From the relative eclecticism assumed by the Robbins Report (1963), the system began to respond to a newly sharpened instrumentalism, which espoused economic and consumerist values, at the same time as it decreed selectivity, particularly in research grading and funding, which had excellence as its leading criterion. Whilst expansion, fuelled by increased student demand, was a dominant factor in causing change, it pulled into more rigorous public policies a domain that had hitherto been trusted to do good by doing what it thought to be good. The demystifying of academic work, and reduced confidence in professional groups in society as a whole, went along with increased numbers and severely cut units of resource. In Chapter 4 we address policy movements that have so deeply affected the working of higher education. We append to Chapter 4 a chronology of the main milestones of the period of reform.

The ending of the funding for five years at a time (the quinquennial system), the move towards markets, change in the mechanisms of funding, the build-up of selectivity and the enhanced stratification that resulted, and the assertion of quality assurance policies, were emphatic evidences of a changed government approach to higher education. The changes in scale and perceived objectives were accompanied by changes in macro structure and particularly the supersession of the binary by the unitary system, which we consider in Chapter 5.

Shifts in policy led to changes in governmental structures and the policy-making and planning processes in which they engage. The policy restlessness evinced by successive governments from the mid-1970s to the mid-1990s gave rise to different relationships between the state and higher education, and several changes in the machinery of both central government and its intermediary bodies, the grants, funding and research councils. The long-standing body that administered grants to the universities, the University Grants Committee (UGC), was replaced in 1989 by the Universities Funding Council (UFC) which in turn was superseded in 1993 by the Higher Education Funding Councils (HEFCs) for England, Scotland and Wales. In the other half of the binary system, the first funding body, the National Advisory Body (NAB), existed from 1982 until it was replaced by the Polytechnics and Colleges Funding Council (PCFC) which ran from 1989 until the introduction of the HEFCs. Structures reveal more than formal relationships and these changes display the new vulnerability to policy of the higher education enterprise at large. This is the substance of Chapter 6 which also analyses how far ministers or civil servants have been the principal drivers of policy.

Chapter 7 carries the themes of power and autonomy into our consideration of the impact of changes in the state on institutional government. In our companion volume Mary Henkel has considered how institutions structure the choices and behaviour of their members, in whose professional lives they increasingly have become strategic entities. We consider here how institutions position themselves in the polity, and attempt to conceptualise their changing role and identity.

These largely historical chapters (Chapters 3–7) feed the more analytic treatment of some of the underlying themes of the nature of the policy system and the state. Chapter 8 gives an account of changes in the policy systems relevant to our themes. We examine the policy process, and the ways in which particular groups have exercised influence. This chapter, based on detailed interview work, considers the role of the groups, in elites or networks or policy communities, who have been involved in policy making and implementation.

In Chapter 9 we venture on some emerging conclusions. In that chapter we note how higher education is a subset of larger public policies and systems but also idiosyncratic in the way in which it has been allowed to develop. We reflect on the extent to which policies have been discontinuous and the extent to which higher education is a case of policy exceptionalism. We finish by considering how far there has been organic evolution or imposed change.

APPENDIX TO CHAPTER 1

Methods

The methods for the whole project have been:

- i) joint identification by the three teams of the substantive content and methods of the national studies and hence of the comparative study. This process was conducted through workshops and the exchange of drafts;

- ii) study, by the teams, of policy documentation to create a systematic tabulation of changes in the governing structures of higher education;

- iii) selected interviews with past and present key informants on changes in the policies and structures of central government in relation to higher education. In recent methodological debate about policy networks (Cavanagh, Marsh and Smith 1995) it was noted that it was important to conduct interviews to understand the significance of contacts between government and interest groups in a way that could not be achieved from merely examining lists of who was consulted;

- iv) studies of a representative group of English institutions and their component faculties, fully reported in Henkel. (forthcoming). The range includes: four 'new' universities, two technological universities, a 'green fields' university, a civic university, a provincial university, a college of London University, and Oxbridge;

- v) within the English project institutions, studies have been made through documentation and semi-structured interviews within the following subject areas: biochemistry, chemistry, economics, English, history, physics and sociology.

The interviews of particular importance to the concerns taken up in this volume were conducted with mainly two types of informants: policy formers and other key informants about policy formation. At the same time, we were able to benefit from interviews with both policy makers or observers and academics conducted for our contemporaneous evaluation of the Foresight Initiative, funded by the Nuffield Foundation (Henkel forthcoming).

The total number of those interviewed specifically for the study of policy formation was 90. However, many of them occupied more than one role and the list below therefore adds up to more than that number:

- 11 former ministers and those currently in office at the time of interview
- 6 chairs of the Committee of Vice-Chancellors and Principals (CVCP), 4 chairs of the Committee of Directors of Polytechnics (CDP) and 5 senior officials of the two bodies
- 4 chairs and 8 chief executives and other senior officials of funding councils
- 11 chairs and chief executives and 17 members and senior officials of research councils
- 4 former permanent secretaries and 15 other senior civil servants
- 1 chair and 5 Fellows of the British Academy (FBAs)
- 11 Fellows of the Royal Society (FRSs)
- 28 institutional leaders
- 13 senior academic commentators on higher education
- 3 journalists specialising in higher education policy
- 2 union leaders
- 5 industrial leaders or representatives.

This was not, of course, a full population sample, and was, to some extent, created opportunistically. However, it incorporated a reasonably large proportion of those involved in many of the most important policy movements, and some seasoned observers of policy formation.

In addition, we have drawn on the over 300 interviews carried out as part of our study of the implications of policy change for academic identities, values and modes of working. This part of the project comprised two case studies of quality assurance and the Enterprise in Higher Education Initiative, as well as a study of the impacts upon academics of the whole raft of reforms carried out in our period. The case studies incorporated interviews with those involved at national level in the two specific policy areas, as well as with members of senior academic management teams and administrators in seven universities and academics in seven disciplines. The more general study was based largely on interviews with individual academics from six disciplines in four more universities. The main findings from these are reported by Mary Henkel in the companion volume to this book.

All of our empirical work has been placed on a data base (NUD.IST) which has enabled us to read across interview, documentary and secondary material under discrete thematic headings. The analysis of material was assisted by the creation of detailed coding frames against which our data could be recorded. The recording has been an onerous task, and if we have any counsel to offer it is to be relatively parsimonious in the coding heads selected, and to avoid over-allocation of empirical sections when creating the codes.

Chapter 2

Our Project
and Theoretical Position

The overriding objective of our project is to examine the ways in which the policy changes characterised by their authors as 'reforms' affected the values and working of English academics. In this volume we are particularly concerned to analyse the nature and cause of the reforms, the changes in government machinery that they entailed, and the nature of the groups who had a role in causing or otherwise affecting change. To achieve these objectives we have to contend with a web of conceptual problems.

As we have noted, our project began with a strongly comparative intention which required us to establish the common conceptual and thematic bases of the three studies. These will be set out in more detail in a volume to be written in collaboration with colleagues from Norway and Sweden.[1]

Use of theory

Throughout our study we have been concerned to keep an adequate balance between a strong empirical base and exploiting and contributing towards theories relevant to our field. We endorse Page's belief (Page 1995, quoting Sartori 1970) that the whole of political science is a trade-off between configurative or detailed discussion of one case or a few cases and broader and more abstract theoretically based generalisations which 'are best seen as a continuum rather than as categories of comparison'.

Archer (1979) has noted that it has proved virtually impossible to make an adequate match between micro analysis, in which the verities

---

1   Kogan, M., Bauer, M., Bleiklie, I. and Henkel, M. (forthcoming) *Transforming Higher Education: A Comparative Perspective*. London: Jessica Kingsley Publishers.

of close-grained empirical studies can be demonstrated, and macro analysis, in which more generally applicable propositions can be announced and interrogated. The world of knowledge has increasingly accepted that more than one incommensurate or apparently inconsistent proposition can be advanced simultaneously. In the social domain, in particular, reality does not pile up in well-connected hierarchies of paradigm and theorems.

Some of our closest colleagues in the field (e.g. Maassen 1996; Goedegebuure and Van Vught 1996), however, urge the necessity of stating hypotheses from previous accumulated knowledge and testing, and verifying and adding to them (Kogan 1996). If that were to be our dominant intellectual and research procedure, we would be subscribing to a major hypothesis which is dubious in its own right. The presumption would be that there are sufficient regularities in social experience for them to be capable of being incorporated into overarching frameworks and hypotheses. Such an intellectual procedure is both possible and necessary in the physical world, although natural phenomena, such as some to be found in metallurgy, biology and biochemistry, are not always capable of subordination to assumptions of regularity. In the social arena the data emerge in topological rather than progressive arrangements. Whilst we can certainly look for juxtapositions and thematic comparisons, and attempt to find causal explanations, we will be strapping ourselves into an unnecessary bed of nails if we try to direct our research on the basis of prestructured hypotheses. Where there are usable hypotheses, let us enjoy them. Otherwise, there is plenty of good work done at the level of thematic comparisons as our Dutch colleagues' own work amply demonstrates. It is wrong to assume that without hypothesising there is no theorising.

Our UK study faced a further obstacle to making a clear connection between hypotheses and actual outcomes in that in the UK at least, and less so in our two Scandinavian counterparts, overarching government policies (for example, the intention to roll back the frontiers of the state) were not consistently carried through in the policy area of higher education.

Our own approach

We have used methods that are historical (that is, the juxtaposition of sometimes competing evidence over time sequences) but also those taken from political science. We have not assumed that there is a generally applicable comparative framework but demonstrate that it is possible to enlist salient theories in the descriptive analysis and comparison of key political and academic phenomena; this process could be the first step in attempting to create a comparative framework.

The main theoretical issues of concern are as follows:

- changes in the role of the state and of the place of the universities within it;
- the extent to which contexts or individual actors cause change;
- higher education policy making: dual processes, elites and interest groups;
- continuity and discontinuity in policy.

The historical movements against which we have played these theoretical concerns include the nature of the reforms created by government and changes in the mechanisms of government. Specific issues which have highlighted our themes are the expansion of the system and the end of the binary system. Our analysis serves as a background to the parallel study (Henkel forthcoming) of the impacts of the reforms in terms of the epistemic identities and working practices of academics in a range of disciplines, and in a range of institutions. This also contains an account of the generation, application and impacts of quality assurance policies and the Enterprise Initiative as a means of identifying the dynamic between the macro, meso and micro levels of working or between government and some of the main interest groups.

We give here an account of our positions on the four sets of theoretical themes listed, which are addressed further in later chapters.

Changes in the role of the state and the place of the universities within it

The starting point for our three national projects was the evident changes in the role of the state promoted by national governments. As major public institutions, universities can be considered either as subsystems of the state or as independent institutions that nevertheless are strongly affected by the nature of the state. A primary task is therefore to locate universities among the range of British public institutions, and to assess how they can be related, if sometimes uncertainly, to a continuum of views about the appropriate role of the state.

Viewed as a set of public institutions, universities hold a particular place, shared by only a few others, within the range of British governmental arrangements. The British state mediates its policies through what can be described as an organisational zoo in which the different species can be typified in terms of the functions they perform, the power or authority characteristics and the forms of control and dependency which they employ, and the kinds of knowledge on which they depend for their functioning.

At one end of the spectrum of state mechanisms, some public institutions, such as the armed forces, the tax authorities and social security, have direct lines of command to a national authority. This hierarchical structure may be mitigated by the use of wide discretion, as with tax authorities, but, essentially, such organisations act within legal and managerial structures which can be fashioned to meet exclusively policies which are determined on high. Then there are those in an intermediate position, the most obvious of which are local authorities, which are intended to carry out national policies (which have become increasingly prescriptive since the early 1980s) but with regard to the wishes of their local electorates and on the base of a high component of professional judgement. At the furthest end of the spectrum are charter institutions which include the BBC, the national museums and the universities. Their status has been that of almost wholly independent institutions but deferring to public policies which largely constitute the conditions under which the bulk of their resources have been secured. Much of our analysis considers whether, if the discretion allowed to universities and the academics who constitute their working base has been increasingly circumscribed, the central tasks of universities (i.e. research and teaching–learning) remain the domain of the prime practitioners, rather than the governing structures.

As with the range of institutions, so normative accounts of the appropriate extent of state action, or the values and purposes of the state, can be placed on a spectrum. This goes from the minimalist position advocated by Nozick (1974) in which the state does no more than to protect the natural rights of individuals, through more traditional liberal and conservative thinking, to the maximalist communitarian or absolutist views both of which grant maximum authority to the collectivity. Arguments about higher education's autonomy may have, indeed, not been too far from the Nozickian view in that they have sometimes included demands for complete freedom from public control, to the extent of arguing for exemption from public audit of the funds originating from the national purse (Kogan 1969).

Recent UK Conservative governments adopted a neo-liberal rhetoric about the desirability of limiting the role of the state. However, this was not entirely consistent with previous conservative thinking; it is worth recalling Scruton's statement that 'the conservative is recognisable as a political animal by his reluctance to effect complete separation between the state and civil society, and that it is as deep an instinct in a conservative as it is in a socialist to resist the champions of "minimal" government' (1980, p.48). This ambivalence is reflected in, for example, the fluctuations of policy on the extent to which research should be funded from the public purse and directed into 'economically useful' areas.

Views about the appropriate arrangements for specific institutions are not always consistent with opinions about the degree of state action that is appropriate in the society as a whole. In general, the particular nature of higher education, or higher education essentialism, means that in most societies universities have a rather special place.

Normative theories of the university

Of all public institutions, the university has been subjected to most analysis of its idiosyncratic nature. In the theory of the independent institution, albeit in receipt of substantial subventions from the public purse, institutional and professional freedoms are regarded as essential for the pursuit of its purposes.

Clark's triangle (1983), as extended by Becher and Kogan (1992), refers to the way in which higher education policy and the systems resulting from it are the resultant of a triangle of forces: professional-collegial; governmental-managerial and market. Becher and Kogan, adapting Premfors, added a welfare state force. This could also be expressed as a civil society force which might accommodate community, distributive and other welfare functions of higher education. An important subset of Clark's hypothesis is that academics have a dual accountability to their 'invisible colleges' of fellow academics and to their institution.

On the basis of this heuristic, it is possible to compare systems and, at any one time, to denote the extent to which one force, e.g. managerial as against collegial, or civil society as opposed to market criteria, is driving a system. In fact, in the UK, power seems to have shifted from the level of the working academic to that of the institution, the national authorities and the market. This irregularity of pattern in itself demands explanation. The UK began at an opposite corner of Clark's triangle from that of its continental counterparts. It is shifting towards state control, whilst other systems are moving in the opposite direction. It is possible that similar contexts are impelling them to a median position.

The normative theory of higher education is further reinforced by consideration of the relationships between the types of knowledge generated and the higher education organisation required to sustain them (Becher 1989; Bernstein 1963). Forms of knowledge, hard or soft, the collected or the integrated curriculum, affect and are affected by its social or organisational forms. Thus, the 'collected' curriculum is likely to be regulated by less hierarchical structures than would be the 'integrated' curriculum. Where a form of knowledge is provisional or contestable (soft) and not based on pyramids of paradigms and clear evidence (hard), the system governing it will be less determinate. The movement away from disciplines towards areas of study weakens subject boundaries and the forms of academic control over them. It follows that higher education organisation, such as decentralisation, binary systems, more power to rectors, are/should be determined in part by the extent to which they are applicable to the knowledge structures implicit in teaching and research.

So, too, does the assumption, taken from Geertz (1964) and Archer (1979), that forms of knowledge, feeling or value become shaped and structured into procedures, processes and structures, supporting the traditional theory of higher education. There is thus a basic generative process in higher education. It links the relative freedom of the individual academic, to follow their own curiosity and exercise their own expertise, with institutional requirements for collective decision making and rule setting. Henkel *et al.* (forthcoming) have noted how government-steered science policies had in the past often been met with academic scepticism on the grounds that they conflicted with the norms of scientific activity and with well-established beliefs about how science works (Polanyi 1962).

Scientists, philosophers of science and economists tend to stress the logical relationship between epistemologies, the values of scientists and other academics and the distinctive organisational structures within which they work (Dasgupta and David 1994; David 1996; Polanyi 1962). Sociologists of science, though initially promoting these ideas (Merton's classic statement, 1973), later emphasised the influence upon academic values and agendas of dominant societal values and of authority and power and reward structures (Mulkay 1977).

Clark's triangle does not, of itself, entail particular normative positions, but his general corpus of writing falls in with the position taken until recently by that of virtually every other scholar in the field. These entail the socio-technological assumption (Woodward 1965) that the primary modes of production in higher education, as in any other field, determine the social, and hence governmental, arrangements for that field. Since higher education's main activities – research, scholarship and teaching – are essentially individualistic, and depend on the expertise and commitment of creative individuals, its governmental arrangements fall best within the collegial format. A collegium is a minimalist organisation constructed to control standards of entry, to allocate essential common tasks and to distribute resources to its members whilst avoiding control over the amount and nature of the work to be done. By contrast, managerial and hierarchical arrangements assume that there will be policies and objectives set on high which will be disaggregated by academics to whom tasks would be allocated. The professionally led model assumes that collegial arrangements, in which authority and power are shared by academics, are the appropriate way to organise universities. 'Many special characteristics of academic organisations are rooted in the structure of academic work ... the parts of academic systems have grown to be quite fragmented and independent with extreme division of labour and complicating mutual influences on each other' (Hölttä 1995, quoting Birnbaum 1989 and Clark 1983).

Clark extended these assumptions to his account of the change mechanisms of higher education. These are driven by the way in which knowledge is produced through ever-changing and increasing specialisation which constantly generates new forms and boundaries, subdisciplines and domains. This all happens with scant regard to national government or institutional management. Institutions may develop their own portfolio of values and lay down their own criteria of excellence (Becher and Kogan 1992), but more salient are the criteria and judgements of the international disciplines or the national guilds to which academics belong. Hence, process determines structure.

Much the same themes are celebrated by a succession of authors on the organisational and decision-making characteristics of universities. The diffusion and complexity of patterns of authority give rise to the dominant organisational models which accompany the normative political theory of higher education. Collegial, bureaucratic, political and organised anarchy models 'are found in universities, but in different parts, different issues, and at different points in time' (Hölttä 1995). The collegial model is compatible with the model of disciplinary self-governance. In it, decision making is characterised by consensus. The bureaucratic model, in which the institution creates rules, regulations and hierarchies to regulate procedures and processes which might assure accountability for the performance of public purposes, is also present in virtually all higher education institutions. Within the political model (Baldridge 1971), however, the university is assumed to be fragmented into specialised groups with divergent interests and preferences and the system therefore depends upon mutual dependency groups and on social exchange. The organised anarchy model (Cohen and March 1974) predicts that organisational action at university is virtually unintentional. Decision making and organisational choice are characterised by the 'garbage can' model (Cohen, March and Olsen 1972). The choices available are determined by the use of the garbage can into which various problems and solutions are dumped by participants. Decision making is individual rather than organisational. At the same time, a university behaving on the model of organised anarchy 'also has formal structures, roles, and external regulation mechanisms for educational and administrative activities' (Hölttä 1995). Against this traditional normative model we can increasingly set models derived from managerial concepts of higher education, from the pursuit of social concerns derived from access or lifelong learning policies or from the burgeoning quality industry. These find expression in some of the prescriptive literature on quality assurance and on effective management on institutions.

It is not easy to distinguish normative from empirical statements in this area. Whilst many of these (mainly American) statements were intended to be analytic descriptions of the nature of higher education based on their understanding of the governmental arrangements demanded by the essential nature of higher education, the analysis usually started from acquaintance with the most prestigious research universities and did not encompass the 'less noble' forms of higher education, such as teacher training institutions or military academies, also usually but not always defined into higher education. The analyses also tended to understate the extent to which some basic units in some subjects were led in hierarchical and even authoritarian ways. It would not be unfair to say that the collegial or anarchic models were based as much on wished-for states as on states that were discoverable in the whole range of institutions. They constituted ideal pictures.

At the empirical level the nature of higher education institutions has, however, seemed to justify unique relationships with the state and perhaps to strengthen the case for claiming a degree of higher education exceptionalism. These features include the central role of knowledge generation and transmission in higher education institutions. We have already noted that the basic argument for autonomy is that the very nature of knowledge generation requires freedom from direction if it is to result in the disinterested and critical search for knowledge. 'The underlying dynamics of knowledge organisation are difficult for the state to contain' (Clark 1983, p.179). However, it is also argued that new forms of knowledge generation increase steerage opportunities (Gibbons *et al.* 1994), although an earlier tradition of 'finalisation theory' (Van den Daele, Krahn and Weingart 1977) maintained that the willingness of a field to be steered depended on the paradigmal stage that had been reached.

Further claims for exceptionalism rest on the long history of some of the institutions which predate the existence of national states. This provides them not only with a historically based moral right to autonomy but also considerable immovable assets which provide a degree of protection from state control. In many societies links between universities and other elites defend them from lay interference. There is the perceived importance of higher education to the success of modern economies and the resulting pressures on institutions (see, for example, Becher and Kogan 1992; Salter and Tapper 1994). Some outputs are used directly as consumption benefits and others as part of the production process (Cave *et al.* 1997). Higher education can thus be seen as contributing to both production and consumption as used in Cawson's 1986 model of corporatism (Cawson 1986). The increasing emphasis on the role of graduates in the economy means that higher education can be increasingly seen as part of the supply side of the economy.

But many of these arguments are two-edged. Thus, the very importance of universities to the economy favours a stronger degree of public policy influence. Arguments derived from the nature of knowledge production work in favour of autonomy, and arguments from its use argue in favour of state intervention. Moreover, arguments over control need to have some appeal to their political constituencies. In the UK the political constituency coming to higher education's aid and arguing its case for continued protection has been weaker than for the top US universities, which seems to imply that exceptionalism is not entirely carried by force of moral argument but also by the characteristics of the political environment. Students of higher education government must, in fact, look out for a range of normative theories which will develop and change in response to changes in higher education tasks. New Public Management and the Evaluative State start with largely managerial preoccupations. Assumptions about governance connected with powerful drives towards lifelong learning and wider access can be expected to develop and contest the space hitherto occupied by the traditional academic-professional theory.

As we noted above, comparisons of the state's role in relation to higher education in different countries follow closely the style of Clark's triangle (e.g. Frederiks, Westerheijden and Weusthof 1994). Analysis of the grip of the state has also utilised Neave and Van Vught's (1994) continuum, which has a controlling role for the state at one end and a more liberal supervising role at the other (Richardson and Fielden 1997). These international comparisons usually suggest the UK gives more autonomy to its universities than most other countries.

Universities in Britain: their position and autonomy

Normative theories can be applied to an analysis of traditional university autonomy in the UK and how the position has changed. Berdahl (1977) noted that academic freedom and institutional autonomy are not the same thing, and this distinction is borne out by some of our interviewees who believed that the power of the institutions has grown at the expense of individual academic freedom (see also Tapper and Salter 1995). Berdahl distinguished between academic freedom which belongs to the individual academic, substantive autonomy which is the power of the institution to determine its own goals and programmes, and procedural autonomy which is the power of the institution to determine the means by which its goals and programmes will be pursued. The extent of autonomy can be identified by analysis on several dimensions (Frazer 1997). These include the legal status of an institution (is it recognised as a separate entity; is it free to own property); academic authority (can it make academic awards); mission (does it determine its own goals); governance (who appoints its governing body); financial (is it free to make expenditure decisions); employment (does it employ its own staff); and academic decentralisation (does it determine student admissions; must it seek approval for courses; does it determine its own curriculum; has it freedom to pursue research). Frazer points out that autonomy must be qualified by some attribute of the institution. Thus, in some systems it will be the faculty rather than the institution that possesses the autonomy.

On almost all of these criteria UK universities scored high. The concepts of academic freedom and institutional autonomy, as exemplified historically by the role of the University Grants Committee, were strongly embedded in the British political culture. The traditional autonomy of UK higher education was bolstered by thinking from a wide range of positions on the extent of appropriate state action.

The traditional liberal view of restricting the role of the state in fields such as higher education was stated by John Stuart Mill, who claimed the 'most cogent reason for restricting the interference of government is the great evil of adding unnecessarily to its power' (1962, p.244). Even for the conservative Scruton, with his belief in a role for the state, it is important that universities are autonomous and 'focused on internal aims' (1980, p.160). Elsewhere in the book (Chapters 6 and 8) we describe the strong links between universities and other bodies in which members of elites can be found, such as those existing between the UGC and the Treasury. This played an important part in bolstering the autonomy of universities. Another aspect of this that is seen to be stronger in Britain and other Westminster systems than elsewhere is the role of buffer bodies standing between the state and the universities.

These considerations form part of the more general assumptions about the role of the UK state. Neave (1986) suggests that in the Continental European countries the revolutions of the late eighteenth and nineteenth centuries ensured that the university was incorporated in the national bureaucracy. By contrast, in the UK 'the status of academia as a property owning corporation of scholars, the purest expression of which was in the two Ancient British universities, was preserved ... Until the First World War ... there existed a broadly held view which regarded education ... as ill-served by state intervention' (pp.109–124). Instead, there developed the idea of the facilitatory state which would provide resources to universities whose freedom would be enjoyed within an area of negotiation largely controlled by the universities themselves. The resulting autonomy was both institutional and individual, and embodied in charters and collegial self-government. It must now be asked whether the weakening of the Millian theory of the state in general has been accompanied by a shift in the normative theory of higher education governance.

Initially, in the twentieth century in the UK the growth of intervention was accepted much more in some public services than in others. Similarly, Keynesian social democracy was concerned more with intervention in the demand side of the economy than the supply side. In general, in Britain the Welfare State was slowly accepted but 'the notion of a developmental state, using its power to give its citizens a more sophisticated set of comparative advantages so that it could compete more effectively with other states, met dogged and uncomprehending resistance' (Marquand 1988, p.147). Accordingly, higher education remained an area of public service which retained a large degree of autonomy.

Reformulating theories of the state: New Public Management and the Evaluative State

Whilst the classic theories of the state gave relatively clear choices between contesting value positions, in our period governments lent support to patterns of governance that seemed to reflect their own ambivalences about the extent and nature of the control that they intended to exercise over public institutions. These ambiguities were fully present in the attempts known as New Public Management (NPM) to both decentralise and to substitute more direct means of control by the package of instruments associated with the rise of the Evaluative State. In the context of British higher education, the total effect was, however, more centralisation. As we will note later, the decentralisation implicit in New Public Management approaches were more appropriate to hitherto centrally administered public agencies.

An element in the rhetoric of the Conservative government was that they were increasing the autonomy of a range of public services by applying the bundle of notions that have become NPM. Its thinking about the administration of public services stresses devolved responsibilities for the delivery of centrally determined priorities. This hardly applied in higher education where there was already devolved responsibility and internally generated priorities. Even in countries such as the Netherlands, where the tradition of institutional autonomy in higher education was less developed, there were doubts whether NPM-type reforms would really lead to greater autonomy

(Maassen and Van Vught 1988). Nevertheless, NPM has contributed to the analysis of reforms in public services.

In New Public Management (Pollitt 1995), eight elements comprise a shopping basket for those who wish to modernise the public sectors of western industrialised societies, although not every element is present in each country, let alone each public service (Pollitt *et al.* 1997). These elements are: cost cutting, capping budgets and seeking greater transparency in resource allocation (including formula-based funding); disaggregating traditional bureaucratic organisations into separate agencies; decentralising management authority within public agencies; separating the purchaser and provider functions; introduction of market and quasi-market type mechanisms; requiring staff to work to performance targets, indicators and output objectives; shifting basis of public employment from permanency and standard national pay and conditions towards term contracts, Performance Related Pay (PRP), and emphasis on service 'quality', standard setting and 'customer responsiveness'.

Many of these changes have been required of higher education but it has been largely exempt from those which concern governmental and organisational relationships: namely, disaggregating traditional bureaucratic organisations into separate agencies; decentralising management authority within public agencies; separating the purchaser and provider functions. This must be because UK universities were already largely free of external bureaucratic structures, and did not need to be decentralised from them, and the UGC as a buffer was, for at least most of its history, an organisation that was seen as being more independent of the government department than any of the new agencies.

There was always a powerful academic evaluative system through which external examiners assessed the validity of examination procedures and results, and the academic world awarded statuses and resources to their peers. Such a system has been part of the trustful relationship and corporatist bargain with higher education in which it was assumed that academics' own exercise of authority, based on their own esoteric knowledge of what constituted quality, was both constitutionally and functionally appropriate.

Much of this remains, but with the rise of the Evaluative State (Henkel 1991; Neave 1988), academic judgements are incorporated into a rigorously administered public evaluative regime which affects reputations and the allocation of research monies and includes the publication of teaching quality gradings. These changes move the state into a stronger regulatory position, and also close to boundaries of what had hitherto been academic mastery on the means of normative control.

The Evaluative State can be considered part of the more general shift in the working of the state entailed in New Public Management (Bleiklie 1998, p.299; Dill 1998, p.361; El-Khawas 1998, p.317). However, UK higher education policy started from a point different from that of other systems where the Evaluative State was a 'direct bid to reduce the ambit of the state and substitute in the affairs of higher education the market for the state' (Neave 1998, p.272). Dill (1998, p.382), drawing on our previous work (Cave *et al.* 1997), appositely notes that 'the rise of the Evaluative State is often interpreted as a shift from an earlier uneasy balance between professional and state control to some new combination of state–market control'.

Both NPM and the assumptions underlying the Evaluative State are developments of the broader range of theories of the state. The emphasis on evaluation chimed in with two other strands of new government thinking – the belief that publicly employed professionals should be accountable for both their processes and outcomes, and the desire to provide information to users of services that might serve as a proxy for pricing in otherwise uncosted services.

The extent to which contexts or individual actors cause change

Theories of the state embody ideologies. Ideologies current at the time of reforms formed part of the context for, and drove key individuals towards, particular policies. But higher education policy was also affected by demographic, economic and social factors. Individuals acting either alone in a position of power or as part of an interest group or an elite acted decisively within these contexts. It would be a fruitless task, and one now virtually given up by historians, to attempt to weigh the relative importance that must be given to broad historical contexts and to individual actors in causing change. For one thing, some individuals, and Thatcher in our period is an obvious example, change the context within which other individual actors work. Thus, ideology, within a particular economic context, and one in which social expectations had changed, drove politicians to change the assumptions on which policies were based. At the same time, as we have noted, the traditional normative model of higher education government maintained a powerful ideological source of resistance to some of the policies; this was reinforced by the assumptions underlying the incorporation of academics into their disciplines and academic identities.

We note in Chapter 3 how, by the 1970s, confidence in the objectives and operational capacities of higher education had already begun to decline. An anti-professional ideology – the general distrust articulated by Conservative governments of special interest groups and professions – combined with the 1979 Conservative government's mandate to roll back the frontiers of the state to add to government's impatience with negotiation. Ideological shifts thus affected the structure of influence.

These shifts in sentiment and influence no doubt contributed to or ensured that there was no wider public and political resistance to reduction in the unit of resource and the consequent proletarianisation of academics (Halsey 1992), as did radical student behaviour in the late 1960s.

The shift from what Salter and Tapper (1994) describe as the liberal elite ideology of universities could also be seen as a shift towards a different range of possible ideologies. Three of these to be examined in Chapter 3 are: a belief in accountability and managerialism; support for the economic ideology of higher education (Salter and Tapper 1994); and a shift towards market ideology. This included an emphasis on consumerism within the market in which consumers with the right information would determine what is provided (mac.16), a thesis opposed to the notion of universities as expert providers of specialised services.

We have noted that the ideological drives behind change were complex and multivalent. Our own preference is to take note of the power of ideology, but not to allow it such an important role as do Salter and Tapper and therefore not to assume it to be always the driving force of change. So although the rise of the economic ideology was important and based on concern about the economy and the place that higher education might play in its enhancement, its conversion into expansion of the system was not the result of a continuous explicit and deliberate policy. Even less was expansion the product of egalitarian impulses. Other powerful contextual factors were at work and ministerial changes were important. Furthermore, expansion itself became the driver of change in the governance of the system, in the governmental demands for selectivity and for quality assurance, and in the ultimate demise of the binary system, although in that case anti-local government sentiment played a major part, too. In time, there can be no doubt that other contextual changes will help to cast the mould for further changes. The perceived changes in the economy and its demands for different kinds of knowledge and human resources can hardly fail to put pressures for change on both the curriculum and on research and development. They have already given rise to two government initiatives – the Enterprise and the Foresight initiatives. Within our study we note a great deal of rhetoric in their favour but, at this time at least, can be less certain of their impacts.

Some accounts (for example, Scott 1995) concentrate on changes in the economic, social and epistemic contexts. Whilst we acknowledge the changing ideological and other contextual factors, we also (see Chapter 6) show how the actions of individual actors are important. We therefore look for no single factor affecting change but for the interaction of actors and their historical contexts and a constant reiteration of connection between them. Intentions were forged partly by belief systems, partly by the power of circumstances, and partly by opportunistic reactions to what might not have been planned or even rationally contemplated.

Higher education policy making: dual processes, elites and interest groups

Changing theories of the state and contextual factors offer a background within which policies are formulated. The next series of questions running through our narrative is: how far was higher education policy determined as a matter of public policy, how far was it created within the system itself, and what part was played by elites and interest groups.

UK higher education is regulated by more than one system: the governmental and the academic. Governmental regulation takes place through the central policy-making bodies and bureaucracies, the allocative bodies and the quality assurance bodies. These provide the frame for the policies for the universities which then seek to find their particular identities and niches within them. At the same time, a different set of policies are formed through the invisible colleges of academics. They decide the award of the more prestigious academic posts and honours, reputational statuses and, interlocking with the allocative systems, the awards and differential allocation of funds.

There are thus two policy- and decision-making systems which have no formal connection with each other but which affect, and generate energy between, each other. Their action can be likened to that of tectonic plates,[2] which shift under the surface of the earth to generate energy between them. These points indicate the exceptionalism of policy making within higher education.

It would be true to say, and is possibly no more than a tautology, that those closest to the official governmental system, through co-option to it, or through close consultative relationships with it, were more likely to agree on the importance of sustaining quality through both selectivity of research funding and quality assessment of both teaching and research. The two worlds of government regulation and invisible colleges connect through co-opted elites described below; in this way, such policies as selectivity can be represented as, and may actually be, the result of central government incorporating views that exist in the academic world, although the policies may not be legitimised by the academic world at large.

Connection between the two worlds is particularly made through the allocative systems which are peopled by the co-opted elite. They retain strong academic membership, who are, however, increasingly joined by non-academics. In these transactions, government policies frame the direction of decision making but do not directly affect the judgements about individual allocations.

Our empirical narrative will show that higher education policy making has always been relatively closed; until about the 1970s government could assume the consent of a beneficiary clientele, and the university system, at least, could largely run itself mainly on professional-elite criteria, all with government connivance. Since then, whilst the professional and elite model still subsists within important strands of policy, government has become top-down, non-participative and non-consultative on its larger policies, although much implementation is left to the funding and research councils. These developments are not necessarily consistent with the assumption that policy making in the central government department was led by bureaucratic determinism (Salter and Tapper 1994; Tapper and Salter 1978) (see Chapter 6). Our evidence is that ministers were the key actors in the 1980s and 1990s.

2   This metaphor has also appealed to Professor Ronald Barnett who used it in his inaugural lecture at the London Institute of Education. This appears to have been spontaneous adoption of the metaphor on both sides.

In much recent writing on public policy making, pluralistic concepts such as policy networks have been a major consideration. Although we shall consider their application to higher education, its exceptional nature means that other theories, particularly elite theories, might be potentially more useful when analysing the generation, mediation and implementation of policies. Some of the main theories available are described below, but for our more detailed examination of these overlapping theories see Marton, Hanney and Kogan (1995) and Bleiklie, Marton and Hanney (1995).

The role of elites

The reason for examining elite concepts is to see if they help shed light on policy making for higher education. The issue can be complex because there is a range of theories, including general ones about the ability of elites to control and contain the policy agenda. This has sometimes been described in terms of non-decision making (Bachrach and Baratz 1963) which might be appropriate for analysing the way in which higher education policy was largely kept off the wider political agenda for many years. The postwar period in the UK was seen as a time of the final flourish of 'donnish dominion' (Halsey 1992) but it 'may have owed as much to a congruence of interests, between political and academic elites as to a principled respect for university autonomy' (Scott 1995, p.62).

Elite theories include analyses of academics in general as a knowledge elite who have a 'near monopoly over the selection, training and accreditation of their own ranks and of other elites' (Etzioni-Halevy 1985, p.17). The links between university elites and other elites in society have in the past been seen as particularly important in the UK where studies have focused on the role of the elite universities, Oxford and Cambridge (Oxbridge), in educating the wider elite (see, for example, Wakeford and Wakeford 1974; Wiener 1981). This linkage does not remain a secure description of the way that groups have interacted and exercised influence during our period. Tapper and Salter's account of the challenge to the traditional liberal university ideal presented by the rise of an economic ideology is described in terms of a split between different parts of the elite (Tapper and Salter 1978, p.150).

When consensus breaks down, however, academic elites can also play an oppositional role (see, for example, Jenkins 1996, p.136). Ozga (1987) suggests that some ideas from elite theory warrant further study in higher education policy, namely the opposition of elites to the proliferation of state power, the idea of service being the obligation of elites, and the basis of elite power in non-economic sources, i.e. through ideological and moral leadership. In terms of higher education policy making, however, such an oppositional role, whilst potentially important for the health of the society, could serve to alienate the government from academics. To some extent this happened with the letter from 364 economists criticising the economic policy of the Conservatives.

As a knowledge elite, academic elites also play an unusual role in that, using Crewe's terms (1974, p.34), they could be defined in terms of being 'the best' and not necessarily, as are other elites, according to their power base. A range of elites, rather than a single elite, can be assumed to operate within higher education and to make some impact on the dual policy process. Whether all those discussed below can be described as 'elites' has been challenged by some of our respondents and certain groups could equally well be called leadership groups. They divide into several types: the *academic elites* as represented mainly by fellowships of the Royal Society and the British Academy – these are the true knowledge elite; the *institutional leadership elites* as represented by vice-chancellors of the 'old' universities and the newly incorporated universities (formerly polytechnics); the particular *leadership elites in Oxford and Cambridge* as represented by the heads of colleges; and the *co-opted elites* appointed by government to lead or act as members of the funding and research councils.

The idea of *co-opted elites* has been used in understanding higher education policy making (Becher and Kogan 1992; Kogan 1992). Co-opted elites can operate in three directions: they form part of the government decision making when they act through government appointed bodies; they internalise, interpret and help implement government policies through their own power and authority networks; and they create hierarchies of resource and esteem in their own domains, partly on licence from government. Becher and Kogan suggest that it is the co-opted elites that provide the link between the normative and operational modes of working (1992, p.59). Elites could exist coterminously when the same group of people (elite individuals) held positions on research councils, at the elite institutions, at leading scientific and arts societies, and on committees responsible for developing and implementing government policies. At least in relation to science policy, we shall examine how far a role was played by some of the leading members of the co-opted elite who were often also members of the academic elite. Such people were usually selected on the basis of their personal attributes and views rather than because they represented any interest group. More generally, in elite theory, some emphasise that there is no single elite group which has control over policy making in the society (Dahl 1956, 1961; Schumpeter 1956). This view, often called democratic elite theory, involves the concept of multiple and autonomous elites and would also incorporate the looser notion of polyarchy (Dahl 1956) which, as we shall see, could be applied to competition between groups of elite scientists for control over science policy.

Corporatism

Like elite theorists, corporatists (Grant 1985) believe there are a few small groups of power holders who determine political outcomes in society. Under corporatism, political exchange is limited to a few participants who are insulated from external pressure. These participants, usually business associations and unions, receive a representational monopoly from the government, in exchange for the organisations delivering their members' compliance on government proposals. In some countries, including Sweden, corporatism is seen as working across the board of public policies, but even in countries such as Britain which are seen as weak cases of such macro-corporatism, 'particular policy areas are often highly insulated from competitive group pressures and subject to joint determination and implementation' (Cawson 1986, p.2). This means that corporatism could be operating in specific policy fields. Corporatism has been defined in various ways, and the exchange relationship which ruled until the late 1970s in British higher education may also be expressed as a 'corporatist bargain' (Cawson 1982; Kogan 1988) through which the state will give freedom, funds and legitimacy in return for discernible contributions to the public good by way of advanced education and new knowledge. It implies a degree of co-option and incorporation in government. In some ways corporatism does not necessarily seem to be associated with university autonomy. Various explanations can be offered, however, of this apparent anomaly. The political culture was such that there was an acceptance by those in power that their closeness to the world of higher education should go along with not challenging its autonomy.

There was a 'trusting relationship', and funding was provided to meet all deficiencies. Dependency was mutual and took the form of an exchange relationship (Blau 1964; Ranson 1980; Rhodes 1981) both between the state and institutions and within the universities themselves (Blau 1973). In this relationship higher education depended upon government for its resources and, to some extent, legitimacy. Government depended upon higher education for the training of its skilled human resources and for the creation and dissemination of knowledge. Reform, in such an exchange relationship, would be negotiated and not imposed, although for the universities there was traditionally comparatively little public policy making.

Policy networks

The term 'policy network' is defined as a generic label for the different types of state/interest group relationships which exist in the policy process (Jordan and Schubert 1992; Raab 1994; Rhodes and Marsh 1992) and it is widely used in assessing public policy making. Although there are few empiricised examples of pluralistic influence in higher education (Kogan 1992), some recent literature supports the use of the policy network concept when analysing higher education policy making (e.g. Marshall 1995a; Sanchez-Ferter 1997; Van Vught 1985).

The policy network concept can be seen as a continuum on which policy community is placed at one end and issue network at the other (Daugbjerg 1998; Rhodes and Marsh 1992). The criteria for analysis are membership, integration, resources and power. A policy community would thus be categorised by its limited membership, frequent interaction with shared basic values, all participants having a resource base and the ability to deliver their members' support, and power among the network members relatively equal in distribution. On the opposite end of the continuum are issue networks, categorised by their large and/or wide range of affected interests, fluctuations in contacts, access, and level of agreement, unequal resource distribution combined with varying abilities to deliver members' support, and unequal powers among the groups. The extent to which policy networks can explain policy changes has been questioned by Dowding (1995) who suggests that 'policy community and issue network are merely labels attached to an explanation of differences between policy formation and that labels do not themselves explain the difference' (p.142). Even if the terms are useful generally in public policy making neither typification seems to fit closely the situation of British higher education policy making, although we shall attempt to see how far we can observe a shift, similar to that described by

Marshall (1995a) for Australian higher education, from a policy community to a more recent issue network.

Continuity and discontinuity in policy

Whilst the policy changes discussed were substantial and had considerable impacts, some originated from factors present before the large changes of the 1980s. A principal force for continuity was the presence of particular groups in particular roles. '...History has its continuities as well as its breaches; continuities contained within the experience of generations' (Trevor-Roper 1992, pp.xii–xiv). For some generations, the ablest have secured admission to elite universities. This builds up enduring academic cadres, sharing similar approaches to academic values, work and statuses. The academics deriving from the more elite centres have occupied the key academic, institutional and system leadership jobs, even if they no longer have a monopoly of them (Halsey 1992). Over one-third of UK vice-chancellors in post between 1960 and 1996 had attended Oxbridge (Smith *et al.* 1999). The traditional academic ideals persist in both research aspirations and teaching practices (see Henkel forthcoming).

Universities' position in the system is conditioned not only by current differential flows of revenue, but also by fixed capital, in buildings and equipment, and financial resources, that they have inherited. This is true not only of the sciences and technologies, but also of the humanities and social sciences where the location of the major libraries strongly affects research potential.

There are, however, some conditions that must be placed against this account. Some institutions have succeeded well in rising within the hierarchy of esteem. Overall institutional success in the competitive race is conditioned by discipline distributions. Resistances to change reside in what has been called essentialism. Many academics are attempting to defend what they regard as the core academic values of the disinterested search for truth and particular forms of power and professional relationships from the social demands created by government and other sponsors. Academic identities are formed in both undergraduate and postgraduate experiences (Becher, Henkel and Kogan 1994). They remain a basis of belief in essential procedures for the creation of knowledge.

Those in leadership positions in the former public sector do not come exclusively from traditional elites and they now carry countervailing weight in funding and quality councils. But they have hardly penetrated the peer groups upon whose judgements allocations for research by research and funding councils depend. There is thus a dialectic at work between traditional academic values and those stemming from concepts of public utility. Continuity is embodied in the values promulgated and the powers exercised in traditions that far antedate the heroic ministers of the Thatcher era.

Conclusion

Our theoretical position will be seen to be that of eclecticism. We eschew general hypotheses but look to political and other social theory to illuminate and help us to classify the experiences undergone by higher education in the UK between 1975 and 1997. In doing so, we have brought theorising about higher education governance into the mainstream of normative theory about the nature of the state.

PART II

Changing Nature of Higher Education

Main Policy Movements

Our theme in the chapters which follow is that of how a set of highly idiosyncratic institutions, employing perhaps some of the most individualistic of public professionals, started from a position of privileged dependence on the state, which they largely enjoyed on their own terms, and increasingly came to experience the consequences of the radical conservative revolution of the 1980s and 1990s in relationships between the state and public institutions.

Chapter 3

The Reform Movement:
Contexts and Massification

We begin with an analysis of the changing contexts within which
reform was advanced and give an account of the factors behind the
expansion of higher education.

I HIGHER EDUCATION AND BRITISH PUBLIC POLICY

First, we note how higher education was subjected to many of the
policy changes that affected the whole of public policy from the early
1980s. In depicting these changes, several linked assumptions can be
tested. Thus, Margaret Thatcher's determination to roll back the
boundaries of the state and substitute the working practices of the
market for those of the Welfare State have been taken to go alongside
that untidy bundle of policy premises known as the New Public
Management (NPM) (e.g. Pollitt 1993), described in Chapter 2. For
the most part, but over time and not systematically, the premises of
NPM were applied to higher education policy. At the same time, the
main lineaments of the Evaluative State (Neave 1988) were put in
place.

To some extent, the universities were being treated to prescriptions,
particularly on funding practices, that had always been applied to
other services, but the treatment felt correspondingly more
unfavourable because of their previous autonomy. The relative
affluence of the 1960s and early 1970s gave way to cumulative cuts in
resources allowed for each higher education student place, to the
point where standards of provision, such as staffing ratios, were
drastically reduced. In general, those of our interviewees who
commented on the point thought that higher education was not
singled out but was treated in much the same way as other institutions
in pursuit of public funds (e.g. mac.42).

Yet, in important respects, whilst the changes may have been greater than those faced by other sectors, higher education was able from the mid-1980s to exempt itself from some of the changes imposed elsewhere. For example, no university was closed and no employees had to 'apply for their own jobs', as was the case in local government or the National Health Service (NHS).

There was dramatic expansion of student numbers, as is described later in this chapter, and higher education's gross expenditure increased substantially. Whilst staffing ratios deteriorated and in comparative terms salaries slipped, the degree of exceptionalism enjoyed by higher education is illustrated by Table 3.1 which gives figures comparing the growth of higher education expenditure, in current not constant prices, with that of other public services between 1977/78 and 1996/97. Between 1977/78 and 1985/86 (when the demographic trend was mostly upwards) higher education had the lowest percentage increase in expenditure. However, between 1985/86 and 1996/97 expenditure in the UK went up more in higher education than in all education, or on the armed services, the police or even health and social security. The contradiction between the general backlash against the Welfare State and the growth of higher education has been even more marked in the UK than other European countries (Scott 1995).

Table 3.1 Public expenditure on public sector services (£million)

Expenditure	1977/78	1985/86	1996/97
HE	667	1359	4132
All Education	8341	17,283	39,133
Armed Services	5827	15,066	16,122
Social Security	15,150	46,246	106,958
Police	1037	3147	6896
Health	6823	17,889	43,199

Source: *Office for National Statistics (ONS)* from *The Blue Book*: Table 5.4 (1998) (Macro-Economic Statistics). These figures show current not constant prices

This growth of expenditure showed a willingness to spend more, but on a system facing greatly increased demands and expected to meet them with considerably lower standards of provision. As with other public services, the government aimed to shift the dependence of higher education on public funding to different forms of market earnings.

At the same time, it imposed various forms of accountability, the most important of which concerned the insistence on quality assurance. Whilst centralisation and accountability were imposed rigorously in higher education, this affected different institutions differently. In important respects, the former polytechnics became more free than they were before incorporation under the 1988 Act; the controls exercised by their local authorities were removed, as were those of the Council for National Academic Awards (CNAA) by the 1992 Act. The 'old' universities, however, experienced more external pressure than hitherto. It is claimed that under the government of John Major, 'Thatcher's centralisation gathered pace: ... it extended further in to the running of the NHS, the new police authorities, housing, the railways, the schools and universities, and the administration of justice ... League tables and audit comparability proliferated ... she may have intended to "take power to cede power", but she never got round to the second half of that remit' (Jenkins 1996, pp.15 and 21).

Furthermore, although it is generally believed that policy marked a severe break with what had gone before, two caveats can be registered in the light of the evidence that we present. First, radical change may have already been implicit in previous policy moves; many of the changes were already taking place in the later 1970s (Ziman 1995). Second, whilst the policies might have been radical, they may not have as radical effects as has been supposed. Our analysis will attempt to show how far there have been 'real' changes, and their extent. As we saw in Chapter 2, the answers to those largely empirical and historical questions lead the project to ruminate on the deeper issue, namely, whether the continuing intrinsics of higher education, its essentialism, make it less likely that change in the essentials will occur. We shall return to this issue in Chapters 7 and 9; it is a central theme of Mary Henkel's book.

Whilst the changes in higher education do fit into the wider range of reforms in public services, it is useful to analyse the reforms in higher education in various broad time segments, for the period 1945 to 1997, that are specific to the system:

- *1945 until 1963* – a period of growth in demand and provision but essentially continuing a pattern in which research-led universities were divided from non-university and teacher training institutions, all within a highly selective system. The non-university sector itself, other than teacher training, was somewhat undifferentiated and included technical and further education colleges offering courses of advanced study at the same time as they offered craft and technician training.

- *1963 until 1975* – a period stretching from the legitimation of expansion, but under roughly continuing conditions, by the Robbins Report (1963). During this time, the non-university sector grew in parallel to the universities and gained strength with the creation of 30 polytechnics. Numbers continued to rise but the participation rate levelled off and there was increasing financial stringency.

- *1975 until 1981* – the ending of the quinquennial system in 1973/74 was a decisive turning point, with 1975 marking the start of the post-quinquennium period.

- *1981 until 1997* – a period of change in which the finance, government and substantive content of higher education were subjected to the radical changes to be noted later, but in which also, from the mid-1980s, there was a return to rapid expansion.

II CONTEXTS

In identifying the major shifts in policy and structure that might affect academic workings and values, it is possible to identify the contextual frames within which changes took place. Some of the changes in policy and structure themselves became the contexts of further change. For example, whilst the expansion of the system was led partly by policy, partly by demography and partly by changes in social attitudes, it was itself a strong factor in causing many of the subsequent principal policy changes. Demography, changes in the economy and in society, developments in the nature and transmission of knowledge and in ideology constituted the contexts within which change took place.

Demography

Higher education policy has always been sensitive to the numbers of potential students. Educational demography has two components – that created by the numbers in the main age cohorts from which students are recruited, and that created by a combination of student demand and governmental, institutional and employment incentives. For the most part, the total size of age cohorts has been a less potent factor in driving up the size of the system than have been changes in the proportion of age groups, and changes in the kinds of age groups, that have sought and been allowed admission (see our later discussion of massification). The 1978 Brown Paper *Higher Education into the 1990s* (DES 1978) showed that the number of 18-year-olds in Great Britain fluctuated considerably but that they increased from 700,000 in 1960/61 to reach 906,000 by 1965/66. They then dropped sharply to 741,000 in 1969/70 before gently rising again throughout the 1970s to reach a peak of 941,000 in 1982/83. Numbers declined significantly to 622,000 in 1995/96 before once again starting to rise.

When these figures are compared with the growth of student numbers in Table 3.2, the paradox emerges that the greatest expansion in the entry of 18-year-olds occurred when the number of 18-year-olds was dropping. This accounts for the odd shape of the graph of the Age Participation Index (API) (Figure 3.1). A partial explanation is provided in the detailed Confederation on British Industry (CBI) analysis (CBI 1986) which showed that whilst the total number of 18-year-olds would decline by 240,000 between 1988 and 1995, the numbers in the top two social classes, which provide many of the recruits for higher education, would fall by a much smaller proportion – only 35,000 in total (CBI 1986). The highly significant factor that birth rates in the social classes from which students are still mainly recruited would fluctuate less than in the lower socio-economic classes seems to have been overlooked by policy makers in the early 1980s despite some mention of it in the analysis in the 1978 Brown Paper.

Table 3.2 Higher education students enrolled, 1965/66 to 1995/96 (000)

	1965/66	1970/71	1975/76	1980/81	1985/86	1990/91	1995/96
Universities							
Full-time	173	235	269	307	310	370	1108
Part-time	13	43	82	101	120	154	612
Total	186	278	351	408	430	524	1720
Polytechnics and colleges							
Full-time	133	221	246	228	289	377	
Part-time	110	121	137	191	216	274	
Total	243	343	383	419	507	652	
All HE							
Total	429	621	734	827	937	1175	1720

Sources: *Statistical Bulletin* (DfEE 1993) and *Annual Abstract of Statistics* (1997) 5.12

We will consider later in this chapter some of the more detailed attitudes towards, and consequences of, expansion of the system and discuss how political responses to predicted trends may further explain the apparent contradiction between the pattern of expansion and the demographic trends.

The economy and society

In spite of recurrent currency crises and a continuing slide in productivity and international competitiveness in the 1960s, the economy was thought capable of sustaining increased numbers at fairly generous subsistence and educational levels. The capacity of the system to sustain increased numbers was not in doubt at the time of the Robbins Report (1963). This preceded by two years the publication of a National Plan (DEA 1965) which assumed a 5 per cent increase in the gross national product for the foreseeable future. Expansion was legitimated at a time of confidence of the link between educational investment and economic growth.

It was the oil crises of the 1970s which first changed both the reality and the perceptions of uninterrupted growth of expenditure on higher education on the deficiency funding model, whereby institutions could expect to receive public funding to meet all of the costs for which they could not find funds themselves. There had already been some pulling back on public expenditure in the early 1970s after a period of prodigal growth. But from 1973 onwards the reductions in resources per student began to make themselves felt – although not on the drastic scales that were to come.

But if the retrenchments of the 1970s could be explained by problems in the 'real' economy, the later reductions in unit costs sometimes took place in years of economic growth and were as much the product of political preferences for reducing the role of the state and decreasing taxes. Whilst the government recognised that forms of advanced training might contribute to economic growth, they promoted the notion that the market must fund that from which it will benefit.

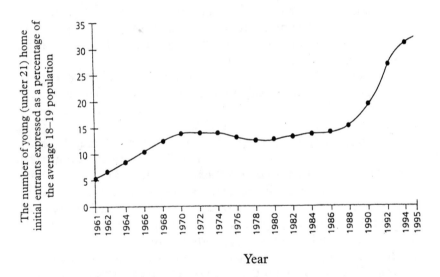

Year

Notes: Initial entrants are those entering a course of full-time higher education for the first time.

1961 figure estimated using Robbins Report App.2A, Table 3 (Percentage of the population of each age receiving higher education GB Oct 1961).

Due to minor change in definition, the years 1961 to 1970 inclusive are not strictly comparable with later years.

Due to minor change in definition, years from 1980 onwards are not strictly comparable with earlier years.

Figure 3.1 Higher Education Age Participation Index (API) – GB Institutions

As we will see later, the commitment to higher education increasingly included a strong instrumental strain which argued that higher education should change its curriculum and research towards the pursuit of economic competence to enable the UK to compete in global technologically driven markets. This helped account for such initiatives as those of Technology Foresight, inaugurated in the White Paper of 1993 (OST 1993), as well as the many appointments to higher education and science policy bodies of industrialists, businessmen and industrial scientists who, it would be hoped, would convert institutions from their assumed academicism.

The relationships between changes in higher education and the economy are not easy to track empirically and are likely to be complex. It has been maintained (e.g. Scott 1995) that social and economic factors influenced demand for higher education in specific ways, in that new occupations for which the applied social sciences and business and management studies are appropriate preparation have become increasingly important as traditional industrial occupations have declined. Therefore, it is argued, 'the "pull" of the economy has been more powerful than any "push" from within the academic culture' (p.59).

In particular, the jibe that the polytechnics, instead of becoming technological institutions, expanded mainly in the social sciences 'is based on a failure to appreciate the scale of these changes in occupational structure' (Scott 1995, p.59). It is true that some polytechnics sought to anticipate new occupational demands. In the view of one observer (mac.220), this may have resulted in part from external pressure, because that was expected of them by the regional advisory councils and inspectorates responsible for approving advanced courses. The CNAA, too, in scrutinising courses for approval, took seriously the question of employment outcomes for students and had assumed that 'they should be a concern of institutions in appraising their course proposals ... Subject boards ... laid considerable stress on the "market research" aspects of course proposals' (Silver 1990, pp.98 and 266). The take-up and remuneration of their graduates in these areas were, in fact, less impressive than those of university graduates, although polytechnic graduates in certain specific areas (e.g. accountancy) did better than those in non-specific subject areas (Brennan *et al.* 1996). For that matter, several universities also offered courses in business and management studies. Even where, as in recent reports from the CBI, the needs of the economy are cited as a major factor in the demand for continuing expansion of higher education, claims have been made that such an analysis does not in fact reflect the true needs of the economy. Thus, it was recently suggested that 'at least in numerical terms, current graduate output more than satisfies demand from employers for graduates to fill traditional "graduate jobs"' (Keep and Mayhew 1996, p.92).

Changes in society both cause, and are intensified by, an increase in access to higher education. Later in the chapter we discuss how expansion was associated with the growing bourgeoisification of society. Furthermore, on one important index the equality function began to be successfully served: the number of undergraduate places taken by women rose from 25 per cent to over 40 per cent between 1960 and 1988 (Fulton and Elwood 1989), although the social class composition of recruitment hardly changed. The proportion of women and men studying for a first degree had become equal by the mid-1990s, and, as significant, women no longer predominantly enrolled in the post-1992 universities or on part-time courses (Coffield and Vignoles 1997). The rate of participation, however, of those from lower socio-economic groups and those with disabilities continued to lag behind the improvements shown for ethnic minorities, women and older students (Robertson and Hillman 1997). Whilst the majority are now over the age of 21 years and 30 per cent are over 30 on entry to higher education, 65 per cent of mature students are to be found in the post-1992 universities (Coffield and Vignoles 1997, para. 3.1 and Table 3.1).

The impact of new knowledge

Changes in the nature of education and of research can also be considered as both the outcomes of, and the contexts for, change. Whilst our empirical work (Henkel forthcoming) will show some of the accounts of these changes (e.g. Gibbons *et al.* 1994) to be exaggerated and insufficiently empiricised (for an authoritative critique see Godin 1998), certainly there have been substantial changes in the knowledge landscape. In the late 1960s and 1970s, there were onslaughts from the sociology of knowledge that challenged the authority and legitimacy of academically anchored knowledge. This undoubtedly had an effect on the status of academics and on their forms of governance that had been almost wholly professor-led. It is claimed more recently that the mono-disciplines have yielded territory to trans-disciplinary working (Gibbons *et al.* 1994). The extent of that shift is obvious in different degrees in different subjects and different levels of the system. On the whole, the most secure and elite parts of the system have been able to accommodate such new formats without disturbance to their disciplinary hegemonies. The newer parts of the system which earn their status by attention to application were more likely to respond to the new formats.

The increasing importance of domains (Trist 1972) and Mode 2 knowledge and the modularisation of the curriculum have had effects in several directions. Movements in the organisation and transmission of knowledge may have been enhanced by the attempts of the government and of the European Union to create programmes which cut across disciplinary boundaries and national research programmes. They have also strengthened academics' intention to secure money from a wider range of sources.

These movements have left academic groups at the base of the system, less well boundaried than hitherto. They have made them more prone to institutional interventions because they have implied a weakening of the power of their disciplines whose expertise provided protection from non-academic influence. At the same time, academics in some subjects may work more strongly within extra-institutional networks. The 'invisible colleges' which connect academics within subject areas (Clark 1983) have always competed for their loyalty with the power of the institutions. The authority and critical locations of knowledge are now less certain, although, to judge by many of our interviews with senior academics, faith in the essential functions of the academic system remains firm. A familiar point of view was that whilst changes in knowledge are represented by such developments as technology transfer, science parks, and teaching company schemes which are driven by non-academic objectives, they depend upon university-created knowledge and university-trained graduates.

Ideologies and policies

Some of the ideological shifts related to the way in which society and public services in general should be organised. Others stemmed from the government's attitudes to public institutions and particularly those claiming autonomy on the grounds that they acted as hosts to work which depended on professional freedom.

The reduction of professional hegemony

There had been such a growth in state activity by 1979 that Thatcher's call to roll back its frontiers received wide support. There are claims that in many services the power of the state was not, in practice, reduced (Jenkins 1996). In higher education, in particular, the suggestion that the Thatcher reforms increased autonomy seems unsubstantiated. Instead, our proposition is that as a result of these policies of the government and their agencies, and institutional leadership, there was a shift from academic control towards both the market and to the incorporation of universities in the generality of state control. But there remain plenty of pockets of opinion that sustain the traditional theory.

It was an open question whether in the period from 1945 to 1980 higher education had constituted a system in more than a notional sense: the linkages of value and authority were relatively loose, and universities' autonomy was deemed to be entrenched in their charters. This philosophy of institutional and individual academic freedom was in place for other major public institutions, too, particularly local authorities and schools. The state ideology of higher education and the quinquennial system of grants to university were the *a fortiori* example of a belief in professionally led, but publicly financed, institutions which could fulfil their obligations to society through a process of trust and negotiation. Within the corporatist bargain (Cawson 1982) freedoms were accorded in return for working with the state. The traditional doctrine as applied to universities had seemed the stronger by virtue of the contrasting treatment in the controls over course approvals and resources in the public sectors of higher and further education. It rested on an implicit acceptance of higher education's essentialism, a belief that the nature of its tasks required particular forms of organisation and control.

Now, however, the boundary between what should be funded publicly and what earned privately shifted, so that the acceptable sources of higher education funding became multiple and virtually unbounded. In the late 1940s and 1950s, the UGC were still regarding money coming straight from government or private sector sources for specific purposes as tainted; only the purification by process of untied block grants to be distributed by academics to academics would preserve academic integrity. Until the 1970s, government assumed that what academics thought to be good research and teaching was likely to be good for the economy and society (although there were always parts of government that disagreed). The judgements of government converged with those of academics co-opted through membership of the central bodies. Throughout the 1970s the traditional assumptions about the Welfare State – of which higher education formed one element – remained firm, if somewhat battered by economic hazards and growing lack of confidence in the capacity of public systems to deliver services with sufficient responsiveness and economy. But the first casualty within assumptions about the Welfare State was less its distributive policies than its assumptions about the state's duty to support public professions largely on their own recognisances.

By the 1970s, confidence in the objectives and operational capacities of higher education had begun to decline. With increased uncertainty in the economy at large, the demand for graduates stopped growing (Williams 1984) and with it the pressure for places. Radical student behaviour of the late 1960s contributed further to public questioning of the value of higher education. As a former chairman of the CVCP and vice-chancellor described it:

> When the select committee investigating student unrest in 1968 visited Essex, one student, backed by others from all over the country, interrupted the chairman's remarks at the final session ... he wanted to know, he said, what right the committee had to be there. Universities were autonomous institutions ... When he refused to sit down, the chairman adjourned the session and the committee returned to London. The Speaker referred the incident to the Committee of Privileges and I was summoned to appear before it.

Although the period of disruption involved only a small minority of students, for a long time – perhaps as long as 20 years – its aftermath was thought to affect the ability of some of the better UK universities to recruit able students, and to affect the attitude of both politicians and the general public towards higher education. The first pressures produced by the economic uncertainties and demographic fluctuations of the 1970s were the justification for changing patterns of governance and more explicit planning mechanisms at the centre (mac.44, 5), for the insinuation of particular educational and research objectives by government, and the requirement that institutions become more efficient through the strengthening of managerial structures and techniques. These were to be the policies of the 1980s but they were already emerging in the 1970s.

Even before the 1980s the government was articulating and in many cases initiating changes. As the financial system and spending became larger, the Treasury, the Public Accounts Committee and the press began to ask if the resources were being spent properly. An early harbinger of these shifts in attitude had been the decision of the government in 1966 to place the audit of university accounts under the purview of the Comptroller and Auditor-General. The decision was significant in itself, but the furore surrounding it was even more revealing about the assumptions then governing state–university relations (Kogan 1969). In the 1980s there was increased pressure from parliamentary select committees.

An anti-professional ideology had been building up for some time, some of it emanating from right-wing academics (mac.26) which by the late 1970s articulated itself as a general sentiment of both conservative governments and their predecessors that universities were too secure and self-congratulatory at work in their responsiveness to the needs of the community. Hence demands for stronger accountability (mac.16). The 1979 Conservative government arrived with a mandate to reduce the functions and powers of the state. Whilst every previous government went through at least the form of working with the policy communities affected by changes of policy, this government was impatient of negotiation and protests on the effects of drastic changes (Young 1989). One minister expressed government's dislike of 'vested interest groups'. He preferred people who would challenge orthodoxy and he would not get this from the representatives of organised groups: 'I am very suspicious of all advisory bodies. I'd cut them all out, and take soundings according to the circumstances. You're far better going through the telephone directory of the universities and just marking ten people ad lib and sending for them' (mac.8).

Further actions from the universities alienated ministers. A vice-chancellor noted: 'That certainly led some Conservatives to ask … why should we be giving more money to people who are wasting their time and the taxpayers' money, our money? … Keith got flour thrown over him at Essex and never let me forget it.' And Rhodes Boyson: 'I had riots wherever I went, I began to have little faith in higher education at all … they wanted a good life did the dons and they liked having all these students from abroad … since that time I have taken much less thought for people permanently in higher education.' Oxford's refusal to award an honorary degree to Margaret Thatcher added to ministers' belief that the universities were too strongly influenced by left-wing ideologues (mac.201).

The universities found no constituency prepared to come to their aid (mac.205), even when they were subjected to the consequences of the most drastic government ideology. The Labour Party and its parliamentary Opposition conducted internal discussions of how to make higher education open to more people, and the importance of strengthening the science base (Salter and Tapper 1994), but provided no clear opposition to either the 1981 cuts or to later reductions in the unit of resource.

By the early 1990s, many of those working in universities were feeling undervalued and out of political and social favour, a phenomenon common to other European countries as well (Taylor 1987). The Carnegie study on the academic professions showed that British academics felt this most strongly (Fulton 1995). This feeling persists among some of the most highly regarded humanists (mac. 211, 214). In higher education, at large, staff considered themselves underpaid even in comparison with those in other publicly funded occupations; rightly so, as we shall analyse later.

The reduction in public and political regard and the consequent proletarianisation of academics (Halsey 1992) was in part reinforced by the sheer growth of the system, which demystified academe and made its operations and practitioners commonplace. Science had grown too large for its own good: 'Every professor expects two of his brightest students to become professors. There is no primogenitor. Costs have expanded. The system has been growing steadily for 300 years but could not go on doubling. If there is a shortage of resources people set up control and bureaucracy' (mac.207; Ziman 1995).

There was then a decisive shift from the traditional view that higher education was important for its own sake and that left largely to itself out of it might come all of sorts of benefits (mac.16), and from the traditional conservative belief in the sustenance of free institutions able to survive on the recognisances of their own expertise. There was a shift towards a range of ideologies which we describe below.

Accountability and managerialism

The accountability of universities and their academic staff had always been regarded as something for which they would take responsibility for themselves. The polytechnics were a different case, coming as they did under the government and financial control of their local authorities and the academic vetting of the CNAA. Even in matters of financial propriety, as we have noted, it was not until 1966 that the universities came under the purview of the Comptroller and Auditor-

General and even then clearances by the universities' own auditors were to be taken on trust (Kogan 1969).

The introduction of NPM throughout government represented a shift towards managerialism in the public services: 'Thatcherism included a clear political commitment to reduce the size of the civil service and increase the efficiency of government ... An Efficiency Strategy was inaugurated ... A powerful combination of careful planning and ideological commitment provided the driving force ...' (Metcalfe and Richards 1990, pp.1–2). A powerful Efficiency Unit, based in the Prime Minister's Office, conducted scrutinies into many aspects of the work of government departments.

The strengthening of accountability mechanisms is noted at several points in our narrative. In Chapter 7 we note some of the changes concerning the growing legalisation of higher education. The emphasis given by the central departments and the funding and research councils to corporate planning and performance indicators (PIs) became stronger. So did institutional leadership, reinforced as it was by the doctrines contained in the Jarratt Report (1985) (see Chapter 7).

The patterns of accountability between universities and the state thus became tighter. But the substantive issues of the curriculum and of research objectives and methods, though affected by funding or other forms of government influence, remained almost wholly within academic discretion. Otherwise, however, the accountability of academics reflected the changing state–institutional patterns. They were constrained less by formal requirements than by the tightening of the boundaries of resource and expectation within which they work. The need to both pull in research resources and attend to larger numbers of students put pressure on discretionary time. Hitherto, university teachers were expected to do their agreed share of teaching, administration, assessment and pastoral work. This left the bulk of their time free for their own research, scholarly or consultancy pursuits. As pressure of resource and quality assurance grew, so a head of department, also under pressure from the institution, was required to consider each academic's contribution to the gradings and earnings of the department. This converted the role from that of a convenor of a collegium into that of a manager of resources. We take up the changing relationships between the state, the institution and the academic base more fully in Chapter 7.

Instrumentalism and the economy

Economic instrumentalism had always been a component of higher education policy, but was generally considered adequately provided by the offer of liberal education that would equip students for a wide range of occupations; some two-thirds of graduates took up occupations unconnected with the fields of their undergraduate studies (Pearson 1985). The universities were thus assumed to be offering transferable learning skills (Boys *et al.* 1988). In any case, the polytechnics had been created to afford an equal place in higher education for applied and vocational education (Crosland 1965; DES 1966). Now, however, these desiderata were to be fashioned in explicit government inducements for the whole system. Less was now to be left to chance. Even before the change in government in 1979, a stronger instrumental emphasis was beginning to be explored for the whole of higher education, at least within government (mac.39; Roizen and Jepson 1985; Tapper and Salter 1978). On becoming Prime Minister in 1976, James Callaghan had told Gordon Oakes that he wanted it to be directed towards the needs of the economy.

The interest in this theme of Margaret Thatcher and the Policy Unit at Number 10 derived from an assumption that the UK was falling behind economically (mac.14) and that higher education had failed to furnish the economy with the right skills and attitudes. The writings to that effect of Wiener (1981), whom Mrs Thatcher used to quote (mac.100), and Correlli Barnett (Barnett 1986) had some influence on a range of ministers including Lawson, Heseltine and Joseph. In 1987 a White Paper restated the 1985 Green Paper's new policy emphases: 'Higher education should serve the economy more effectively ... and have closer links with industry and commerce and promote enterprise' (DES 1987). Universities that followed this prescription were to be rewarded.

One minister denied this policy preference: '... if you go through the participants here – for example, previous holders of my office – I don't think you will find you have a lot of a calloused horny-handed gentlemen who decided they didn't want all that bloody nonsense, that we are going to produce a much more literalist or a teleologically driven system ... but ... there is interest in competitiveness in the market system' (mac.7). It is in fact true that the government did nothing to discourage work in the less useful subjects, as long as it was excellent.

The economic objective was perceived in the institutions as being the most powerful. There was 'a strong government wish that the university system should serve society and the economy by contributing to wealth creation through training as well as educating graduates who are able to go into the community and make an immediate contribution to successful businesses and administration … There was a realisation that the old economic and manufacturing activities of the UK were not going to survive, and the need to offer more sophisticated products made necessary a well-educated, trained and retrained workforce. This led to pressure to increase the system both for economic pay-off and to meet the expectations of the young, and, increasingly, of older groups, of a university education' (mac.16).

In the next chapter we will examine how the drive towards instrumentalism was evident in the attempts to create new emphases: in the curriculum through such initiatives as the Enterprise Initiative; and in research funding through Technology Foresight (mac.101, 102) and by developments in the Science and Engineering Research Council (SERC)(mac.17).

The growth of instrumental approaches may be associated with the way in which the scientific elite became involved with industry. An increasing number from industry now occupied key positions as director-generals of the research councils and as chairs and members of research councils.

Yet, witness evidence shows that there was no obviously direct pressure from industry for changes in the curriculum: 'We just used to moan about it. Ministers were reporting what they thought industrialists ought to want rather than what industrialists said they wanted' (mac.104). It is not clear whether the CBI urged the government to require the research councils to be more orientated towards industry (mac.105). At any rate, the economic strain of policy was not thought by some to be the result of a dialogue with industrialists. 'Researchers at the National Institute of Economic and Social Research probably had more influence. The message that more university graduates should be better focused on the skills and attitudes needed from business and industry was institutionalised in the Council for Industry and Higher Education (CIHE) and reflected in the universities in the increasing role given to their lay councils' (mac.23).

Although there was a growing belief that higher education should serve the needs of the economy more specifically than it had done in the past, there was no consistent thinking about how this could be achieved. Policies were a confusion derived from instrumentalism, a belief in market ideology and acceptance of the need for basic research. One leading scientist described the sequence of policy changes as follows:

> In the early 1980s researchers were encouraged to go and do something useful – Many did, but around 1984/85 ... the government realised that was inconsistent with the principles of the market, i.e. that it was probably not right for the government to fund near-market research in areas that might be applied. So there seemed to be a sea-change when the Thatcher government realised that the proper place for government funding in public institutions was where there was market failure ... as in basic science and therefore they began in the late 1980s to focus on basic science and that caused a lot of confusion amongst the science community ... (and) led to near-market reviews of institutes ... In the last eight to nine years there has been the recognition that we had to become useful not only by doing applied things but by networking and making our basic science available and exploitable. That third emphasis came in the 1990s Tory government (and will probably be continued by the present government with a little more emphasis on health and the environment) and means if you do basic science, maybe in strategic areas, you should make sure that anything that arises from that is exploited and the Intellectual Property Rights are fed back. (mac.115)

William Waldegrave, appointed Minister for Science in 1992, relates: 'I was concerned to redefine the doctrines that were left behind by Mrs Thatcher which were not foolish but which seemed to signal a rather paradoxical belief that anything that had application had to be funded by industry, i.e. that only complete market-failure things could be done by the state sector at all.'

The shift to market systems

A major aspect of Thatcherism consisted of a belief in the free market philosophy as developed by von Hayek and the Austrian school (see, for example, Kavanagh 1987). It is claimed that in relation to science policy Polanyi shared these views (Edgerton and Hughes 1989). He was a leading advocate of the internalist view that scientists should be left to determine their own priorities. There is some evidence, according to Edgerton and Hughes, that Mrs Thatcher, or her advisers, were aware of the Austrian tradition as applied to science policy: 'In her Speech to the Royal Society in 1988 Mrs Thatcher stated that the economic rewards of basic science are "totally unpredictable". She indicated that she has "a great deal of sympathy" for the view that "we should be ready to support those teams, however small, which can demonstrate that intellectual flair and leadership which is driven by intense curiosity and dedication"' (1989, p.422). A further key aspect of Thatcher ideology was monetarism, which involved controlling public expenditure so as to ensure inflation was contained and the private sector of the economy was not 'crowded out'. Whilst such views had an impact generally on the Conservatives, they impinged particularly on higher education when their strongest advocate, Sir Keith Joseph, became Secretary of State for Education.

Markets have taken on several meanings in higher education. In the 'real' market, universities sell services in competition with each other or with such other groups as private management consultants, or costed groups within industry itself. But the metaphor of the market has also been extended in two other ways. It can mean competition for limited resources within bidding systems set up by funding bodies. It can also mean an internal market within institutions where different groups secure resources in return for discernible outputs, such as the numbers of students taught, or buy services from each other and from the central institution.

Part of the objective behind the market modes was to privatise what some would consider an overprotected sector of public activity and to force its activities into open commercial competition. The formal justification, however, rested on social and economic arguments. Thus, the Confederation of British Industry (CBI 1986) argued that a market-led system was required if optimum returns were to be achieved and supply brought into balance, although 'some government intervention will be necessary both because higher education has wider benefits to society and because government has a role to correct possible market failures ... in, for example, providing long-term capital infrastructure or helping students of backgrounds that might deter them from entry ... The size and nature of higher education should be largely determined by the demands of the customers.' It thus opposed rationing. Developments in the labour market, fuelled by the growth of high technology, were creating new needs and opportunities for highly educated manpower, of a kind which higher education existed to provide. There was therefore an economic case for a further rapid expansion in graduate output. The costs of such expansion could not, without unacceptable increases in government expenditure, be met from the public purse. The system must be broken of its heavy dependence on taxpayers' money, and required to sell itself to its immediate clients, the intending students and the employers of graduates (mac.34).

The market was to help both government and institutions become free of their dependence on the deficiency grant system (mac.7, 9). Some saw this in terms of empowerment. Others said, 'Perhaps some believed that.' Institutions were expected increasingly to sell their teaching and research in a real market where a price was struck, sales made and a profit realised. Almost all now sold short courses and consultancies. Some, including some of the richest, had science parks to which commercial firms were attracted by the offer of possible research collaboration with relevant academic groupings. Many did not make a good return on capital, and unless academics were prepared to negotiate their research emphasis, connections were largely symbolic and nominal (Dalton 1987), but the 'Cambridge phenomenon' (Segal, Quince and Partners 1985) has been widely viewed as a successful model (mac.116).

Richard Bird, deputy secretary responsible for higher education in the Department of Education and Science (DES) throughout the 1980s, thought the obvious candidate for consideration as the guiding philosophy behind the action of ministers was the 'promotion of some sort of "market" whose functioning compels greater attention to the customer' (Bird 1994, p.83). In practice, he continued, 'I have always found it hard to discern any clarity of theme or practice which would justify an assertion that a "market approach" (never mind just who are the customers!) was being pursued. In detail there was not always consistency.' In the next chapter we describe some of the attempts to introduce a market system.

Excellence

Policies reflected the multiple and sometimes competing purposes and sponsors of post-school education. There was ministerial support for encouraging excellence (mac.116). The sponsoring of excellent research, in particular, research selectivity, and the restratification or confirmation of existing stratification that went with it, were radical in their explicitness but they were a continuation of traditional policies. So was the assumption that higher education should continue to train an elite for society, the economy and the world of science and learning. The change in policy was that providing for an elite was to be the avocation of a minority of universities. The paradoxical result of massification was that what had already been elite institutions became even more highly meritocratic. 'There are now no leisured dolts at Cambridge. 2 As and 1 B are the rock-bottom qualification, and many have 3 or 4 As. There is now an anxiety that Cambridge is giving too many firsts. The very large number of upper-seconds worries us less in view of the high level of entry' (mac.211).

But this went along with all but general agreement that higher education should continue to expand. The universities and their leading elites were content for this to happen on the assumption that the system would differentiate between different forms of higher education within either a binary system or a differentiated unitary system. Christopher Ball described how: 'I had to think about this question when, as an Oxford don, I was suddenly made chairman of NAB. My friends in Oxbridge said, "They can't possibly be doing higher education, because they are not doing research." I had a personal crisis about it eighteen or nineteen years ago and could not make up my mind about it. Either I take the view that they must do research to be "real" HE and resign or I take the view that research is not essential to teaching. I took the latter view ... But teachers in higher education should be scholars. However, you don't need specific funding for scholarship.'

Egalitarianism

Egalitarianism in higher education had always been a complex and ambiguous issue. Throughout the postwar period it was the prime example of what Anthony Crosland typified as the soft or weak or opportunity concept of equality (Crosland 1962). The access implied by Robbins was to be for those qualified on high criteria by the international standards. This did not, of itself, address the issue of those held to be limited in opportunities of access by social or educational background. Nevertheless, the policy that all qualified applicants would find a place within a highly variegated system of education was an article of faith first expressly legitimated by the Robbins Report (1963). However, it had been conceded by successive governments in the preceding years, and assumed by the UGC in the late 1940s (UGC 1948). It was this principle, somewhat reformulated in 1984 by a statement by the UGC and NAB (UGC and NAB 1984), which legitimated continued expansion, backed as it was by student demand, and it persisted until the mid-1990s when expansion was held back. By the end of our period, the Age Participation Rate was 33 per cent.

If, however, expansion and increased access brought with them greater equality of opportunity, it was not an explicit agenda item. Politician interviewees, but only when asked, maintained that expansion was partly motivated by belief in equal opportunity. When asked whether he recalled, as is stated in Kenneth Baker's auto-biography (1993), that opening opportunity was really the underlying motive, a former minister was uncertain: 'I think that's right. I think it was so. Possibly not.'

One senior policy maker said that throughout all of his time in all of his roles, equality had hardly been mentioned as a factor (mac.14). Policy makers whom we interviewed did not volunteer it as a current policy theme. When asked, most agreed that it was not one that had ever been raised.

One interviewee (mac.2) noted that the Robbins objective of social cohesion, 'a common culture and common standards of citizenship', had been disregarded and was still not being addressed in 1995: 'You can create a sort of meta-unity, but our unity is in our diversity. But we have not found a way of articulating that.' The concern was now much less with generating a more socially just, fair or coherent society, although there was a residual belief in the distributive function of higher education underpinning the support for an expanded system (mac.14, 1).

III MASSIFICATION

Almost all of our interviewees, at all levels of activity, identified the growth of the system as the key factor behind the other major policy changes. It also became a key policy issue in its own right. Given the decline in the unit of resource for core functions, which was accentuated if not created by expansion, the case for selective distribution of research funding became stronger (mac.17). Massif-ication – to use the American neologism – raises the question of whether expansion was a product of other, exogenous factors, or whether it derived from the internal logic of higher education, or whether it was driven by conscious policy intentions. We return to these questions in Chapter 9.

Stages of growth

The standard definitions of different stages of system growth have been those of Trow (1970), who described elite systems as those catering for up to 15 per cent of school leavers, up to 40 per cent recruitment as constituting a mass system, and proportions beyond that creating a universal system of higher education. These figures are contestable: for example, few would have considered the bottom end of the British system which catered in all for 15 per cent of school leavers in 1970 as elite. Also, the proportion of mature students now recruited makes the model less applicable. But if one uses Trow's definition, it can be said that the UK system was on the brink of becoming a mass system by the early 1970s and became such in the latter 1980s.

As noted earlier, the UK had begun in 1945, as did most European systems, with a tiny university population, catering for three per cent – just over 60,000 – of the school-leaver age group. There was a non-university sector located in those technical colleges which offered degree-level work and a further small teacher training college sector. From 1945 to the early 1970s, massification resulted in a virtually spontaneous five-fold expansion to 15 per cent. In the 1970s there was a halting of the expansion in the Age Participation Index (API), probably due to lower job expectations on the part of school leavers, but student numbers drifted upwards with the rise in the number of eighteen-year-olds. In some years, the API even drifted down slightly, but from the mid-1980s there was again a large pick-up in the API as numbers rose, to the surprise of some, despite the downward demographic trends reported earlier. The numbers rose to an eventual 32 per cent in 1995. Figure 3.1 shows how the Age Participation Rate Index for full-time students climbed steadily from 1961 to 1970, after which it levelled out until 1984 and began to climb steeply after 1986.

The numbers in higher education increased from 321,000 in 1962/63 to 1,597,000 in 1995/96[1] (Dearing Report 1997, Chart 3.4) and nearly 1.7 million by 1996/97, although those figures are substantially enhanced by the inclusion of the increased proportions of part-time students and by students attending courses that would not have rated as being of higher education level in 1945. It does not, however, include some 200,000 students undertaking higher education courses in further education institutions. Table 3.2 contains figures (drawn from two sources) which are not entirely consistent with those quoted in the Dearing Report but, nonetheless, confirm the general trends which that report analysed. Higher education had shown that it would take in more students without a proportionate increase in funding, though protesting all the while that a reduced unit of resource would result in lower standards. Efficiency gains of 3 per cent a year were demanded in many years.

not have rated as being of higher education level in 1945. It does not, however, include some 200,000 students undertaking higher education courses in further education institutions. Table 3.2 contains figures (drawn from two sources) which are not entirely consistent with those quoted in the Dearing Report but, nonetheless, confirm the general trends which that report analysed. Higher education had shown that it would take in more students without a proportionate increase in funding, though protesting all the while that a reduced unit of resource would result in lower standards. Efficiency gains of 3 per cent a year were demanded in many years.

The number of universities increased from 24 to 43 between 1945 and 1967 and, on the collapse of the binary divide, to 105 in 1997, a figure, incidentally, well above the OECD norm of one university for one million of the population.

The nature of student demand

The figures above incorporate substantial changes in the composition of the student body. Over time, both the absolute and proportional figures of postgraduate students went up substantially (Dearing Report 1997, Chart 3.3; *Statistical Bulletin* 1996, Table 1). By 1997, nearly 309,000 postgraduate students were in courses. Expansion was also due to a broadening of the range of demand. Whereas early planning assumptions had always predicted the numbers of school leavers entering higher education (mac.5, 14), and a vast upward swing did indeed lead to the 31 per cent rate by 1993/94, the growth to a population of 1.6 million and beyond in the whole sector also depended on the recruitment of many more older entrants and the growth of part-time education. Between 1982 and 1992, the number of full-time equivalent mature students in the first year of courses in British institutions rose by 135 per cent from 66,000 to 155,000 (DFE 1992). As we have seen, the numbers of females entering from all age groups increased.

In the first phase of massification, until the early 1970s, it was assumed that there was a constant replenished reservoir of talent, 'a widow's cruse' in Robbins's term, that given an opportunity could profitably find a place within universities that were research-led or polytechnics that would provide for equally able people but with a more applied bent. This assumption was fed by research on the pool of ability (e.g. Douglas 1964; Floud, Halsey and Martin 1956; Robbins Report 1963). The successive raising of the age of compulsory retention in schools from 14 to 16 years between 1948 and 1972 increased the available pool of those going on to take A levels. In the early 1960s it was already clear that more A-level passes in the schools meant greater pressure for places, and this belief was explicitly articulated by their spokesmen on official bodies (e.g. the Secondary School Examinations Council 1963). The transformation of 75 per cent of secondary schooling from modern to comprehensive schools created different vistas of possibility for many more people. Reforms of O level and the introduction of the GCSE improved staying-on rates and this increased the supply of people able to qualify for higher education (mac.22). The lengthening to three years, in 1962, of the two-year teacher training course added greatly to the student numbers, counting as degree-level students who would contribute to the justification of the polytechnics resource base.

During the first years of expansion, the material standards of what the universities provided were rising: increasing numbers of students were able to be accommodated away from home and staffing ratios improved from 1:10.2 in 1939 to 1:8.6 in 1952, and then to 1:7.2 in 1957. The resulting increases in cost led inevitably to more control over resources (UGC 1958). We have noted earlier the subsequent declines in standards of provision.

The expanded system of the 1970s still sustained traditional concepts of an elite university system, alongside which non-university higher education was allowed to grow, first as part of an advanced further education system and then, from 1966, as the public sector-led polytechnics. In almost all other Western European, American and Australasian systems, both sectors would have been deemed to be university, and, indeed, in ultimate profiles, most became undistinguishable from international concepts of universities, albeit within a steep hierarchy of resources, esteem and proportion of effort expended on recognised research.

The golden age began to crumble from about 1974: with economic and oil crises, rising inflation and concern that the APR had stuck at about 14 per cent (mac.109). Expansion of student numbers was certainly not in the sights of the universities in the late 1970s and early 1980s. 'The government was saying that the number of students would go down and the chairman of the UGC said that he had six universities in his top drawer that had to close because there would not be enough students for them' (mac.46). An earlier chairman of the UGC, Sir Fredrick Dainton, had emphasised the need to protect the unit of resource (mac.44). In 1981, at the time of the cuts, the UGC was told that ministers did not mind whether the cuts would be in students or unit costs; they opted for cuts in student numbers (mac.44). Both Joseph and his junior minister Waldegrave (later to become Minister for Science) were surprised that excluded students went to the polytechnics, and their ability to do so without constraint caused the Treasury to wake up to the fact that student grants were a potentially open-ended commitment. As the need to sustain a viable place in the system became more acute, in the 1980s universities mainly ended their resistance to expansion. 'All civic universities knew they had a physical problem [but] that from being cosy and circumscribed were now being obliged to open up and be more heterogeneous' (mac.17).

We have seen how the economic demand factor is more difficult to connect with either student demand for places or pressures for change in courses and the curriculum. One interviewee (mac.104) referred to pressures coming from industries for, for example, postgraduate provision because of changes in technologies, which made it necessary to switch support from new graduates to older people needing support in the 1980s. This would certainly explain in part the expanded demand for part-time masters' courses evident throughout the system from the 1980s onwards (Becher, Henkel and Kogan. 1994). But it hardly affected the minds and actions of school leavers. Indeed, whilst undergraduate numbers as a whole went up, the demand for places in the hard sciences and technologies remained dauntingly low. Whilst the economy was a factor in the expansion, it was not clear that the long tail of graduates were skilled as a result of going to university or that they could transfer their economic role (mac.107). The main driving force, probably, was youth unemployment – students could sustain an identity and be eligible for at least meagre subsistence grants – and the intuition that in a hardening labour market qualifications might give an edge over competitors for employment.

If the earlier expansion, until the early 1970s, was a largely inert response to demand, so, to a large extent, was the continued gentle expansion of numbers which followed throughout the 1970s as the number of 18-year-olds went up. As Table 3.2 shows, the universities' expansion was much greater than that in the public sector in this decade, which probably reflected student demand. One senior contributor to policy making puts it like this: 'Policies at the end of the 70s were limited in conception.' There was 'no perception of mature and part-time demands. All was based on full-time young students' (mac.5). The analysis was made, therefore, on the narrow basis of numbers of school leavers. The metaphor of 'tunnelling through the hump', that is, a policy of keeping student numbers stable in the early 1980s until increased age groups had passed through the system, implied that as the numbers of 18-year-olds fell back, any feasible increase in the Age Participation Rate would be insufficient to maintain student numbers at the level they would have reached in the peak year of 1982/83. It also implied an unchangeable composition of participation that must be accepted as a planning given. When the going got tough later on, the Department was not ruled by manpower needs but by costs and by the growing criticism of the softer edges of higher education provision. It was assumed that they could 'massage their way through without any major change in policy'. The second wave of expansion which gathered momentum in the 1980s incorporated broader assumptions about access and neither destroyed nor depended on elite concepts of student recruitment and scholarly avocation. Nevertheless, different factors must have been at work in shaping these different phases of expansion.

There were growing expectations on the part of an increasingly prosperous population; in the view of one official (mac.47), expansion was due to deeper social factors and 'the deeper, less quantifiable things like the arrival on the scene of people who were the offspring of the first generation of parents to go to university in any number'. Increased juvenile unemployment made the imbursement and status of student desirable to more young people. There were perceived demands for higher levels of education from the economy: 'To ration a good like higher education was not sustainable. The aspirations of middle-class parents made it impossible to keep it up. Expansion meant the democratisation of access to the economic world' (mac.32). 'The most important factor was the growing bourgeoisification of our society, and the spread... throughout the middle classes and the working class, of the assumption that if you are able to, you should pursue education after 18' (mac.25).

At the same time, proposals were made that the funding bodies should reward institutions which recruited applicants with lower A-level scores and those with non-traditional qualifications (Fulton and Ellwood 1989). The academic gold standard implied by Robbins's principle of social demand would thus be abandoned. British higher education would move from the borderline between an elite and a mass system to being well on the way towards a universal system. With it, the case for an explicit stratification of institutions,

Much of the expansion in higher education consisted of the mainly spontaneous response, especially of the polytechnics, to the growing student demand. One of our interviewees (mac.109) further noted: 'Universities were promoting themselves in a way that they had never done before ... there was latent demand but it also showed that there were huge numbers of people willing to be asked and not needing much convincing.' There is some evidence that demand rises to meet the places available to meet it.

Political attitudes towards expansion

Not only in the 1960s and 1970s was an expansionist doctrine being promulgated throughout the OECD countries (Templeman in Kogan 1975), but leading politicians were putting their shoulders behind higher education as part of economic growth and opportunity, from the 1956 White Paper which promoted technical and technological education (Ministry of Education 1956), through to the appointment of the Robbins Committee (1963). The Minister during the first key period of take-off was expansionist to his marrow. David Eccles, more than any other politician, initiated the pressure for expansion – he was already making the case for it in a speech in the House of Commons on the Crowther Report on secondary education in 1960 (Eccles 1960) – and launched the series of events that led to the setting up of the Robbins Committee. It was supported by the human capital arguments put forward by economists and fully argued in the Robbins Report (1963, paras 620–630), which legitimised the expansion that was already happening and made explicit the policy that all qualified applicants should find a place somewhere within a highly variegated system.

One interviewee noted that politicians began to respond to the social changes and that, for example, the Tory parliamentary group on education in the 1970s saw expansion as a response to unmet demand rather than economic need and thought it particularly important to mothers 'wanting things for their daughters' (mac.17).

The first official questioning of demand-driven expansion had been in the Brown Paper (DES 1978) which opened a public debate on ways of containing or at least planning the demographically driven expansion that might occur in the next few years. The 1981 cuts were originally intended to reduce university expenditure rather than the number of students. In the early 1980s, 'Sir Keith Joseph was prone to question the policy and this was because of a concern to save money rather than a positive attempt to reduce numbers. He quite often said,

"And I don't rule out having to close institutions." At the same time, his reluctance to sponsor expansion and ... his view on higher education [was] ... influenced by the reception he got from left-wing students when he went round universities and polytechnics ... he thought expansion meant more and more left-wing people being in university who really weren't getting the kind of education which would help the economy' (mac.105). He 'had the Kingsley Amis attitude towards higher education ... that more was likely to mean worse ...' (mac.9).

Whatever the explanations for expansion, a purposive and continuous policy in its favour is not one. The expansion of the 1980s was 'a policy that we stumbled on more by accident than design, although there will be a lot of people wanting to take credit for it after the event, but you have to ask yourself, how many people actually intended to do what they were doing, in the sense of creating a conscious policy move. A typical British muddle' (mac.2). In 1984 the merger of small departments was taking place, and at that stage 'there wasn't the belief that participation rates would increase dramatically. We were still talking about the contracting system' (mac.103) but policy on expansion was still confused. Nothing was done to inhibit the expansion of the polytechnics and, indeed, at least one minister believed they should expand (mac.40), but the overall policy for the two sectors taken together had hardly been thought through and at the time '... when NAB was being created, [Joseph] pointed to the downward demographic trend. He said we've got about 30 polytechnics in England. By the end of the decade we'll probably need half of that number ... There was no sense that this was an opportunity to widen access. We argued back with him ... You'll find it in NAB writing the new principle of providing for all who are able to benefit, which, in the end, may mean everybody!' (mac.2).

The NAB made much of the running and issued a joint statement in 1984 with the UGC. This reformulated the Robbins axiom and stated: 'Courses of higher education should be available for all those who are able to benefit from them and who wish to do so.' Although this reformulation was included by Joseph in the 1985 Green Paper, it was accepted only with 'important caveats' (DES 1985, para. 3.2). Nevertheless, Christopher Ball argues:

> From that moment onwards, we had won the access argument with ministers and were able to refer back to it. Ministers did not quite know what it meant. They had not thought through what they are now discovering about the ability to benefit. Robbins was

right about the widow's cruse. That there is no limit to the pool of ability. We knew that and the question was how fast we could move towards increasing access while maintaining quality ...

Joseph did not see that the change from 'qualified' to 'ability to benefit' was the sea-change ... the binary division helped him. He could be fastidious about university courses because that was 'real higher education' whereas here was this NAB thing pushing forward and expanding vocational polytechnic courses, if you did not look too closely. Of course, that wasn't what was really happening: we were expanding access to a wide range of general and specialist courses of advanced learning and massively increasing participation in higher education. It was NAB that converted Britain from an elitist system to mass higher education. And a good thing, too.

In spite, however, of the acceptance of a reformulated Robbins principle, the Green Paper still referred to falling student numbers. This assumption was criticised by the CVCP (1986) and the CBI (1986). They challenged both the figures and the policy assumptions contained in it.

If the degree of consensus on the rightness of expansion was strong and became stronger rather than weaker as time went on, it was based on no systematic analysis of social or economic need. For most of our period, ministers and officials let it happen, almost as if it were a force of nature that could and should not be contained. But this would be at a price: 'Over all looms the old notion which emerged with Shirley Williams long ago that the staff ratios in universities were all wrong. So the Treasury would say yes to more people but only on condition that each cost a great deal less' (mac.46).

Rather than a dominant expansionist ideology, it is more likely that political attitudes towards it were varied so that, of the two Secretaries of State for much of the 1980s, Joseph was sceptical whilst Baker was positive. The thinking behind the changing attitude was complex:

There was always demand – not very well considered – from the academic community for expansion. The change was a reflection of changes in ideals and values in the wider society which led to an increased focus on formal qualification and learning as being important in career opportunities and life chances. These are a part of bourgeoisification ... The value shifts were not uni-directional. People are not motivated by a desire to achieve equality of opportunity but by the desire to achieve opportunity ... Bourgeoisification is in the interest of the Conservative Party. More people coming from HE and moving into professional middle-class positions in society means more Conservatives, part of the erosion of Labour's working-class base. (mac.25)

and

You were finding pathways for merit and opportunity, a wider, more flexible attitude to access. That looked very much a Tory agenda and to an extent a Major-ite classless society. (mac.43)

and

'Kenneth Baker's speech at Lancaster in 1986 was the clearest expression of political support for expansion. He said that the UK should plan to double its participation rate over the next 25 years. At the same time, there was no significant pressure from the sector to expand, and only limited demand from students for additional places. The speech represented a personal aspiration from Baker. The Treasury were informed and were not concerned given the long-term horizon' (mac.108). Kenneth Baker was later to note that his main motivation was to open up higher education to more people. 'He was determined to do it ... he was opportunistic and expansionary by nature' (mac.40). At that time, Conservative Party managers thought the expansion policy initiated by ministers was good (mac.100).

There was also a view that in the mid-1980s the Treasury were convinced that there was a case for expansion of higher education to match other countries' levels of participation. For Richard Bird, 'Treasury reluctance was lessened by the experience that more could be had with an apparently steady squeeze on the unit of resource; by the changed demographic outlook; and by recognition that frustrated students frequently swelled the ranks of the unemployed. In this setting all the political arguments might seem to point towards giving positive messages on student numbers. These began, then, in 1986/87' (Bird 1994, p.76). Thus, when demand for graduates seemed to be growing, the downward demographic forecasts, and yet the continuing demand for places in higher education, probably made it easier and more pertinent for ministers to argue the expansionist case. The position had changed dramatically from that in the late 1970s and early 1980s when, as we have seen, the assumption was that the falling demographic trend would inevitably result in fewer students and excess capacity if the system was allowed to expand too fast.

Kenneth Baker claimed that in his 1989 Lancaster speech he 'set a target in one in three by the year two thousand' (Baker 1993, p.235). However, the suggestion in the 1991 White Paper of a one-in-three participation rate by 2000 was not thought of as a target but an extrapolation or estimate of the consequence of this demand-driven process. 'There was no central model that said: "Thou shall recruit." There were incentives, but responding to incentives didn't have a long track record ...' (mac.7). The participation rate was achieved in two years and those involved were surprised by the size and speed of expansion and extent to which funding encouraged expansion or, in the view of the Treasury, over-delivered it (mac.7, 9, 108). 'For quite a long time I don't think any of us really believed that numbers would take off the way that they did' (mac.7,4). In spite of doubts entertained by some ministers, Baker's expansionist assumption remained unchallenged until the mid-1990s.

The market mechanisms worked much more rapidly than the politicians had expected. The expansion was, however, suddenly halted by the decision in 1993 to change the funding arrangements (described in the next chapter) and introduce a Maximum Aggregate Student Number (MASN) for each institution. This meant that the numbers entering universities levelled off, although the total number of students continued to increase for a few years as the entry figures established in 1993 worked their way through the system.

In 1994 a visit to Malaysia, where a challenge was lodged by those used to sending students to the UK, caused the Secretary of State of the time to raise the question of graduate standards in the expanded system. This led to Higher Education Quality Council (HEQC) exercises on the subject, as described in Chapter 4. In 1996 a minister responsible for higher education expressed doubt about the policy of provision meeting demand (Forth 1996).

Attitudes of industry to expansion

The CBI's response to the 1985 Green Paper (CBI 1986) maintained, on the basis of careful analysis, that the government had underestimated future demand and that a higher proportion of the UK population should benefit from higher education (para. 3.14, p.12). However, the notorious difficulty of recruiting a single view from industry on any important matter is reflected in the evidence from policy makers and academics about employers' view of expansion. Some thought politicians were pushing for expansion more strongly than industry. 'In many cases, employers appeared to be more interested in graduates as a source of talented recruits – because the more able school leavers increasingly went into higher education – than they were in the value of higher education itself.

education – than they were in the value of higher education itself. Ministers felt that businessmen would be keen on the expansion of higher education. But I never remember any senior businessman urging the case for the expansion of higher education with the same enthusiasm as the politicians who advocated it. My impression is that many businessmen felt that the money would be better spent raising standards in the schools' (mac.22). 'The Department of Industry put an interpretation on what they thought industry ought to want. There were differing views among the CBI and Engineering Employers' Associations' (mac.105). There was not as much pressure from industry for an expansion of higher education in the 1980s as there was to provide a mix of people trained and educated to change with industrial changes. They wanted a secure supply of able technicians (mac.101). 'Industry did not feel there was a shortage of people. Both the expansion and the ending of the binary system got a head of steam without a lot of substance to them' (mac.16). The leading role played by the CBI in attacking the 1985 Green Paper seems to be overlooked in comments such as: 'Once it became fashionable, bodies like the CBI, (Institute of Directors) IOD and Chambers of Commerce are very good at retaining and repeating views which they have derived from someone else. Investment in human capital was a second-hand view to peddle' (mac.206).

The view coming from industry was not consistent. 'CBI has changed its views a bit. In the early 1990s they were highly instrumental. They have now moved into core skills, and understand that intellectual capacity is the most important core skill that you can have ... (mac.206) There was pressure from business reflecting their views of the changing nature of work and the qualifications required. Pressure had built up since the Black Papers, Callaghan's Ruskin College speech to consider the implications of the education system for competitiveness.' (mac.25) One leading policy maker observed that employers were, in fact, divided in their support of expansion: 'The CBI and the Engineering Employers' Associations often had different views, the Engineering Employers were looking for more HND-type technicians than graduates, whereas CBI were looking for graduates in particular spheres; yet when one talked locally to employers and the CBI regional branches, they had different views from that at the centre – there was no one view from employers but the government on the whole listened to the CBI.' With not much consensus coming from industry '... the number of graduates, let alone PhDs, in control of industry, was minute, whereas in Germany it was over 50 per cent ... that was the great difference between the industries of the two countries at the time in the 70s and 80s – manufacturing industry in this country was going to its nadir ... and the DTI felt we needed better-educated management in manufacturing' (mac.105).

The Council for Industry in Higher Education explicitly made the case for expansion. In the 1990s the CBI argued first for a recruitment of 40 per cent, then for 50 per cent, to be achieved by the year 2000. At any rate, 50 per cent should be qualified up to level 3 (CBI 1994). They consulted their members on whether post-school expansion should be in further education or higher education and members opted for the expansion to be mainly in higher education, but demand-led (mac.34; CBI 1994).

Institutions' views

Much of the 1980s expansion was the spontaneous response of the polytechnics to student demand. This started in the early 1980s, at a time when the UGC were determined to maintain their unit costs. Some claimed that the government deliberately channelled expansion into the polytechnics at the time of the 1981 cuts (mac.40). Another version is that the NAB-planned expenditure levels for 1984/85, which were devised during 1982–83, 'had been bounced on them ... by the expansion of individual institutions: NAB was really dominated by local authorities; the DES – the people who held the money – they would not have promoted expansion ... individual entrepreneurial skills [were] exercised by individual polys ... Much of the expansion took place in the social sciences which were cheaper to provide' (mac.105).

Christopher Ball recalled that the NAB 'took a conscious decision to keep that inflationary mode in being, suspecting that it would encourage institutions to continue to recruit. During the 80s we kept a light hand on the tiller to ensure that the expansion was reasonably responsible, regionally balanced, that it did not go so far that quality was put at risk, listening carefully to HMI and CNAA, doing enough over planning to persuade the government that we were being ferocious whilst at the same time allowing a drift upwards in expansion.'

Expansion elicited conflicting responses from the institutions. In facing the expansions of the 1990s and the reduction in the unit of resource, the older universities expressed anxiety about the quality of what was being provided in the new universities. A ministerial view of this was: 'Whilst the universities had remained fairly static and expected the same units of resource, the polytechnics had expanded dramatically and had concerned themselves with education that was adjacent to training. They had developed new courses which seemed relevant to students and to industrialists. They had willingly made mixtures of subjects that would appeal to students. The universities could have been far more open' (mac.1).

The approach of the public sector was unequivocally expansionist (mac.49). It was not simply that the funding systems encouraged expansion. Expansion catering for a problem-orientated, student-centred kind of education was ventilated at seminars held by the CDP with eminences from HM Inspectorate such as Sheila Browne, Pauline Perry and Eric Bolton. Metaphors flowed freely. In the polytechnics, as cuts first affected the universities in 1981, they were determined to 'turn the burner up' (mac.6). William Stubbs recalls saying in a lecture: 'The universities were like galleons; they were strong, they were symbolic of power and wealth and they could sail the globe, but the polytechnics were caravels, they could come in shore and they could shift with the wind. Be responsive to opportunities. Not for them the imperial routes, more the trade routes.'

It was later in the 1980s and into the 1990s that the polytechnics and, increasingly, some universities looked to expand most rapidly. At the institutional level, the PCFC system of funding places for students encouraged expansion in the polytechnics, where the largest expansions took place. Although the system-wide fees-only policy cut across this PCFC methodology (mac.15), it also was a key factor in access for polytechnics as well as universities. It involved unfunded student numbers or the ability to take on students for whom institutions collected only fees, not grants (mac.27). These later became recognised as part of the baseline on which grants were allowed. 'This drove a lot of expansion.' At any rate, 'every time they expanded, higher education demand increased' (mac.2). Many universities expanded dramatically in the early 1990s.

The consequences of the changing scale of the system

Faculty numbers

As the Dearing Report crisply put it, 'historical information on academic staff numbers across higher education as a whole does not exist'. The number of UK academic posts increased from nearly 42,000 teaching and research staff in the universities in 1989/90

(Halsey 1992, Table 6.2, p.132), or 38,300 full time equivalent teaching staff if one takes the DFE figures (HE Statistics 1993, Table 23), and 25,000 higher education teachers in non-university institutions in 1989/90 (HE Statistics 1993) to 91,000 teachers (of whom 20,900 were part-time) and 33,300 researchers (of whom 3700 were part-time) in 1996/97 (Dearing Report 1997, Table 3.1, p.29).[2]

Staffing ratios

Standards of provision changed under the impress of expansion. The ratio of full-time students to full-time university staff rose from 8.1 to 11.2 between 1971/72 and 1989/90 (Halsey 1992, Table 4.5, p.99). In the old universities the ratio of full-time equivalent students to full-time staff fell from 9.5 in 1981/82 to 14.0 in 1993/94. In all universities in the unified sector, the ratio reached 17 in 1994/95. Moreover, by 1994/95 52 per cent of academic staff appointed were employed on fixed-term or other insecure contracts (AUT 1996).

Funding

Funding under the HEFC heading for the UK (including Northern Ireland) in 1995/96, that is provisions made by both local education authorities (LEAs) and central government, came to a total of £5,907 million[3] (including mandatory awards made in respect of students in non-HEFC institutions) (Office of National Statistics *Annual Abstract of Statistics* 1997, Table 1.1). The grants plus fees for full-time equivalent students in Great Britain were predicted to fall, however, between 1995/96 and 1998/99 from £4,904 to £4,305 (in real terms), a drop of 12.2 per cent. This drop was higher in England (at 12.8%) than in Scotland (10.3%) or Wales (8.1%) (AUT 1996).

Academic salaries suffered considerable attrition when compared with those of comparable groups. The Association of University Teachers (AUT) suggested to the Dearing Committee that whilst university salaries remained unchanged in real terms from 1981,

2   Only those teachers and researchers on more than a 0.25 contract are included in these official figures. Those undertaking extramural work are thus excluded.
3   Again, we have to note conflicting official figures. The figure given by the Office for National Statistics for 1996/97 is £4,132 million (see Table 3.2). The Dearing Report (Table 17.1) shows public sources of funding, 1995/96, as £4,452 million but £7,123 million from total public sources including fees, research grants and other public sources.

comparable groups had seen increases from between 18 and 50 per cent. The CVCP, evidently using different bases of comparison, observed that while university teachers' pay grew by 8.6 per cent in real terms between 1961 and 1993, non-manual male workers in general saw their pay increase by 37 per cent (Dearing Report 1997, para. 3.47, p.32).

It was this relative worsening of salaries, staffing ratios and general esteem that gave rise to the concept of the 'proletarianisation' of the academic profession (Halsey 1992; Salter and Tapper 1994).

CONCLUSIONS

The historical account in this chapter illuminates some of the contexts within which policy changed and, in particular, the great expansion of higher education which constituted both context and consequence of policy change. In Chapter 4 we go on to address the other main policy movements that have so deeply affected the working of higher education. We append to that chapter a chronology of the main milestones of the period of reform.

Within the contexts provided by demography, changing economic and social circumstances and the changing nature of knowledge, we have to reckon with changing belief systems or ideology. The free-standing and independent institution, and the profession that it housed, was not wholly replaced by an ideology that enhanced the role of a nationally directed system. Indeed, by most international standards, British universities continue to enjoy considerable degrees of freedom. But there was certainly a shift. There was a change in boundary between the public and private domains. The trust placed in professions gave way to, at best, a testing and, at worst, a mistrusting relationship which entailed political alienation from the universities. In Chapter 7 we will give an account of pressures for growing accountability and managerialism within the universities. Throughout, there was shift towards instrumentalism and the advancement of claims of the economy and to market behaviour. Egalitarianism, an explicit motive in the 1960s, was hardly on the agenda, except inasmuch as widened opportunity provided one form of it.

From our account of the genesis of expansion, we can say that it was not wholly expected, let alone planned. Some interests, and notably the polytechnics, saw advantage in it, both for their potential clients and for themselves, and eventually reaped rich rewards. Those in command of the public sector, as institutionally expressed in the

NAB, lent support. Expansion gained support from ministers, by no means throughout the 1980s, but at critical points in policy evolution, and, in retrospect, it was seen as a contributor to the bourgeois-ification process that the ruling Conservative Party would endorse.

The growth of the system is commonly regarded as triggering off many of the changes that occurred in British higher education in the 1980s and 1990s. It is assumed by many of those interviewed to have opened up higher education to vigorous public policies, to have led to the creation of structures for quality assurance, the reduction of funding for each student, more government control, the implosion of the binary system, and more explicit stratification and selectivity. These related policy developments are taken up in Chapters 4, 5 and 6.

Chapter 4

The Reform Movement: Objectives and Policies

I MAIN POLICY MOVES

Within these contexts, part policy-created, part emanating from the changing nature of society and the economy and part resulting from changes in ideology, there have been major shifts in government policies. A rationalistic account of policy formation would seek to show some linear relationship between these changing contexts and ideologies and the formation of policies which are then given operational form in statements and the pursuit of objectives. But as our example of the moves towards expansion (discussed in Chapter 3) shows, for the most part the changes were not preceded by any attempt to evaluate higher education to see if it was in need of reform and sometimes not even by systematic working-out of, or pronouncements on, policies. Similarly, in the 1980s: '...most of the significant developments of the decade happened in piecemeal and pragmatic fashion. There were certainly some overall trends of policy, though these could by no means be assembled into any kind of grand strategy' (Bird 1994, p.83). So although we begin our description with the policies that emerged, not always systematically, from the policy makers, we cannot produce any convincing and comprehensive account of their links with objectives.

Moreover, policies did not all emerge as consistent with each other. For example, the somewhat deterministic science policies, intended to enhance the link with economic productivity, did not fully accord with policies of a free market government. Nor did they easily sit with the continuing belief in sponsoring academic excellence for its own sake, as incorporated in the working of the research assessment exercises. Thus, the research and the funding councils pursued somewhat different selectivity criteria. If policies were shot through with ambivalences, could that be defended on the grounds that government made constructive use of ambiguity in that it enhanced diversity or eclecticism while pursuing broadspan ambitions for the expansion of opportunity?

Until the advent of the Conservative government in 1979, the objectives of higher education, by which was largely meant university education, were those expressed in the Robbins Report: '...instruction in skills suitable to play a part in the general division of labour ... what is taught should be taught in such a way as to promote the general powers of the mind ... the advancement of learning ... the transmission of a common culture and common standards of citizenship' (Robbins Report 1963, paras 25–28). These objectives became more complicated and often potentially contradictory as time went on. 'The hierarchy of objectives must change its balance overall when you move from an elite system for 4 or 5 per cent to a more or less mass system ... With that sort of participation rate, transmission of values ... and ... transmission of a dominant culture become a rather different concept. Research for the majority of those 40 or 50 per cent of the population going through HE is simply a spectre' (mac.40).

Associated with expansion were reduced funding for each student and changes in financial systems, including attempts to introduce market approaches. With expansion and economic considerations might be associated the concern for selectivity and the development of the powerful new quality assurance policies. Each of these policy developments is analysed in this chapter and, for completeness, we allude to the conversion of the binary into a unitary system, the changes in government and planning, and the shift from collegial to managerial power, at both the national and institutional levels. However, these three issues are so important that each is incorporated into its own chapter – Chapters 5, 6 and 7 respectively. We conclude this chapter by considering the attempts to change the substantives of higher education: the curriculum and research.

The ending of the quinquennial system, changes in financial systems and moves towards markets

We have seen how changes in the funding arrangements were a product of not only expansion but of changes in the political and economic environment and in ideology. The inevitability of growing and demand-led expenditure was thus more easily questioned.

Looking at the period overall, university grants per student suffered from a 10 per cent reduction in the 1970s through failures to compensate fully for inflation; between 1980/81 and 1989/90, unit costs in the universities fell by 5 per cent and in the polytechnics by no less than 21 per cent (Williams 1992); between 1976 and 1998, the reduction in funding for all higher education was over 46 per cent per unit of funding (Dearing Report 1997, para. 17.16). A former secretary to the UGC noted how the Robbins Report had failed to consider the costs of increased numbers, even on the scale that they had predicted the system would reach (Carswell 1985). The value of student assistance went down progressively, and by 1997 it seemed inevitable that tuition fees would be charged and that the system of maintenance grants would be radically changed. These changes were in fact introduced by the Labour government that came into power in 1997.

1972–77 was the last period in which even the illusion of advance and largely unpredicated quinquennial funding of the universities had been sustained. In 1973/74 there were particularly fierce cutbacks. In 1974 the award of a committee on public sector teaching salaries (Houghton Report 1974) created for the first time – if temporarily – higher salaries in the public than in the university sector and the government's reluctance to remove this anomaly was evidence, perhaps, of changing attitudes towards the universities.

1974/75 became the last year in which substantial capital funds were available through the UGC (Moore 1987). And from then the quinquennial system of funding, which had already began to falter, came to an end. One vice-chancellor quoted Dorothy Sayers at the UGC in 1973 that their latest letter was 'like the thirteenth stroke of a grandfather clock which sheds doubt on all those that preceded it' (Kogan 1975, p.197). In 1977 the UGC had to report a conclusive downturn in the process of growth and a series of ad hoc decisions related to changing national pressures: 'As a result there is a deep and damaging sense of uncertainty which can only be removed by the restoration of the long term planning horizons' (UGC 1977) – a viewpoint repeated in the Croham Report (1987) ten years later. It was accepted that the taxpayers should receive full value for money.

The quinquennium was fleetingly replaced by the triennium, which 'was thought to be the one triumphant thing to emerge from the chaos of the IMF' (mac.41). Step by step from the mid-1970s, the universities' almost unique freedom in finance was reduced, and by the end of the 1970s the notion of a sacrosanct unit of resource was coming under criticism (see Chapter 6).

In 1979 the process of charging overseas students a higher fee than that required of home-based students, begun in 1967 by Anthony

Crosland, was carried to its extreme and also used as a further means of cutting government subsidy. Institutions lost funds on the assumption that they could be recouped by recruiting the same number of overseas students in 1980 as before, even though fees would be much higher. The government was widely criticised for its lack of consultation (mac.30), a criticism made specifically by the House of Commons Education, Science and Arts Committee (Williams 1981, p.41), and for its lack of regard for the way in which it discriminated against institutions recruiting many such students or for the more general effects on Britain's role as a major world provider of higher education.

It was, however, not until 1981 that the framework policy premise, namely that higher education would be driven by student demand, that all qualified students should get a place, within relatively steady units of resource, came under challenge. That assumption was challenged by the first drastic reductions in funding for universities, made at a time when student numbers were projected to rise – it was the government's good luck that the polytechnics showed themselves willing to admit the applicants thus displaced. Taking together the reduction in recurrent grant for overseas student fees and the cuts imposed in 1981, the universities lost between 13 and 15 per cent of their income over the following three years, depending on how many overseas students were recruited. It took some years to restore these overseas student numbers, which finished up being redistributed differently between institutions (mac.25).

The 1981 moves to reduce the financial commitment to higher education were the first to lead to staff reductions and the closure of university courses. They resulted less from specific higher education policy than from a general Treasury-led movement to limit public expenditure (Kogan and Kogan 1983; mac.110). This was seen as a product of Treasury thinking and particularly that of such permanent secretaries as Peter Middleton, as much as anything coming from Number 10 Downing Street. All the evidence is that ministers responded to a Treasury demand for reductions in expenditure with no clear thought about their effects on the ultimate balance of the system, though at least one grew to approve of the cuts (mac.8): 'The Treasury were pushing for the cuts ... I thought they were fair: I wasn't worried about it ... HE at that time was a privileged pursuit – it's less of a privileged pursuit now ... in many cases they were better off on pupil/teacher ratios than they were in America. That's an exaggeration.' He would have liked a system of generous scholarships for the most able but with emphasis on the subjects likely to be useful to the nation. The rest would have to pay economic fees.

There are contested accounts of how government viewed the changing balance of numbers brought about by the 1981 cuts (mac.8, 41). Our interview evidence is that whilst government accepted that the decision was to be wholly that of the UGC (mac.30, 41, 48), it had expected that they would keep to the same level of admissions but reduce unit costs. The consensus is that the UGC were left to determine how to administer the reductions, which appears to be an abdication of central government responsibility, but that, afterwards, ministers were unhappy at the decision to cut numbers rather than the unit of resource – the universities hoped that the reduction would persuade government to restore some of the cuts. Keith Joseph phoned the chairman of the UGC, Sir Edward Parkes, at breakfast time to beg him not to cut the number of university places (mac.18). In a much criticised decision (for example, Kogan and Kogan 1983), they decided to reduce student numbers by about 20,000. It has been argued (Moore 1987) that had this not been done the government would have thought the UGC to be failing in its main function. In the event, nothing approaching that reduction occurred, because of the continuing high demand for places and the difficulties of removing so many staff positions.

1981 was a year of drastic policy change and marks the start of the final period of our analysis (see Chapter 3). 'July 1981 was the crucial date. Before then, there was very little government policy for higher education. After 1981, the government took a policy decision to take policy decisions, and other points such as access and efficiency moves then followed' (mac.44).

The cuts were visited differentially on the universities. They were done so on broad judgements made from diverse sources on research quality, and more objective data such as the level of A levels. The criticisms that followed concerned the lack of transparency about the criteria used (Salter and Tapper 1994), the fact that there were huge differences in the amounts lost by some universities and the fact that most technological universities did badly. Some universities, such as Keele, fell foul of the policy criteria which particularly penalised those institutions with a bias towards the arts and social sciences (Stewart 1989). One result was that some new universities, including three technological universities, were given good gradings which established them publicly among the ranks of well-established institutions.

The effects of the tightening of resources on the universities were complex. One official (mac.31) described how the universities cut back substantially on student numbers because they had been led to believe that the total of vote-funded higher education was cash limited. The large cutting of grants and selective distribution of them fell particularly on the more vocational universities, and those that were most squeezed were the ones closest in character to the polytechnics. Students who would have gone to those universities turned to the polytechnics.

The new Conservative government had already turned its attention, in 1979, to the public sector's funding arrangements. These consisted of the Advanced Further Education (AFE) pool which was theoretically an unlimited commitment of resources from which local authorities could draw to fund their polytechnics and colleges. Ministers, according to one of the officials involved, 'seized on the need to eliminate the open-endedness of the pool. That this process came to be known as "capping" is proof of the potency of the mixed metaphor in Whitehall' (Jones 1983, p.2). Following discussions with local authorities in the summer and autumn of 1979, the necessary legislation was enacted in the 1980 Education Act. This provided that the Secretary of State should determine the size of the AFE pool in advance for each year and after consultation with the local authorities. The way that distributions from the capped pool were made illustrates inconsistency between the two parts of the DES dealing with higher education. 'Authorities putting together pool claims for 1981/82 had without difficulty been able to read the "unit cost" writing on the wall and had without difficulty concluded the way to produce a forecast and a claim implying a low unit cost was to bid up the student number element. This they duly did' (Jones 1983, p.12). So although unit costs were being squeezed in the polytechnics, the system encouraged them to take extra students at the time that the universities were facing reductions. This also created a climate in which polytechnics realised that they needed to come together in some sort of a planning framework. It contributed to the move in favour of the creation of the NAB.

As we have seen, the polytechnics rapidly used their freedom over admissions to recruit many of the students who were unexpectedly refused university places (mac.6). By the end of the 1980s there was an enormous growth in some polytechnics. They brought in many more students, on the assumption that eventually they would enhance their resource base. At any rate, the universities, it can be seen with hindsight, had made a major strategic error in not sustaining student numbers.

The Secretary of State for Education, Sir Keith Joseph, was concerned more than any other spending minister to reduce levels of public expenditure, driven as he was by a monetarist ideology. According to a senior civil servant at the time: 'By the mid-1980s preoccupation over the scale on which resources were having to be devoted to HE was undiminished. Joseph, indeed, often proclaimed privately his disposition to assist the Chancellor by cutting back expenditure right across education and invited his senior officials to come up with proposals accordingly. But, in addition, questions were being voiced by ministers and some of their advisers over whether much of the HE output was economically valueless and even "damaging to the spirit of enterprise", and whether therefore HE should be both reduced in scale and somehow drastically reformed. Officials at the time detected a belief that expert opinion would necessarily be skewed to reflect and protect the interests of producers at the expense of the community, and a related reluctance to receive and consider it. Accordingly, serious dialogue with academics was essentially disavowed, and evidence supporting prejudices, such as that against sociology, given excessive attention' (mac.5).

The UGC allocations in 1981 were significant in that they incorporated differential quality judgements, thus beginning the explicit stratifying of universities and departments which became more open in the 1986 research assessment exercise (RAE). In the latter, the UGC graded cost centres (clusters of subject disciplines) in four bands, and published the results, a procedure repeated with variations in 1989. Some 14 per cent of UGC funds to universities were to be distributed according to the hierarchy of esteem established by such gradings. The notion that all British universities formed part of an elite group was thus called into question.

As we have seen, by the time the Conservatives were in office, confidence in the capacities of higher education to manage resources began to decline. 'In fields where the government was articulating and in many cases initiating changes, the demands for accountability were predominant. The system was bigger and spending more, so the Treasury, Public Accounts Committee and newspapers began to ask, "Is it spent properly, are financial controls tight?" In some ways, more significant is the general distrust articulated by Conservative governments of special interest groups – this applies to all professions – feeling they easily slide into self-congratulation and comfortable security with declining responsibility to the community. This led to demands for them to account for what they do' (mac.16).

Within the UGC in its latter days and the HEFCs later on, there were shifts in the emphasis and methodology of funding (mac.103). The funding methodology had been thought to be a mystery until 1985. It seemed to be based upon, simply, the adding to historic commitments. The UGC, however, moved increasingly towards a more transparent and objective methodology in which, in broad terms, students in a given subject matter would get the same money wherever they were, but that research funding must be based upon quality assessment (mac.45), as referred to above and described in more detail in the next section. Alongside reductions, changes in the production of information on cost in departments sharpened the awareness of accountability and were related to judgements made on quality (mac.31, 40). Financial forecasting models were developed. There was a move from the exclusive focus on subjects towards institutional focusing and demands for strategic plans. There were also attempts to consider funding and distribution on a regional basis.

In the 1980s the Public Expenditure Survey procedures were already dominating the annual expenditures of funding and research councils (mac.204). Each year a policy scrutiny was required which made it imperative for arguments in favour of sustaining existing levels, or ensuring that cuts were not deep, or for additional money, to be made so as to accord with what was perceived to be government policy. Both the reduction in unit costs and the pressures to pursue government's preferences were, no doubt, among the reasons why increasingly in the 1980s the universities applied effort to securing external funding (mac.208). 'External sources of funding for research are important. Last year [1996/97] the external resources grew by 7.8 per cent. The year before by 7.7 per cent. And in the years preceding those rather more' (mac.208). The search for money, however, went alongside an increase in productivity as measured by, for example, publications in the technological subjects, of which 80 per cent came from universities (OST 1997).

In various ways, there had already been moves in a market direction. There was a competitive search for new sources of potential student recruitment through reformulating basic units and degree programmes. This was particularly marked in relation to courses leading to a professional qualification, such as accounting and nursing studies, where the interest groups concerned were generally successful in persuading institutions to offer graduate status to entrants to the profession and to create chairs in the subjects. It also applied to traditional disciplines which might find themselves merged in communications, business, information or tourist studies (Boys *et al.* 1988).

Ministers encouraged the new funding councils that started operating in 1989, the Universities Funding Council and the Polytechnics and Colleges Funding Council, to introduce market mechanisms. These were to be in addition to the system, referred to in the previous chapter, of fees-only students for whom institutions did not receive grants but which would become recognised later as part of the baseline on which grants would be based. The PCFC approach was that the institutions were in the market bidding for funds and it would promote the characteristics of a market. To the criticism that it was not a real market because there was only one buyer, the answer was 'it's not quite that because the students are buyers too'. The methodology enabled those polytechnics which were ahead of the game, even at low unit costs, to prosper (mac.31). The approach adopted by the PCFC, which entailed institutions bidding for extra funded places beyond a certain baseline, was viewed favourably because it made a particular effort to identify certain programmes of 'outstanding quality' and to reward the institutions providing them by favouring their bids for places (PCFC 1990). The council also employed a 'moderation factor' to limit the rate of growth which might otherwise have been attained by institutions tendering low prices per student in the 1990/91 exercise. Thus, an explicit attempt was made to both reward quality and to limit the risk of quality degradation to which the tendering process might otherwise lead, and to preserve some institutions tendering at very low rates from the consequences of their actions: 'This approach, combined with gradual introduction of tendering by the PCFC, seems calculated to generate some of the efficiency gains from the process whilst avoiding some of the more obvious risks' (Cave, Hanney and Kogan 1991, p.164).

Whilst the chief executive of the UFC was promoting policies of rationalisation, his chairman, Lord Chilver, was promoting a market approach: 'He said he believed that unhampered market forces could achieve the ideal world by about Tuesday week. He was passionately opposed to any kind of planning and he genuinely wished to see the UFC abolished' (mac.45). 'I never understood how Lord Chilver expected this market to work and I feel I was not alone. It's not a true market because the taxpayer pays the bill' (mac.22). In higher education, as in most 'reformed' public sector enterprises, 'pure markets are more a theoretical construct than an empirical reality' (Goedegebuure *et al.* 1993). The UFC's initial attempt to introduce a bidding system, under which universities would offer to provide places for students at a certain price, failed because institutions got to know each other's prices, and only a small number of institutions were prepared to bid. The UFC wrote to the institutions in the following terms: '...although universities bid for expansion, the Council was disappointed by the scale of economy offered by the universities' bids over the 4-year period. The Council is unable to accept this position. The Council is committed to increasing effective and efficient use of resources and wishes to consider the options further' (UFC Circular Letter, 29/90). The CVCP were told in 1991 that 'for 1992/93 and beyond, additional student numbers would be allocated on a competitive basis with the main determinant in the competition being performance in recruiting fees-only students' (Davies 1991). The Minister for Higher Education, at the same time, avowed that in the post-binary system 'the central issue for the universities in the 1990s will be how to maintain quality while expanding rapidly and economically' (Davies 1991, para. 11).

Although the HEFCE started with an expansionist policy, as was noted in Chapter 3, the Treasury were alarmed at the cost of success of market policies in achieving an APR of over 30 per cent; this resulted in a dramatic change of policy. The HEFCE reported: 'In view of this rapid expansion, the Government announced a policy of "consolidation"' under which controls on the growth of student numbers would be applied in order to limit public expenditure ... The Government expects to maintain the participation rate of young people at just over 30% through to 1997–98' (HEFCE 1995). The policy reduced considerably the amount of marginal funding available for growth and required the council to set upper limits on the number of students funded. Each year the council notified institutions of the minimum number of students they were expected to teach for the available grant, and any shortfall would result in grant being withheld. Furthermore, a Maximum Aggregate Student Number was introduced for each institution, and they were also threatened with reduction of grant if they went more than fractionally over this number. This policy seems to have been driven by the Treasury for financial reasons but, as we have seen, there were also increasing doubts about the quality of what was being provided in so rapidly expanded a system. The strict restriction on numbers was referred to by several interviewees as an example of the increased control imposed on the universities.

Some of the best-regarded universities could take in their stride the demands for productivity and relevant research but found the system of allocation laborious and artificial. It was said to be dominated by formulae, but whereas these had begun with a liberal use of intuitive judgement by those who were able to apply them with full knowledge of the implications, they now represented 'a system out of control' (mac.213).

Stratification and selectivity

The build-up of selectivity policy

There have always been status differentials in UK higher education. Whilst, in part, they were related to historic positioning, accumulated wealth, the social status of students and political affiliations, increasingly their position in the academic hierarchy relied on research achievements. In an earlier research project (Boys *et al.* 1988), our team noted nine different types, roughly cascading in status order, of higher education institution. The hierarchy of universities was denoted by research records, qualifications of staff (Halsey 1992) and qualifications on entry of students. But until the 1980s, in what had been the larger part of the system (the universities), equality in formal terms, at least, was assumed in terms of roughly equal funding per commensurate unit, the expectation that all teachers would be researchers for about a third of their time, and the common standards putatively ensured by the external examiner system. This was reinforced by the funds provided through the UGC which was the part of the dual funding mechanism supposed to ensure that there were well-equipped and funded laboratories in all universities. Research council funding was the other part of dual support.

The argument about selectivity had begun much earlier than the 1980s (mac.48). As far back as 1965, the Department of Scientific and Industrial Research in its final report had come out in favour of selectivity, and then in 1967 the Council for Scientific Policy stated 'there will have to be further progress towards specialisation at selected centres together with concentration of resources in some fields of science' (Council for Scientific Policy 1967, para. 57). The general letter of guidance issued by the UGC under Sir John Wolfenden in 1967 again raised the question. The case for selectivity was spelled out a few years later by the Science Research Council (SRC) in *Selectivity and Concentration in the Support of Research* (SRC 1970) and by Brian Flowers (Flowers 1970), even if by 1990 he thought it had gone too far (SERC 1990). Our evidence is that some parts of the academic community, and in particular the 'hard' scientific elite within and outside some of the research councils, were advocating selectivity before, and supporting it after, government acted (mac.40).

The degree of stratification, existing well before present policies came into place, was described by a leading policy maker:

> If one goes back to 1971 at five-year intervals, of the top 15 earners of research council funds there are eight who are there every year. The others are in and out and the order changes; it is not a fixed league. The new funding arrangements will make hierarchies less fluid but it was never all that fluid ... After Robbins there were brought in two groups of universities, the greenfields and the former CATs [Colleges of Advanced Technology]. The greenfields universities went out and built research universities in the image of Oxford, Cambridge and Imperial. They went and bought these very bright young people. Bath and Surrey inherited staff, and they made themselves research universities by changing the cohort ... Surrey said all of our academic appointments for the next 25 years are going to be researchers. They now finish up middle of the second division, after 25 years of pretty generous research funding. (mac.19)

Despite the pressures for selectivity and concentration, senior policy makers were concerned to sustain a broadly based system. A chairman of the Science Research Council and his two predecessors (who 'knew each other very well') aspired to the same overall policy:

> There were two strands ... First, to maintain the dual support system: to have a strong and effective research council system, we believed there had to be well-found laboratories in the universities, and that could only come from having an adequately funded UGC ... The second principle was that, certainly by 1975, the universities had become the custodians of basic research, that research in industry and in government laboratories had become strongly mission orientated – in one case because of international competitiveness, in the other because the government labs had ever-widening horizons and had to begin to focus in order to work effectively. So we saw ourselves as the custodians of British basic research, and the principle when running British research councils was to maintain a coherent research base spanning the active

areas of scientific and technological research but also integrating that base into the world at large, e.g. we were very strong supporters of being in CERN ... We all saw that engineering was not strong ... our policy under the second principle was to build up engineering in the universities and our research establishments ... we invested ... grants to build up the research base of the UK and for that selected areas of research but, even more importantly, also maintained a steady flow of trained scientists and engineers with PG experience.

The policy of research councils such as the SRC and the SERC throughout the 1970s and into the 1980s was to fund the best proposals wherever they came from. The SERC was becoming more selective and increasingly identifying areas in which to launch programmes, but scientists in any department could be funded to work in them. This had been highlighted when the SRC established a committee in 1973 to advise on the encouragement of postgraduate training in the polytechnics, and a few years later the committee's remit was broadened to include advising on how the SRC should encourage polytechnics to develop a distinctive role in research (SRC 1977). In 1980 the Advisory Board for the Research Councils (ABRC) and the UGC appointed a joint committee under the ABRC chairman, Sir Alec Merrison, following concern about the health of the dual support system for research in universities (Merrison 1982, p.1). It found that these concerns were real, and one of its main recommendations, in addition to a call for more money, was that 'universities will need to concentrate funds into selected areas'. The Research Committee of a university 'would come to conclusions about the areas on which the university should concentrate' (pp.27–28).

The demand for explicit selectivity was triggered off by the progressive reduction in the units of resources allowed by government, as we have seen (Chapter 3), a policy already set in train by the severe cuts of the 1970s. One senior policy maker believed that reductions in the 1970s had cut out the fat and therefore the consequences of cuts in the 1980s were more severe (mac.117). It had not been considered necessary to be selective hitherto in awarding core funds to universities, i.e. those coming from the UGC, for teaching and the research infrastructure. From the mid-1980s individual selectivity by the research councils, however, became partly overridden by cost centre selectivity by the UGC. After some hesitation, it was decided not to rate universities as a whole in the

RAE but only by their component parts. Nevertheless, as we discuss below, proposals were soon put forward by the chairman of the ABRC, Sir David Phillips, for the stratification into R (research), T (teaching) and X (mixed) institutions. The influence that the RAE began to have on funding from 1986 was described in the previous section, but the policy's origins were complex.

The research assessment exercise

Government ministers began pressing the UGC more firmly than before. In 1982 Sir Keith Joseph asked it for advice on the development of a strategy for higher education. This eventually resulted in *A Strategy for Higher Education into the 1990s* (UGC 1984), which stated: 'We propose to adopt a more selective approach in the allocation of research support among universities in order to ensure that resources for research are used to best advantage' (para. 1.9). Although Joseph had written, in a letter to Parkes in 1983, that greater selectivity 'may be necessary' (UGC 1983, Appendix F), this had been supported by very few institutions in the UGC's consultative exercise (UGC 1984, p.61). Some saw Sir Peter Swinnerton-Dyer, the new chairman of the UGC, as reading the situation as to what was politically necessary and the junior minister, William Waldegrave, suggested that Swinnerton-Dyers' known preference for excellence and stratification contributed to his original appointment.

We have some insights into who made the running on these radical policies. 'Selectivity was science-driven. The Treasury was behind the demand for concentration because of the black hole of money being spent on research. It started with science and got extended to the rest. Swinnerton-Dyer's mathematical formula then got repeated through the rest of the system. It was not employer-driven' (mac.213). Other interviewees gave witness to Treasury pressure for greater clarification of how the funds provided by the UGC for research were spent (mac.117; Bird 1994). Within the UGC, research assessment was put forward primarily by Peter Swinnerton-Dyer but with the support of the committee. The assessors from the research councils and officials from the Department were in favour. If the UGC had not taken the initiative, the government might have done so. The industrial members of the UGC were not taking the lead and the academic elites in the honorific academies were not pushing for it, although they did not oppose it. They were worried whether departments would be able to get back once they had been given a low grade. The research councils wanted research selectivity because they thought that they should run it. This was part of the pressure on the UGC to introduce it (mac.44). Another interviewee thought, however, in relation to the recurrent notion that all research funding should be transferred to the research councils, that there was no pressure for it from the research councils (mac.102).

Christopher Ball has given a vivid account of the RAE's genesis, which is worth quoting in full, as follows:

> Peter Swinnerton-Dyer, David Phillips and I used to have dinner together, and plan our ... strategy. One evening, Peter said, 'I have a problem ... I can no longer defend the funding of universities through my leg of the dual support system without real account-ability to government. Here you are saying, David, from the ABRC point of view, the UGC is distributing massive research funds, we don't know where they are going, whether they are being properly used, and here is Christopher saying NAB is producing good higher education without research funds, why does the uni-versity system need all these unspecific research funds? I am caught in a pincer movement between the two. I want the system to be more rational so that polys could bid for some research fund-ing, even though they may not get much of it,' David wanted the whole lot transferred to the ABRC because he thought he could distribute it more sensibly. He was in the TRX mode at that stage, and wanted more for the R lot. So we discussed it and I suppose at that dinner we invented the research selectivity exercise. Peter said, 'I think I know how to do it for science, technology and medi-cine, the bigger worry for me is social science and the arts.'
>
> I said, 'I don't think you should do it in these areas at all ... the funds there are relatively little. What you need to account for is the massive medical and engineering spends. Anyway, the job was done for you when we invented the Copyright Libraries. Massive funding was put to create research libraries in Oxford, Cambridge, London, etc. They don't quite match up to modern conditions but it was not a bad shot. All you have to do is to continue to fund five brilliant research libraries and to use modern technology to make them accessible. So don't do it [i.e. the research selectivity exercise for these disciplines]. The cost will be so enormous, it won't be justified by the redistribution of funds that will result.' A month later, when I met him again, he said, 'I liked your advice but I am not going to follow it. I have been to the heads of the disciplinary groups in social studies and arts, and they said if there is going to be a selective exercise, arts and social studies can't be left out. It would appear to the public that our research is unimportant. The dons want it. What do you say to that?' I said, 'They are bloody

fools, and they will live to regret it.' (Christopher Ball has added that his memory tends to dramatise events in retrospect – but he believes the gist of this account to be true.)

Some maintained that research selectivity was linked with autonomy on the grounds that the old research premium on student numbers was 'part of a top-down planning system in which it was difficult for any institution to develop its own policies ... The variability of research funding connects with performance which would then enable a university to decide how to grow its research income' (mac.25). This assumes that institutions can, indeed, determine their own research fates, and ignores the extent to which academic behaviour and priorities have been affected by the RAE exercises.

Since the first RAE in 1985/86, there have been further selectivity exercises in 1989, 1992 and 1996. There has been strong political support for the policy but also wide consultation about the mechanisms to use and how to improve them in the face of considerable criticism (see, for example, Cave *et al.* 1997). In the most recent HEFCE consultation, only one institution replied that it did not think there should be another RAE. The consequences of the RAE have become progressively more severe. The first exercise determined the distribution of almost half of the UGC's research funding. This proportion was being increased but the 1991 White Paper made clear that in the post-binary system student numbers would no longer play a part in the allocation of research funding, and thus dashed the hopes of some in the former polytechnics. Initially, the HEFCE allocations resulting from the 1992 exercise provided no funds for the cost centres given the lowest of the five grades. There was discussion among the research elite (see, for example, the report from the National Academies Policy Advisory Group 1996) about increasing the number of research grades, whilst being more selective about which should attract funding. In the 1996 exercise seven categories were used, but those cost centres graded 1 or 2 received no research funding. Thus, the public funding system provided support for research in a decreasing proportion of the unified system and created even steeper hierarchies of esteem and resource.

R, T and X

There were variations in thinking about how differentiation might operate. The two linked issues were whether higher education could be conducted in institutions where research was not a prime activity and whether universities should be divided into those conducting research (R), teaching without research (T), or a mixture of both (X). One interviewee provides an account of the growing support for a policy of stratification:

> There was an emerging consensus that there should be concentration in 1983. Peter [Swinnerton-Dyer] organised a dinner to talk about research concentration with about 12 people there, people like government chief scientists and two or three industrial research leaders, such as Roberts of UCL, who really knew the industrial point of view. I said that I had always been in favour of a small number of research universities. It will take us some time but we will finish up with 12 to 15 research universities. Peter then made us do an exercise, write the names of the 12 universities. Peter added them up and said, 'You are all softies, you have chosen 15 universities, and when we do it there will be less than 12 because we can't afford more, but you have named only 20 between you.' Even at that stage the limited number was emerging, and people were thinking about institutions rather than departments. At the moment that we were creating the departmental model, we were thinking of moving forward towards the Phillips model, although I had grown up believing that research funds went to the gifted individual. People are now thinking of the institutional model and I think one can see that went back to that conversation in 1983/84 – if not earlier. Everybody knows that money is going to be pushed towards the major research institutions. In one-to-one discussions with universities that would probably not be well favoured, they would say: 'Yes, but I hope it's not going to happen in my time.' There was an intellectual consensus about the inevitable. (mac.2)

A leading proponent of the RTX scheme was the chair of the ABRC, David Phillips, and an ABRC report *A Strategy for the Science Base* (1987, paras 131–135) not only laid emphasis on Interdisciplinary Research Centres (IRC) but also stratification into RTX. Another move towards selectivity and stratification was a series of reviews in different subject areas conducted by the UGC (Shattock 1994). In the end, it did not make a major impact outside a few subjects, but it was relevant to the debate about R, T and X. Although the Oxburgh Report on earth sciences had proposed that support for earth science departments should be at one of three levels, and this was referred to in the ABRC Report, the eventual recommendations from the earth sciences committee were for a four-type classification quite different from that proposed by the Oxburgh Report (Shattock 1994). This indicated that R, T and X would be impracticable. The alternative to

RTX was to enable individual cost centres to receive funding, irrespective of institution. Some were troubled that weaker departments in strong institutions could otherwise become complacent and coast along (mac.22). One research council had always seen funding as being selective, but not exclusive to anyone, and that policy had stuck (mac.108). This was to be the winning formula, although the operation of the grading system for research has meant that there is indeed a hardening into something near an RTX pattern. More than one interviewee predicted that there will be R, X and T departments and that there is likely to be a reshuffling of the order of the newly expanded group of universities; some at the end of the list of the 'old' universities will gradually change places with those at the top of the former polytechnic list.

For Robert Jackson, the problem with the UGC funding being allocated in an insufficiently selective way 'was that a much higher proportion of research council money went to selected institutions than was the case of UGC ... The ABRC was influential in pointing out the waste factor involved. There was an opportunity cost. Not only was public money being wasted, but also money that could have been used better was being spent in the wrong place. Their solution was a dirigistic one. Part of the culture of the top-down planning: let us grade universities so that you are for all time in category X, R or T. I was instinctively opposed to that on my autonomous grounds, it was too inflexible, and gave no scope for aspirations and achievements of particular universities, but, nevertheless, you could achieve the same results on an organic and revisable basis through the means we adopted (i.e. research selectivity), to some extent under my influence.'

Different perspectives on selectivity

The RAE primarily aimed at enhancing quality, whilst other policies aim at relevance. To some extent, the research councils aim for the relevance, whilst retaining rigorous and competitive standards, and the funding councils for quality. 'We [HEFCE] absolutely reject any attempt to dilute selectivity criteria with considerations of relevance. The only criterion in the exercise is quality. On the other hand, we have said that just because research is relevant it should not be discounted. We have said as well that universities must take account of the Foresight Initiative; we were pressed very hard by OST on that. But that's a long way from making research assessment exercises influenced by relevance' (mac.3).

The majority of the policy makers or policy influencers whom we interviewed either believed that selectivity and the resulting stratification were inevitable or that the policy was right in principle. 'Standards must not be watered down; the polytechnics were doing different work from the Cavendish' (mac.1).

There were some differing perspectives, but most with a voice in the matter took up expected positions. 'The Royal Society and British Academy had made the point that if you spread the fundings in some equitable fashion across the system then you end up not being able to do anything usefully' (mac.28). The CVCP was more cautious because it would lead to concentration and an attack on the teaching and research link. The vice-chancellors from leading research universities were pragmatically for it.

Unlike many other European universities, the British have always been concerned about the link between teaching and research. The specific issue of dividing the UGC funding between teaching and research 'made people become aware that there was some rationale in UGC funding; before then the UGC funding was a total black box. What was moving Swinnerton-Dyer was not a feeling that teaching and research ought to be separated or that there should be increased selectivity but simply that the UGC had to have some rationale for the way they allocated their money and that he might have to defend that in public, and being a logical, mathematical type he thought there should be a formula' (mac.102).

Other forms of selectivity were coming into place. The ABRC were encouraging the introduction of Interdisciplinary Research Centres. The SERC followed this policy, but stated in their 1989 corporate plan: 'It would not wish the proportion of research grant funding invested in IRCs to exceed 20% of total grant funding unless there were, in the longer term, positive indications that the Council's expectation of their success was justified' (SERC 1989, p.6). The creation of Interdisciplinary Research Centres was thought by at least one leading scientist to create problems because 'all centres of excellence decay in time, because of the lack of mobility of good people. A good dual support system would enable good centres to move around following the good people. The base does not have enough money to promote fluidity and mobility, whilst the research councils have been forced to identify centres' (mac.101). However, 'there was no pressure on the ESRC [Economic and Social Research Council] to direct its funding more selectively. Warwick, Oxford, Cambridge, London and Manchester got most of the money, but there was a long tail of successful and funded researchers in many other institutions' (mac.110). The effects of stratification were not always what was desired. 'The dual support system would ensure that all would continue to receive essential core funding but it then became underfunded' (mac.101). The 1987 White Paper stated that the obligation to secure selectivity in research funding lay with the research councils, the ABRC, and on universities guided by the UGC. It suggested that a good start had been made (DES 1987).

The academic effects of selectivity are the subject of our separate study (Henkel forthcoming). It would be fair to say that whilst most of the elite and policy-making interviewees who participated in our study were in favour of the principle, many were concerned about some of its particular impacts. Whilst the scientific elite to a large measure supported selectivity, they were anxious to sustain the essentials of the system (mac.101). 'The FRSs and FBAs weren't actually pushing for research selectivity; rather, once it had become clear it was going to be the policy, they weren't going to oppose it. Some had said that every university must be given adequate support to maintain its research and thought that their leadership should put pressure on government to provide more money to make that possible' (mac.45).

'Those leading the research councils found they mostly had substantial support from the presidents of the Royal Society. George Porter, as a member of council and later as PRS, fought long and hard for the responsive mode and did not want big science and engineering to be promoted too much. In this, the fight was thought to be against the government and some of the officers of the research councils. The Royal Society was good at commenting in general about policy but being a champion for everything it was difficult for the Society to be selective' (mac.101).

Attitudes towards selectivity varied among interviewees in leading positions (mac.207). The strongest defence was this: 'Research money should go behind the elite to exploit the breakthroughs. Get rid of the second rate. The contrary should be with teaching. You should put your resources at the weakest point.' Others were more sceptical: 'Stratification has reinforced the place of the elite' (mac.201). 'The RAE is the academic elite strike back' (mac.206).

Some of those interviewed were concerned about the academic impacts, that collegiality might have suffered and that competition between individuals and departments had grown. Many good research departments had suffered from the transfer market.

One academic leader at the summit of the system (mac.42) noted: 'When research grants are given to those within the research council frame of activities, they get more money out of the funding council which enables them to earn more grant. So it's a spiral and its benevolent or malevolent depending on whether you're in it.' In his day, they had spent 10 per cent of resources on developing a few subjects where there were likely applications or rapid scientific understanding, but now it has swung the other way. 'We are approaching the stage where the corporate pressures of the system are overcoming the natural inclination of the individual scholar to follow his or her own values.'

Quality

Anxiety about quality recurs throughout the recent history of higher education. The belief in widening opportunities to enter higher education, now nearly universally held, was not always shared by the academic establishment. In 1948 the UGC was concerned about quality: '...in few other fields are numbers of so little value compared to quality properly developed ... before a student enters the university, intelligence must be trained and the associated personal qualities matured to a standard that we would not wish to see lowered' (UGC 1948). The Committee of Vice-Chancellors and Principals, in a note on university planning and finance for the decade 1947–56, warned that 'academic standards once lowered are not retrievable, and Gresham's law applies to them'. The UGC had not thought it wise to aim at raising the university student population to the American scale 'at the cost of so great a decline in entrance standards'. The UGC would welcome an increase, but it would want to ensure that there would be satisfactory employment for graduates, that accommodation and equipment should be adequate and that there should be no decline in standards. At the beginning of 1953 the UGC argued that the proportions of both the really good and of the really poor students were lower. There were many more second-class candidates. There could not be great increases in numbers without reducing quality (UGC 1953).

Eventually, the universities accepted the fact that expansion would continue, and by the time the system had moved into the mass stage, the boundary definitions of higher education and universities had changed (mac.104), and those academics who might have been most anxious about dilution might have found that their own institutions were immune from it.

In spite of this underlying uncertainty in parts of the system, it was not until the 1980s that government began to press quality assurance. Evaluations, in the sense of detailed judgements of quality and holding institutions and departments to account, had been essentially *ex post*, if they happened at all, and under professional peer control. The exceptions were those sectors, such as British polytechnics, in the pre-university stage; these were subject to scrutiny on both objectives and outcomes by evaluative bodies such as the CNAA and inspection by HMI. For universities, evaluation was connected only loosely to the systems of allocations which were made on a large degree of trust. The universities' own mechanisms were deemed sufficient warranties of standards. Governments' main concerns instead had been structural and input related. Ministers' concerns about standards in schools in the mid-1970s have, however, been identified as a harbinger of similar concerns about higher education (mac.39).

The selectivity and research assessment policies form part of the much wider move to assess quality. Our discussion of research selectivity in the previous section showed how the funding bodies, led by Swinnerton-Dyer, with full ministerial backing (see, for example, 1985 Green Paper), played a dominant part. The HEFCs have continued to lead on this policy, although academics have been co-opted to implement it and we saw that details of assessment procedures having increasingly been a matter of consultation. The lead responsibility and processes of consultation for the remaining quality policies have been much more complex.

UGC Circular Letter 22/85, which set out the new resource allocation procedure for research, stated that 'there are few indicators of teaching performance that would enable a systemic external assessment of teaching quality. [If universities know how to do it] the committee would be glad to be told how to do it' (UGC 1985).

The university system was under pressure to address the quality issue, especially in the light of the Jarratt report, but the CVCP was determined to retain as much autonomy as possible and established an Academic Standards Group, chaired successively by senior vice-chancellors, first by Philip Reynolds and then by Stewart Sutherland. Following the Reynolds Report (1986), the CVCP set up codes of practice on the maintenance and monitoring of standards, including external examining and the arrangements for postgraduate training and research (Reynolds Report 1986). In this respect, as in others, the two sectors began to converge.

The pressures in the public sector were somewhat different. The institutions were pressing for greater autonomy and more flexible and sophisticated forms of institutional and course validation. These began to emerge following the 1985 Lindop Report. At the same time, the public sector funding bodies were looking to incorporate quality assessments into their decisions, including, in the case of the PCFC, their funding mechanisms. The CNAA did not think it appropriate for their information to be used in this way but HMI did co-operate. The Secretary of State made it clear that he expected assessments of teaching to be linked to funding; the former chairman of the council was, as is noted later, happy to pursue this policy without pressure.

In the 1987 White Paper the government had stipulated that the quality of teaching in both sectors should be evaluated. There should be: '...systematic arrangements for ... staff appraisal; evaluation of the results achieved, including analysis of external examiners' reports and students' employment patterns; ... and feedback from students themselves (DES 1987, para. 3.12). The White Paper went on to suggest that the quality of teaching needed to be judged by reference mainly to students' achievements. In 1989 Kenneth Baker stated that 'effective teaching needs to be identified, highly prized, encouraged and rewarded' (Baker 1989). There were several pressures for teaching quality to be assessed and they included not just ministers' and officials' concerns but at least some in the academic community who feared that if research was assessed, but teaching was not, even greater emphasis would be given to research (see, for example, Cave, Hanney and Kogan 1991).

Most within the university system, and explicitly the CVCP, were keen to resist the imposition of external assessment of teaching quality, and, indeed, the chief executive of the UFC, Swinnerton-Dyer, when pressed by the government over quality, thought it should be the responsibility of the CVCP. The Academic Standards Group Report (Sutherland 1989) led in 1990 to the universities establishing their own Academic Audit Unit to conduct audits of institutions.

The 1991 White Paper described quality audit in the following terms:

> The Government accepts the view put to it by some representatives of universities and polytechnics that, in a unitary system, this quality audit role should become the task of a single unit in which the institutions have the major stake. (DES 1991, para. 68)

In the White Paper the Department mentioned reserve powers which would be used if the quality audit programmes were not put in place.

Despite having differing views, the CVCP, the CDP and the SCOP (the organisation for the remaining colleges) developed plans (CVCP, CDP, SCOP 1991) which were endorsed by ministers, and led to the establishment of the Higher Education Quality Council in the post-binary period, although pilot activities started before 1993. Quality audit, which requires institutions to demonstrate that they have their own systems of quality assurance in place, was thus designed by the universities themselves and, although made a statutory requirement in the 1992 Further and Higher Education Act, remained under their control. They 'had their own internal systems and the last thing they were prepared to accept was any reduction in their autonomy or responsibility for control over quality ... they set up a body to do it for themselves whereas the funding council wanted its own independent assessment' (mac.15).

The 1991 White Paper was more assertive about quality assessment of teaching:

> While recognising that the precise arrangements will be matter for the Funding Councils themselves, the Government considers it important that assessment of quality should continue to inform the funding decisions of the new Funding Councils. This is already the case with the PCFC and the UFC ... The role of the assessment units will be for the Funding Councils to determine in consultation with institutions and subject to guidance from the Secretaries of State. (DES 1991, paras 79 and 83)

Some steps had already been taken by the PCFC and the UFC, but the newly established HEFCE, following a letter from the Secretary of State (Clarke 1991) to the chairman of the PCFC, established a Quality Assessment Committee which organised the teacher quality assessments (TQAs). The assessments were to be conducted by subjects, and departments would be graded excellent, satisfactory or unsatisfactory.

There was considerable unease, particularly in the old university sector, about the introduction of the assessments, but by not insisting that they were immediately linked to funding, the government took some of the heat out of the new requirements (mac.102, 108). The HEFCE responded to criticism by mounting a study (Barnett *et al.* 1994) which resulted in an amended system (HEFCE and HEFCW 1994).

A major concern for the CVCP and the funding councils had been government's intentions about the use of HMIs who had inspected public sector institutions. HMI themselves were active in attempting to demonstrate their experience and thus bolster claims for involvement in quality assessment. In practice, however, the hands-off approach was strongly maintained. One former minister said how he shared the CVCP's view that HMIs should not inspect the universities and that the CVCP and the CDP should build up their own systems of evaluation. As a minister, he felt he had no part to play whatsoever in the design of the funding formulae, nor the structure for evaluating research in detail (mac. 24). The resistance from the HEFCE to the employment of many HMIs to assist with TQAs is described later.

Despite all these efforts at quality assurance, the Secretary of State, John Patten, as noted in Chapter 3, faced questioning when in Malaysia and Singapore about whether standards were being maintained. In an address to an HEFCE conference, Patten raised the issue of the comparability of standards (Patten 1994). The CVCP produced an 11-point plan centred on the intention to develop threshold standards for British higher education. This was followed by the establishment by the Higher Education Quality Council (HEQC) of a Graduate Standards Programme.

There was growing resentment in the university system against the combined impact of quality audits, TQAs, and increased accreditation activities by the professional and statutory bodies. This resulted in December 1994 in the new and more conciliatory Secretary of State, Gillian Shephard, asking the HEFCE's chief executive, Graeme Davies, to review the post-1991 arrangements in consultation with the sector. The invitation 'followed sustained lobbying by the CVCP and others about the burdens, duplications and intrusiveness represented by various external quality assurance processes' (Brown 1997). Davies reported (HEFCE 1995), and later that year a Joint Planning Group was established and after considerable debate between the HEFCE and the CVCP, a joint body, the Quality Assurance Agency for Higher Education, was created in 1997.

Further details of the quality policies and their impacts can be found in Henkel (forthcoming). It is possible to conclude, however, that increasingly throughout the 1980s there was a concern to assess the outcomes and processes to higher education. Government's placing of evaluation within publicly prescribed frames led to a reformulation of the nature of academic quality, aided by a veritable industry of definers and prescribers. Thus, the concept of 'fitness for purpose' entailed an assumption about purposes being negotiable. At the same time, the formats were partly, at least, in the form of quantities which make it more possible for academics' performances to be measured and compared by non-academic managers.

The UK thus moved from a position in which the state had virtually no direct interest in assuring quality in universities and in which it delegated quality judgements in the public sector to an increasingly hands-off CNAA to one in which quality requirements were imposed by law. The creation of quality audit, teaching quality assessment and research assessment, and the associated machinery in the funding councils and the Higher Education Quality Council (from 1997 the Quality Assurance Agency), were part of the fundamental shift in the relationships between the state and higher education. For the most part, academics were opposed to the changes (while conceding the principle of public accountability, see Henkel forthcoming), whilst those responsible for the system may have taken a different view. A former chairman of a funding council explained that their feeling was that 'we must do this ... never mind the government, it was our view ... I didn't, as chairman, find the government lobbying me at all. They may have lobbied lower down the line, they may have sent letters' (mac.15). Throughout, there had been discussion with the university system – at least about the details of implementation. The variety of opinions about how quality policies have developed forms part of the discussion in Chapter 6 about the funding councils' relationships with both government and the institutions.

Massification provided a justification for the extensive machinery of quality assurance now in place. British higher education would move from the borderline between an elite and a mass system to being well on the way towards a universal system. With it, the case for an explicit stratification of institutions, differentiating those concentrating on teaching from those concentrating on research, became plausible. Given, however, the general pressure from the government on public services in the UK for the quality of services provided to consumers to be assessed, it is likely there would have been some moves towards quality assessment even had the system not expanded.

The end of the binary line, changes in governance, managerialism

These three key issues are briefly alluded to below and then developed in their own chapters.

The end of the binary line

The unification of higher education into one system was a momentous policy move. Both in its structural implications and as an example of the relationships between central government and interest groups, it constitutes an important case study which is therefore considered separately in the next chapter.

Changes in governance

The creation of a unitary system spelled the end of the local authorities' place in higher education government and management. This was part of a more general reduction in their role. At the same time, although this is contested by some of the players, the great freedom given to institutions that was implicit in the quinquennial system of grants was steadily eroded, by changes to the UGC and by its replacement by a series of funding councils. We shall be examining these changes in more detail in Chapter 6.

Managerialism

We examine some of the characteristics of the moves towards managerialism in Chapter 7. These involved a strengthening of the role of leadership and a corresponding reduction in the powers of academics to contribute to institutional policy making.

II CHANGES IN HE SUBSTANTIVES

Curriculum

The curriculum of higher education has never been part of government's concern or under central control, except in certain areas of professional preparation where, in effect, the professional bodies validated on behalf of government. In the public sector there was appraisal of content, but this became increasingly liberal, and was in any case in the hands of academically membered intermediary bodies. From the early 1980s, government attempted to insinuate particular subject balances – a shift to science, computer studies or business studies – and changes in the research preparation of scientists and technologists (OST 1993). Changes in resources affecting staffing ratios, equipment and accommodation all began to affect teaching. One minister, Keith Joseph, was prepared to go further and fret, ineffectively, about educational sociology at the Open University and peace studies at Bradford (mac.47).

The Enterprise in Higher Education Initiative[1] was the most direct attempt to influence higher education curriculum. It provided grants of £100 million (although that level was not reached) for higher education institutions prepared to 'imbed enterprise into the curriculum' (MSC 1987). This remarkable episode in government–HE relationships had been initiated by two ministers, Young and Joseph, 'who were strongly influenced by the Israeli example of ORT' (mac.14). Lord Young said he and Keith Joseph were 'very conscious of the anti-entrepreneurial bias of higher education. This [EHE] was a way of trying to address that.' It was seen by some as an extension of the Technical and Vocational Education Initiative (TVEI) or extending it to education across the board. Christopher Ball recalls 'the first meeting when we were told about what became EHE':

> It was a cross-higher education meeting called by Keith Joseph and Lord Young. Senior civil servants and a smattering of vice-chancellors, poly directors, Peter Swinnerton-Dyer and me. Geoffrey Holland and I were at one end of the table while the Secretaries of State sat at the other end discussing what they wanted. Geoffrey passed me a note saying, 'Christopher, have you the faintest idea what we should do about this?' I said, 'Not much.' He said, 'Unless someone thinks out what to do, we'll be in trouble.' He and I came in turn and said, 'This is what we think we can do.' We were sent away as a subcommittee of two; Keith Joseph said, 'You seem to know what you're doing.' We were the first people to speak positively about EHE. The others were saying it couldn't be done. We designed certain principles. It must be available to all the students in the institution, even if they study theology – access should not be simply for students of business studies, economics, etc. We should offer money against what institutions wanted to do. I remember Geoffrey saying, 'We don't know what to do, let the institutions come up with good ideas. If they come up with good ideas, we'll give them the money. If there are none, we'll spend nothing at all.'

The public sector again on this issue showed its capacity to meet the current preoccupations of a government determined to induce its own values into higher education. The polytechnics 'lapped it up ... a saucer of cream, wonderful and a very impressive record on the polys' side ... they certainly came leaping towards it in a way which the old

1   A full account of the Enterprise Initiative can be found in *Academic Identities and Policy Change in Higher Education* (Henkel forthcoming).

universities did not, and on the first round they scored extremely well' (mac.43). 'The CDP was involved in it, at least once it got under way; they always had a healthy relationship with the MSC [Manpower Services Commission] and its successors, and we did quite a lot to get the fine print of scheme right – certainly for the second round ... We gave that very strong backing ... it was very much in line with what the polys were doing – they'd got something to build upon and they understood the language in which this was all done, in terms of developing industrially linked or enterprise-linked courses, and staff training and development, and student project-based work' (mac.105).

This polytechnic account may underestimate the extent to which the universities were also, at least, unresisting to the initiative. It came at a time when the prospect of any additional resources was welcome, and many courses in many universities were in any case already adapting themselves, in different degrees, to some of the assumptions which became clarified as part of the initiative (Boys *et al.* 1988). EHE itself increasingly adapted to the ways in which a wider range of higher education styles could adapt. 'The first round was very much trying either to adapt courses or prompt the mounting of courses which were overtly useful to the enterprise culture. The second round was much less face-on ... they obviously had to adjust the system to bring institutions in which hadn't taken advantage, or hadn't scored at the first round. It was much more to be embedded in the institution – not externally directed by MSC' (mac.105).

The EHE Initiative is an example of the DES being placed under pressure within Whitehall. 'At one time, when Keith Joseph was in the DTI, there was talk of trying to screw some money out of it to fund courses because they were courses which bore more directly onto the interests of DTI than what was seen as a rather rudderless, viewless, ineffective, impoverished DES ... there was a feeling that the DES knew about schools ... and didn't know much about HE' (mac.43). The DES was held to be ineffective at the time that the Manpower Services Commission was building up initiatives that would affect work in schools, particularly the TVEI (Kogan 1987), and when one key player described it as being 'raped' by the then Department of Employment (mac.38).

The language of competencies, as opposed to that of certified knowledge, was introduced into higher education through a system of national vocational qualifications. It was hoped that the curriculum would be affected by requirements to meet employers' and students' perceptions of what was needed. Government created a system of National Vocational Qualifications which, in effect, incorporated those qualified by means other than those traditionally required for university entrance: further evidence of the despecialisation of university education in the UK. There was a widening and stratification of entry qualifications and of the ascribed quality of the resulting degrees.

The structure of degrees with tight prerequisite requirements weakened to allow for credit transfer and for the amortisation of subject learning into transferable modules. The arguments for modular courses were those of more economic teaching, greater choice for students, flexibility and transferability within institutions. But critics included some within the new universities (mac.105), who thought that somebody teaching the modular course and doing a modicum of research was unlikely to be at the forefront of his or her subject.

The first full national policy pronouncement on graduate education ever made (OST 1993) proposed reduction in the numbers taking doctorates and that all of them should first take masters' courses from which they could be selected. Masters' courses should include education, in the ways required by external employers, and experience outside university laboratories. This was based on the premise that postgraduate education was dominated by the research needs of universities and not related to a view of what was best for students and society. Whilst the report was labour-market orientated, it said nothing about the labour requirements of higher education which was undergoing such radical changes in its teaching and research patterns.

The joint UGC/NAB 1984 Statement stated that the abilities most valued were the transferable intellectual and personal skills. This was more linked with the thinking underlying the Enterprise Initiative and the public sector than it was with traditional UGC thinking. Moves towards a more student-centred approach were also a product of the expansion, although more traditional universities were doing much to develop student-centred learning.

The impacts of these measures is the subject of our main study, *Academic Identities and Policy Change in Higher Education* (Henkel forthcoming). It can be asked how far these were the results of policy and how far the product of natural responses of institutions to changing environments. The curriculum has always been permeable (Boys *et al.* 1988) and responsive to social developments (e.g. the growth of development economics, business studies, areas studies in place of straight modern languages courses, environmental studies). The dramatic additions to the curriculum, most obvious in the social sciences and to a lesser extent in the humanities, such as the shifts towards hermeneutic approaches, the growth of feminist studies, post-modernist approaches, the year-by-year invention of new subject areas, and the styles of delivery and assessment, were essentially academically led developments. The enormous proliferation of subjects in the sciences and technologies also owed their impetus to academic discovery (mac. 48). In the curriculum there were substantial changes in the universities from the late 1940s, and these were changes made by the universities themselves.

Research

From 1975 onwards, individual ministers had begun to turn their attention to the policy and practice relevance of research council expenditures. Our earlier study of higher education and employment (Boys *et al.* 1988) noted how even in fields such as physics and economics, researchers were finding that the scale and focus of research and advanced teaching were being affected by research council initiatives responding to government requirements for strategic plans for research which embodied economic imperatives.

Policies now tended to shift research agendas to meet the demands of sponsors (Henkel 1995). This was also likely to be effected by the competition for research money (Barnett *et al.* 1994). In the 1970s the bulk of the Social Science Research Council's (SSRC's) money went on responsive grants and very little went on initiatives, although initiatives were started up in the mid-1970s. There is undocumented evidence that ministers made a few appointments to the SSRC to ensure a change in direction. It was now much more determined in stating the directions in which research would go, although it claimed that its themes were so broad that they should not constrain academic enterprise. Some of the research centres pursued fundamental research aspects, but they are pretty policy orientated. A whole raft of policies intended to improve the competitiveness of UK industry through managed programmes of science and technology was initiated from the 1970s. These included the LINK scheme, introduced in the 1980s, which involved joint funding from public and private sources.

The government squared the circle of supporting excellence whilst demanding relevance through the notion of strategic research which would be basic, and leading to the testing and development of theory, but also undertaken with an eye on applicability. It became a strongly expressed and pursued objective in the 1980s. It was this notion which led to support of science and engineering as against particle physics in research council funding (mac.28). The ESRC, in fact, put a great deal of effort into attempting to clarify the relationship between research-related policy and good academic criteria. Increasingly, in the 1980s the membership was tilted towards non-academic researchers. The most explicit move was in the 1990s with the Foresight Programme, which was intended to encourage networking between users and researchers and to identify possible priorities for the development of research according to scientific opportunities and capacities to exploit them on the basis of economic and social demand. The policy was a central theme in the science White Paper (OST 1993) but involved a response to long-standing concerns about the assumed failure of British industry to exploit scientific developments and the need for priority setting. The UK policy was conceived, however, by a small group of science advisers and analysts who were aware of international developments, and gained support from a minister keen to adopt and promote it (Henkel *et al.* forthcoming).

Impact

One important private foundation is 'a great favourite amongst academics because of its generosity, and because it does not have to answer to the government, or exercise thematic priorities ... Quite a lot of scientists make the point that this is the sort of thing which is not currently fashionable or currently supported by research councils' (mac.107). But the research agenda of those in the most esteemed institutions has not changed much, although the links with industry might have done so (mac.16). Nor, unsurprisingly, did those to appointed key positions and memberships on the relevant research councils feel threatened because their basic research was already related to industrial or social concerns (mac.101).

In a *Memorandum for an Incoming Government*, the Royal Society referred to the danger arising from an increasingly short-term and dirigiste attitude towards funding into research. They complained not only of insufficient funding resulting in a weak infrastructure, but the increasing lack of trust between the providers of funds and the research workers and frequently ideologically motivated reviews. They referred specifically to the 'repetitive and disruptive inspections' under the 'prior options' exercise which aimed to assess whether the research undertaken in research council institutes was so near-market that they should not receive public funds. They asked for policy makers to positively recognise the international nature of scientific research and the effective use of independent expert advice (Royal Society 1997).

A note of disquiet from a distinguished theorist of science (mac.207) criticised the very concept of the 'project' which institutionalises the notion of the problem. In the larger professionalised systems, individuals have to formalise their plans to persuade other people to fund them. The articulation of a research objective makes the word 'problem' emerge. But there is no such thing as a problem in the world outside. It is a social construct. It stands for the statement that here is a limited set of research objectives.

The impact of these measures has been significant. Nigel Forman noted: 'What academics are doing now is to the tune of four-fifths of what academics were doing 20 years ago. The interesting change is what happens at the margin, that extra one-fifth where they are allocating their time differently and where their approach is different. They are more competitive and they are more conscious of the lay public, or the need to explain themselves.' A leading Oxbridge academic believed that 'until the late 1970s we felt that we were acting as a society moralised by the professional ideal. Then we had status and respect that we did a good job and that the institution was in a good shape. We could stand international comparisons. What led to extraordinary resentment and hostility to government was to discover that it was felt that in order to achieve what Thatcher claimed would be an enterprise culture was by attacking the professional ideal ... Government did not say to the elite institutions, 'You should put more into business studies, which may not respond to the highest values but nevertheless has a functional purpose.' Instead, what government was trying to do was so hostile to our value system, deliberately rubbishing it. It was perceived that we were under threat.'

CONCLUSIONS

In this chapter we have addressed the main policy movements that have so deeply affected the working of higher education. We append a chronology of the main milestones of the period of reform.

Policy changes were radical and had deep effects on the work of academics and their institutions, although there were also important policy continuities. As we have noted, until the latter 1970s, the universities – unlike the rest of the higher education system – enjoyed state-subsidised independence. This shifted to ambiguous but increased dependence on, and deference to, state policies. The liberal assumptions of the Robbins Report (1963) gave way to economic and consumerist values, yet insisted on selectivity, particularly in research grading and funding, which had excellence as its leading criterion. Expansion, pushed by increased student demand, was a dominant factor in causing change; it pulled into more rigorous public policies a domain that had hitherto been trusted to do good by doing what it thought to be good. The demystifying of academic work, and reduced confidence in professional groups in society as a whole, went along with increased numbers and severely cut units of resource. The changes in scale and perceived objectives were accompanied by changes in macro structure and particularly the supersession of the binary by the unitary system, which we consider in Chapter 5. This, taking place alongside selectivity in funding, was accompanied by the more intense stratification and structuring of the hierarchy of universities through the selective allocation of funds.

But economic instrumentalism was never absent from higher education's agenda, at least from 1945 onwards. The difference was that previously it was conceded by the universities as part of the bargain they had made with the state but wholly on their terms. Quality control, too, had been taken for granted. It now became explicit, public and under increasing state surveillance. The hierarchy of esteem and the differential resources which came with it became steeper and public, and reputations, hitherto almost a matter of private peer group knowledge, became explicit.

Whilst policies were created largely on the hoof, they cumulatively pulled higher education into the public policy arena in which its essentialism, based on the nature of the work that it performed, was in contention with overriding economic and social policy.

The major conceptual issue arising from our account of these policies is whether there is any obvious explanation of how the issues emerged and were resolved. They were not an example of a rationalistic system analysing long-term needs and producing plans to meet them, but, rather, the interaction of the dramatic expansion of student numbers, financial pressures and the ideological positions taken up by ministers and others. These concerns are further explored in Chapters 6 and 8 where policy processes and the groups that influence them are discussed.

As will have been evident from our narrative, the selectivity policies were the subject of micro-political action, but not subject to the operation of clear policy communities and the public deliberation that might go with it. However, in the implementation of the RAE, as with the development of the wider quality policies, there was considerable consultation with the academic community. Within the context of the government establishing that quality would be assessed, there was vigorous debate between competing interests, including the CVCP, the CDP, HMI and the funding councils. The way in which influence operated in the policy zone is taken up more fully in Chapter 8. In the meantime, we turn to the particular case of the ending of the binary divide.

APPENDIX TO CHAPTER 4
Chronology of change: chart of main historical events

1919. Treasury Minute
Established University Grants Committee to provide advice on the financial needs of universities and the grants to be made to them. It reported to the Treasury.

1944. Education Act
Provided for tuition fees and maintenance grants to be paid to students attending higher education and advanced further education courses.

1963. Robbins Report Report of the Committee on Higher Education (Cmnd 2154)
Established principle that places should be available for all who are qualified to take them up. Legitimised expansion.

1964. Government Reorganisation
Department of Education and Science replaced Ministry of Education and assumed responsibility of the research councils and, from the Treasury, for the UGC.

1966 DES White Paper A Plan for Polytechnics and Other Colleges (Cmnd 3006)
Detailed plans for the creation of polytechnics that had been announced in Anthony Crosland's Woolwich speech of April 1965.

1971. Rothschild Report The Organisation and Management of Government R&D (Cmnd 4814)
Suggested applied R&D should be governed by the 'customer–contractor principle'. Findings were largely supported in the White

Paper the following year, and some money transferred from research councils to government departments.

1976. DES White Paper **Public Expenditure to 1978–1980**
Target for expansion of university places by 1981 reduced to 600,000. Figure reduced further in subsequent years.

1978. DES Oakes Report **Report of the Working Group on the Management of Higher Education in the Maintained Sector (Cmnd 7130)**
Recommended establishment of a national advisory body for public sector higher education with institutions remaining within local authorities. On numbers, stated: 'It is clear that the era of rapid expansion is coming to a close and may be succeeded by a decline.'

1978. DES Brown Paper **Higher Education into the 1990s**
First attempt at rational planning of student numbers based on consultation. Attempt to examine likely impact of downward demographic trend of number of 18-year-olds from 1982/23 on demand for higher education.

1980. Education Act
Gave DES powers to cap the Advanced Further Education (AFE) pool.

1981. Public Expenditure White Paper (Cmnd 8175)
Announced cuts of resources which would mean universities losing between 11 and 15 per cent in real terms between 1980/81 and 1983/84.

1981. UGC Circular Letter 10/81
Detailed 1981/82 grant. Gave guidances on how each university might adjust to the reduced level of planned expenditure. Reductions were selective and based on an assessment of quality.

1981. DES Press Notice (November)
Establishment of National Advisory Body (NAB) for Local Authority Higher Education. Role: to advise the Secretary of State on the academic provision to be made in institutions in selected fields and on the appropriate use of his powers with regard to the apportion of the AFE pool and to the approval of advanced courses.

1982. DES Circular 5/82
New advanced courses of further education would be approved only if they met the needs of industry for skilled technological or scientific workers, or were essential in meeting regional or national employment demands.

1983. Public Expenditure White Paper (Cmnd 8789)

Contraction phase would probably be completed in 1984/85. Provision for 1985/86 would be reviewed.

1983. UGC Circular Letter 16/83 Development of a Strategy for Higher Education into the 1990s

Letter posed 28 questions under various subheadings. All universities and institutions required to reply officially to first two questions on resources and student numbers. Other questions could be answered by institutions, groups or individuals.

1984. UGC A Strategy for Higher Education into the 1990s

Explained new approach to the determination of universities' allocations, which would involve selective allocation of research funding. Argued that the opportunity should be seized to improve Age Participation Rate, and contained a joint statement with the NAB which reformulated and thus broadened the Robbins principle; failure to do so would lead to longer term shortages in many specialist skills. Proposed true-level funding in real terms at least until the end of the decade, with longer planning horizon than in recent years. More explicit guidelines should be drawn up to encourage a greater degree of self-funding, or joint funding and other forms of financial support.

1984. UGC General Memorandum of Guidance

UGC preferences on the balance between different subjects and between the numbers of undergraduates and postgraduates.

1985. UGC Circular Letter 12/85 Planning for the Late 1980s

Elaborated on principles in the UGC Strategy Document. Requested from universities information about their academic and financial plans for the four years ahead.

1985. UGC Circular Letter 22/85 Planning for the Late 1980s: The Resource Allocation Process

Letter to universities explaining the new resource allocation procedure. Referred to research performance indicators. Requested ideas about how assessment of teaching could be conducted.

1985. CVCP Jarratt Report Report of the Steering Committee for Efficiency Studies in Universities

Universities and the system as a whole should work to clear objectives and achieve value for money. Made proposals for the functioning of the DES and the UGC. Recommended that the UGC and the CVCP should develop PIs. Made recommendations on university policy and management structures, including: strengthening of role of council; rolling academic and institutional plans; vice-chancellor to be chief executive for the university; small planning and resources committee; budget delegation to appropriate centres; PIs; a more streamlined managerial structure.

1985. DES Green Paper The Development of Higher Education into the 1990s *(Cmnd 9524)*

Rejected an 'over-arching' body for higher education covering both sectors of the binary system. Revoked the concept of deficiency financing to universities (the system whereby universities were allocated funds sufficient to cover their costs). A clear expression of the economic ideology: 'The government believes that it is vital for our higher education to contribute more effectively to the improvement of the performance of the economy.' Subject to important caveats, it accepted the UGC and the NAB's reformulation of the Robbins principle. Predicted that demographic trends would result in a decline in the number of students in the 1990s. Emphasised the need to raise standards and increase effectiveness, selectivity and concentration.

1985. Lindop Report Academic Validation in Public Sector Higher Education *(Cmnd 9501)*

Made proposals for modes of validation to be adopted in the public sector, including stronger moves towards self-evaluation.

1986. UGC Circular Letter 4/86 Planning for the Late 1980s: Recurrent Grant for 1986/87

Gave details of the basis of the 1986/87 grant allocation, and in Part III, Annex 3 published research gradings of universities' 'cost centres'.

1986. CVCP Reynolds Report Academic Standards in the Universities

Set up codes of practice on the maintenance and monitoring of standards, including external examining and postgraduate training and research.

1987. Croham Report Review of the University Grants Committee *(Cm 81)*

Appointed by the DES to conduct a review of the UGC. Proposed the reconstitution of the UGC as a university grants council with broadly equal numbers of academic and non-academic members, a non-academic chairman and a full-time director-general drawn from the academic world. UGC to have 'unambiguous powers to attach conditions to grant'. Other proposals for tightening up accountability of universities.

1987. *DES White Paper* Higher Education: Meeting the Challenge *(Cm 114)*

Stated aims and purposes of higher education. Age participation rate to increase to 18 per cent. Made recommendations for quality and efficiency, including more selectively funded research, 'targeted with attention to prospects for commercial exploitation', and proposed improvements in management of the system. Favoured development and use of PIs. Polytechnics and some other institutions would become independent of local authority control. Proposed establishment of new Polytechnics and Colleges Funding Council (PCFC) and Universities Funding Council (UFC) and new contract arrangements for both sectors.

1987. *NAB* Management for a Purpose. The Report of the Good Management Practice Group

A report for the public sector somewhat equivalent to the Jarratt Report for the universities, but conducted by the National Advisory Body rather than under the auspices of the institutions.

1987. *UGC. The Oxburgh Report* Strengthening University Earth Sciences

Report on rationalisation of earth sciences from which proposals for grading of institutions on research potential have evolved. Not implemented.

1987. *Advisory Board for the Research Councils (ABRC)* A Strategy for the Science Base

Identified a lack of purposeful direction in the deployment of university research effort. Recommended creation of three types of institution (R, T and X) and greater emphasis on programme grants. Emphasis on Interdisciplinary Research Centres.

1987. *Education Reform Bill*

Bill published. Proposed profound changes for polytechnics and colleges which received little attention. Increased the power of the Secretary of State for Education and Science: could make grants to each of two new funding councils (UFC and PCFC) subject to conditions he could determine.

1988. Public Expenditure White Paper

40,000 students added to last published forecasts for the size of the higher education system in the rest of the decade.

1988. Education Reform Act

Provided for incorporation of non-university institutions. Polytechnics and colleges released from local government authority roots going back to 1966 White Paper. National Advisory Body to be replaced by PCFC. UGC to be replaced by UFC.

1989. PCFC Recurrent Funding Methodology 1990/91. Guidance for Institutions

Set out the funding method adopted by the PCFC following a consultative exercise on four options. The allocations to consist of two elements: core-funding based on a percentage of the previous year's allocation – 95 per cent in the first year – and an element for which institutions bid competitively and which would take quality of provision into account.

1989. CVCP VC/89/160A Sutherland Report The Teaching Function. Quality Assurance

Proposals based upon the recommendations of a group chaired by Professor Stewart Sutherland to create a CVCP Academic Audit Unit to monitor universities' own quality assurance. The unit was established in 1990.

1989. UFC Circular Letter 39/89 Funding and Planning: 1991/92 to 1994/95

Explained how the council intended to determine the distribution of recurrent funds in the four-year period from 1991/92. For funding on teaching-based criteria, universities were invited to submit offers of student places. Funding on research-based criteria to be increasingly selective, based on the assessments contained in Circular Letter 27/89 describing the results of the second RAE.

1990. UFC Circular Letter 29/90 Funding and Planning Exercise

Announced the council was unable to accept 'the limited scale of economy' offered by the universities' bids over the four-year planning period.

1991. DES *White Paper* Higher Education: A New Framework (Cm 1541)

Proposed: the end of the binary line; the establishment of new funding councils; research funding to be allocated entirely on a selective basis; quality audit to be the responsibility of the institutions and quality assessment that of the funding councils. Quality assessment was to inform funding. Predicted continuing expansion: 'By the year 2000, the government expects that approaching one in three of all 18–19-year-olds will enter higher education.'

1991. *CVCP, CDP, SCOP* Quality Assurance Arrangements for Higher Education

Paper sent to the Secretary of State describing the quality assurance organisation that the three bodies planned to establish to help member institutions to monitor and improve the quality of their teaching and to develop access. This led to the creation of the Higher Education Quality Council which incorporated the Academic Audit Unit.

1992. *Further and Higher Education Act and Further and Higher Education (Scotland) Act*

Created new funding councils: Higher Education Funding Council for England (HEFCE); Scottish Higher Education Funding Council (SHEFC); and Higher Education Funding Council for Wales (HEFCW). The Funding Councils were required to set up Quality Assessment Committees to assess quality in higher education. The CNAA was to be abolished. University status for polytechnics and all universities and colleges brought within a single funding mechanism operated by the Funding Councils for England, Wales, Scotland and Northern Ireland, which formally took over from April 1993 but started functioning earlier.

1992. *Government Reorganisation*

Responsibility for research councils transferred from the DES to a new Office for Science and Technology (OST), with its own Cabinet Minister in the Cabinet Office. DES became Department for Education (DFE).

1992. *DES Letters of Guidance to the Funding Councils from their Respective Secretaries of State*

Formally requested funding councils to work together with representatives from higher education institutions to build on earlier work and develop performance measures and indicators for both teaching and research. Set out the HEFCE responsibilities for Quality assessment. The councils were free to determine the method of assessment which should be in a form that could be used to inform funding allocations.

1992. DES Letter to CVCP, CDP, SCOP

From Secretary of State encouraging them to set up the proposed quality assurance organisation.

1993. HEFCE Circular 3/93. **HEFCE Assessment of the Quality of Education**

Outlined the purposes and methods of teaching quality assessment (TQA) organised by its Quality Assessment Committee. The purposes included: to ensure that higher education was of satisfactory quality or better, to encourage improvements in quality and to inform funding and reward excellence. Subject areas would be assessed within three categories: excellent, satisfactory and unsatisfactory.

1993. HEFCE. Circular 7/93 **Research Funding Method**

Described the method for funding research in the HEFCE institutions: the scores obtained in the 1992 RAE (1–5) would be translated into a funding scale of 0–4 in the funding allocations of 1993/94.

1993. OST White Paper **Realising Our Potential** *(Cm 2250)*

Set out a strategy for publicly funded research, including introduction of the Technology Foresight Programme. Research council structure reorganised and ABRC to be replaced by a Director-General for the Research Councils.

1994. HEFCE and HEFCW Commissioned Report **Assessment of the Quality of Higher Education: A Review and an Evaluation (Barnett Report)**

Proposed some changes to the HEFCE method of assessment, including universal visiting, summative judgement at the threshold level, and the framing of recommendations for improvement within a limited number of dimensions, so as to produce a 'quasi-profile'. Changes were introduced following the report.

1994. CVCP **CVCP 11 Point Plan**

Produced in reply to the Secretary of State's speech in April, inviting higher education to pay more attention to the broad comparability of academic standards. The plan centred on the intention to develop threshold standards for British higher education. Followed by the establishment by the HEQC of a Graduate Standards Programme.

1995. HEFCE Developing Quality Assurance in Partnership with the Institutions of Higher Education

The HEFCE's response to the Secretary of State's request for proposals to bring audit and assessment together. Proposed that a joint Planning Group comprising staff from the HEFCE and the HEQC would work out how a single Quality Assurance Agency could be developed from that process.

1995. Government Reorganisation

Department for Education merged with Department of Employment to form the Department for Education and Employment (DfEE). Office for Science and Technology moved into Department for Trade and Industry.

1995. DFEE Review of Higher Education

In the face of continued criticism about resources and quality assurance procedures, a departmental review of higher education was announced.

1997. Dearing Report Higher Education in the Learning Society

Established in 1996 to depoliticise higher education issues in the run-up to the general election. It reported after our main period of analysis. Comprehensive review of policy directed to the creation of a learning society. Key recommendations included: further expansion; a framework for qualifications; support for interdisciplinary research and a humanities research council; and radical changes in institutional and student funding.

Chapter 5

The Ending of the Binary System

The origins of the binary system

The ending of binaryism is, perhaps, the clearest example of discontinuity in policy in the British case. Anthony Crosland created the polytechnics in the mid-1960s. In doing so, he pursued what had long been implicit themes of education policy – public accountability in a major part of it, at least for the social and economic functions of higher education, and connection between higher education and the rest of the educational system. The Woolwich speech (Crosland 1965) thus evinced a public moral purpose for these then disparate components of higher education, whilst it somewhat grudgingly took for granted the self-evident virtues of having free autonomous universities meeting quite different functions with support from the public purse.

Unlike his Swedish counterparts, this leading theorist of egalitarianism did not support the more full-blown equality implicit in a unitary system. Instead, he had hoped that separate but equal systems would emerge, quite contrary to his own policies for secondary education. The special identity of the polytechnics was to remain an aspiration and a creed that persisted among some directors of polytechnics until the eve of their transformation into universities in 1992. In spite, however, of earlier advocations of the importance of sustaining their differences from universities (e.g. Burgess and Pratt 1974; Robinson 1968), incorporation as independent legal entities and thus release from local authority control were achieved in 1988, and university status in 1992.

Considerations other than educational lay behind the 1965 policy. It rationalised small into larger and more powerful institutions, though it was apparent that insufficient care was taken to weld them into whole and integrated institutions, and internal integration was achieved through the exercise of the strong bureaucracy that some displayed. Meeting the need to sustain the connection with the schools and with local and regional concerns, by placing them under the local authority control which most of the institutions already enjoyed or endured, also then met the then undisputed objective – shared by the political parties – to sustain local authority function and power. Thus, Crosland chose a path different from that followed by Aneuran Bevan for the National Health Service, who two decades before decisively rejected the local authority option for hospitals.

The DES, and particularly the members of HM Inspectorate concerned with advanced further education, cherished the development of a binary system because they felt it would sustain the public influence over the expanding higher education system, and ensure that the applied dimension would not be overrun by traditional academic concerns. They, no doubt, also felt that it would enable them to have more control over part of higher education than would be possible with the universities. They had, after all, brought them to this point of maturity. In a discussion with one of the present authors, a former senior HMI expressed regret that the former colleges of advanced technology had been later able, as technological universities, to slip away from their applied mission. The implication was that they might have pursued a more virtuous path had they remained in the public sector.

The old system and the Oakes Report

From the early 1970s, the polytechnics were given increasing academic autonomy through the trustful relationships created by the Council for National Academic Awards (CNAA). The provisions of the Weaver Report (1970) had earlier allowed for greater power to the academic boards and thus brought them nearer the style of the universities, although the structures and operations remained more hierarchical and managerial. Decisions on course approvals were still, however, made by regional staff inspectors of the DES and the Regional Advisory Councils. They assessed student demand, possible duplicated provision and the quality of what would be provided.

There was, however, no effective control over monies spent: the LEAs could charge a central pool, to which they all contributed, for the costs of providing higher education through their colleges. The *Report of the Working Group on the Management of Higher Education in the Maintained Sector* (1978), produced under the chairmanship of the Minister for Higher Education, George Oakes, 'focused on finance because the thing was getting out of hand ... local authorities were nominally running it but ... the institutions were running themselves and funding themselves very lavishly ... the government had to fund this, so we had to have some sort of check and basically the Oakes Report was put together to see how we did this ... without impinging on academic freedom: ... and ... which now seems a far-off dream, preserving some major role for the local authorities.' Oakes cited examples of departments in abstruse subjects with no, or very few, students which were impossible to close.

Oakes was a large committee; the AUT, the National Association of Teachers in Further and Higher Education (NATFHE), education authorities, universities and the maintained sector were represented, and each group was fighting for power. Gordon Oakes's own roots were in local government and he sided well with their representatives, including Tories, in favour of some form of democratic control over institutions of higher education. By then, some of the DES people, the NATFHE and the institutions would have been happy to remove local authority involvement. Oakes was supported by the vice-chancellors in declining to give institutions their independence. He agreed the pressure exerted by some local authorities was resented in some institutions but stated, 'My wish was that they would have done more rather than less.' He told local authorities he did not mind them having power, as long as they used it, which was ironic in view of the complaints from institutions in the 1980s about excessive local authority control.

The Oakes working group recommended that a national planning body should be set up for local authority colleges and thus supported the creation of a body analogous to the UGC which would also reduce the quasi-planning role of the DES (McVicar 1989). These proposals were abandoned with the fall of the Labour government in 1979. Nonetheless, in 1980 the new government decided to limit the size of the pool. The operation of the capped pool generated considerable discussions between institutions and the DES (mac.40) and between officials and ministers as to the appropriate mechanisms to use.

The rise and fall of the NAB

The DES produced plans which developed the wishes of the Secretary of State, Mark Carlisle, for colleges and polytechnics to be removed from local control and placed under a national body. When details of the plan, which were somewhat similar to the eventual PCFC, were leaked in the *THES* in early 1981, it 'produced a furore amongst the local authority representatives at national level' (Jones

1983, p.18). The creation of the National Advisory Body and its ultimate demise in 1989 were stages in the progressive increase in central control over higher education. The public sector had been demand rather than policy led. But parliamentary pressure and the manifest need for some planning machinery caused a reversal of this policy.

A convoluted process eventually led to the creation of the NAB (Jones 1983). Officials were not of one opinion, and ministerial changes led to shifts in policy emphasis. The Committee of Local Education Authorities (CLEA) envisaged a national body, similar to that proposed by the Oakes Report, which would be predominantly representative of the local authorities. The government's consultative document (DES 1981) contained the CLEA's proposals as model A and a 'limited centralist approach – similar to the eventual PCFC – as model B. The main concern of ministers was that given the prospect of diminishing resources the overriding need was for "contraction to be coordinated and not random ..."' (Jones 1983, p.17).

In the middle of the consultation process for the 1981 Green Paper, a ministerial reshuffle brought in Joseph and Waldegrave. Three factors weighed heavily with the new ministers: '...a desire for a trans-binary rationalisation and a recognition that a public sector coordinating body was a prerequisite; a desire to move quickly; and an unwillingness to further worsen local–central relations and a consequent unwillingness to contemplate introducing the contentious legislation that model B would have involved' (Jones 1983, p.220). For these reasons, ministers went for something that was nearer model A but with terms of reference and composition that somewhat reflected ministerial thinking.

The NAB was seen as a compromise solution which allowed a strong role for local government, but was one of the few quangos with responsibility to both central and local government. Its terms of reference were to advise the Secretary of State on the academic provision to be made in institutions, the apportionment of the Advanced Further Education pool, and the approval of advanced courses.

A two-tier structure was established. A committee, an essentially political body chaired, unusually, by the junior minister, had six LEA political representatives – local authority councillors – of whom three were Labour, two Conservative and one Liberal. This was placed over a board whose chairman was on the committee and whose members came from the DES, the LEAs and a range of other interests, including the institutions (Booth 1987). The chairman, Christopher Ball, was head of an Oxford college who, as we have seen, played a key role in the policy discussions about the future of higher education at large.

The NAB soon acquired an unusual internal political dynamic: 'At the second meeting, Waldegrave made the catastrophic error of allowing a vote on an issue. It was probably Nicky Harrison, one of the local authority people, who said, "Minister, we seem to be divided on this. I suggest we take a vote." He conceded. The DES officials were absolutely horrified. He had thrown it away. He could never outvote six of them. If they wanted something, they conspired. But by the end of the decade, the Thatcher government won hands down' (mac.2) (see also Salter and Tapper 1994). Waldegrave himself, however, believed in the importance, within a pluralistic society, of local authorities playing a role and told us he saw the NAB as providing one last opportunity for local authorities to show they deserved to have an important place in higher education.

A key function was the rationalisation of courses. This could have been difficult in view of the representative nature of the membership. The chairman of the board recounts: 'We had difficult periods trying to get them to balance their interests. One of the polytechnic directors systematically stopped everything we were trying to do. "Polytechnic directors don't agree with it; it can't happen." We were hung up on getting him to co-operate. At a board meeting I lost my temper with him ... I was ashamed of it, but politically it worked ... In its last year or two, NAB had become very cohesive ... we achieved more than possibly could be expected of us'.

A body which strove to be effective in a policy arena where powerful interests might be in contention inevitably aroused conflicting loyalties. The directors welcomed the NAB as a move towards a national system but were also worried about the influence exercised by the LEAs through it:

> NAB was a creature which they hated and loved ... institutionally it effectively reinforced a local authority grip – a collection of local authorities ... brought to a forum all the local authority perceptions and misperceptions and perhaps multiplied them up. Operationally, of course, it became under X [an official] a pretty ferocious little monster and it was certainly the whipping boy for the screwing down of the unit of resource ... it was seen to be a re-inforcement of all that was bad in local authority control without bringing any great advantage to polys. There was a great debate

about whether we [the CDP] should provide anyone to sit on it. (mac.43)

The presence of the local authorities in such force was irksome to the polytechnics who mostly wanted to be free of them. Some directors also thought some of the NAB staff to be associated with Labour local authority aspirations. They also suspected the local authorities of wanting to spread higher education too thinly, 'presumably to give their own local institution a place in the sun ... many of us in the CDP had had colleges of education thrust upon us. The academic standards of many were less than we would have thought desirable, and to see those colleges outside the polys getting more of the courses that we had pioneered was a bit difficult to swallow' (mac.105). Those representing institutions were thus divided. The considerable unease amongst polytechnic directors at the creation of the NAB was carried over into disputes over its operation (mac.2, 29, 40, 43, 49, 105, 111). According to one official, 'it was a hopeless muddle' (mac.22).

The LEAs owned the institutions but membership of the NAB required them to participate in a national planning frame. They did this vigorously and thus legitimated and were co-opted to the allocation of resources by a national body. They particularly promoted wider access: it was this, as much as local pride, that made the LEA representatives support dispersion rather than concentration of resources. Such conflicts as occurred were between central and local authority perspectives rather than on party lines.

The board's chairmanship was thought to be expert, though it elicited one resignation, but 'one sensed that if Richard Bird or one of his colleagues from DES towards the end of an argument said "But, chairman, we rather think that ministers would not agree with X", that was it, no more argument. So in the end the DES ensured things did not go too far wrong as far as their policy was concerned' ... 'Part of the reason for central government creating NAB was to give it greater control over how the expenditure was organised. With NAB saying exactly what would be the priorities in approving new courses ... but the difficulty was that neither the local authorities nor the central government at that time really understood higher education [or] ... the organic growth of academic life' (mac.105). An alternative view of the relationship with the DES and the board was that the ministerial participation did not make decisive the part played by the DES: 'To the extent that there was central and local government around the NAB table ... and that ministers were not able quite to dictate, nor were local politicians ... there was that negotiating spirit

... the presence, however modest, of institutional representatives was quite important because they were part of that negotiation' (mac.2).

At any rate, ministers held different views of their task: 'Walden hated it. Waldegrave gave every impression of liking it ... Peter Brooke saw it as a job of work to do ... Walden must have reported back that this was intolerable, ministers in the Conservative government being treated like this. That must have been a factor, but it was all part of a bigger debate. The DES had been driving on for a decade to take over. The Thatcher government wanted to emasculate local government' (mac.2). The NAB episode was, in fact, a period of maximum influence which aroused disquiets which eventually contributed to far less power for the local authorities than hitherto. It was structured to be a political arena in which the different parties would be unwilling to give each other much space.

The chairman perceived there to be three main problems to be tackled: what to do about research; what to do about regional strategy; and how to create a quality system. At the end of the decade, he thought much progress had been made on each. There were several cross-binary NAB/UGC planning exercises, and the *Good Management* Report which, it was later claimed, 'reconciled the new managerialism with the best of the old values. Particularly what we were keen on which was pushing responsibility down, the subsidiarity principle ... Putting it to bed was difficult because people had begun to take sides. The new struggle for the heart of local authority higher education.'

The NAB played a key role in changing the content and style of the policy discussion about higher education. Ball's evaluation was: 'We raised questions about what higher education should be about.' The NAB was single-minded about its planning role: 'We were quite a player in helping David Phillips's thesis to become successful – establishing the principle of planning, and making it work ... Our openness went beyond normal higher education practice ... We published all of our papers. Gave them to *THES* and said here is our funding methodology, print it if you want to ... This was only qualified when the reputation of individual institutions was at issue. We faced difficulty in getting the intelligence needed to make rationalisation decisions. But we asked the CNAA and BTEC [Business and Technical Education Council] for judgements on quality. We did not always get co-operation from the bodies who were there to do it. It was more difficult for the CNAA than HMI. That is because CNAA decided it had to give its quality information publicly.'

But the NAB was to come to an end. Salter and Tapper (1994) took the view that by the mid-1980s the NAB's role as a national planning and funding agency was severely constrained by the anarchic politics inherent in its constitution. As a holding operation for central–local tensions, 'it had from the DES perspective outlived its usefulness ... Five years of arduous compromise with the multiplicity of interests had convinced successive Secretaries of State that there must be an easier way of dealing with this sector' (p.146). The contrary view was that the central problem of a planning agency was to get the balance between access and quality right. Thus, Christopher Ball: 'I stand on the record that during the 1980s we succeeded well in getting the balance right. Since then, risks have been taken with quality in those institutions.'

By 1986, tension had built up over the choice between sustaining an acceptable unit of resource and expanding numbers. The NAB published proposals for the 1987 planning exercise showing that, on the resources allowed by the government, 10,000 student places would have to disappear. At a moment uncomfortably close to the 1987 general election, government felt bound to yield by providing an increased allocation: but the episode helped to number the days of LEA control (McVicar 1989).

Incorporation

At the time of the NAB, the public sector, led by the polytechnics, was beginning to draw alongside the universities, but if release from LEA control was being contemplated by some, the unification of the two sectors was on no active agenda. It would have to contend with two major obstacles: the claims of local authorities to play a part in higher education, and universities' pre-emption of a unique status.

On the primary issue of LEA control, in the early 1980s the local authorities were strong enough to be able to condition DES thinking about the creation of any body that would affect them or condition their control. The Conservatives in the early 1980s had a small majority and were losing by-elections. Some polytechnics feared that removal of local authority control, with which they were familiar, might be replaced by that of the DES. The Department of the Environment backed the LEAs. It was only later on that a convergence of views developed between the polytechnic directors and the Conservative government (mac.100).

A minority of members of the CDP remained in favour of the LEA connection but, with the retirement of the first wave of directors, some of whom previously had been principals of colleges of technology and who saw themselves as local authority people, the CDP 'was gradually becoming a different body; the entrenched views which had started right in the beginning were then withering – we were getting a different sense of purpose' (mac.105).

Much of the argument presented itself when directors were considering the place of the LEAs on the national body (mac.105): '... the divide was between those directors whose polys were funded generously with top-up from the local authority and those polys which not only didn't have top-up but had their funds raided by LEAs. They may have welcomed NAB as a step towards creating a national body for public sector higher education (PSHE) but were opposed because NAB was so dominated by local authorities. The great majority of CDP members ... were very much against the domination of local authorities. A few were in favour – the directors of N. Staffs, Thames and Leeds.' For their part, the local authority associations had worked effectively within the Tory Party to persuade ministers to support the option for the NAB that contained more local authority representation (Salter and Tapper 1994). 'Although the CDP, in its response to the Lindop Report,[1] was still referring to the importance of the connection with the local authorities ... it was not expressing a love for them but at that time saying let's go step-by-step towards independence ... we were careful usually not to upset the local authorities which in the end had a veto on various things' (mac.105).

An NAB report (NAB 1987) suggested that local authority controls were inhibiting the development of polytechnics. Its chairman described to us that 'there were three logical positions that could be taken. One was to defend the status quo which gave local authorities control of NAB, if they wanted it. If Chief Education Officers wanted to, they could override the appointments of governors. We said that was unsustainable and got NAB to say so. We went for the middle position of keeping the local authority voice within NAB but effectively removing local authority control from the individual institutions. Institutions would achieve autonomy but with

---

1   The Lindop Report (1985) led to the location of responsibility for academic
     standards more firmly with public sector institutions themselves.

local authority representation. The third position was that of the CDP [which the government adopted] to get local authorities completely out with no representation on governing bodies, and abolish NAB while they were about it. The government made that decision for Thatcherite reasons concerned with the future of local government. More than on the merits of the case. We presented what we thought of as a sensible middle position. It was brave of NAB at the political level to adopt it. The government then used it to support their anti-local position.'

The Committee of Directors of Polytechnics had for some time been pressing for freedom from their LEAs. As Baker recalls, some directors had direct access to Mrs Thatcher. One participant recalls, 'I'm told that someone sat on Mrs Thatcher's sofa at Number 10 and made the case and all was done ... I'm prepared to believe ... that personal persuasion and connection was important but it was nevertheless the case, to go back to the '88 legislation, that the CDP for two or three years put on a very strong collective show at successive annual conferences, to which the Secretary of State came, and pointed out the realities, both political and educational, of the need for a change. So that breakthrough did demonstrate to ministers that there was a collective will – whether that was a revelation to ministers about policies which in any case they were pursuing for other purposes, or were on the move towards making up their mind about, I don't know' (mac.43).

The arguments for release from LEA control – not the same issue as making them into universities – were stated by one director (mac.105): 'The main change was not so much the change of title from polytechnic to university but releasing the polytechnics from local authority control and making them independent bodies in law. Then their governing bodies ... were responsible ... for what went on and were able to bring, particularly as most of the governing body were connected with the employing side of industry, a sense of purpose which hitherto, to some extent, had been much weaker in the polytechnics simply because the local authorities were in control and they were a dead hand, without any doubt, and not least because, for example ... the County Council retained £1m a year of our budget ... supposedly for services rendered, but I could never understand which those services were.'

And another interviewee argued:

Over that whole period ... they wanted to escape from local authority control and they wanted to achieve university status or at

least a status which more overtly acknowledged their comparability with universities, and at various times … we produced a draft charter, a draft model for incorporation etc. … from the very foundation of the CDP … they were uncomfortable with LEA control and felt that the anomalous arrangement of the binary system – not comparable to international systems – ought to be corrected. [The repackaging of polys fits into the expansion or enhancement of access.] … The polys were dedicated to this, and the willingness of government to accede to growing demand and partially fund it weakened the case for leaving polys in a second-class status. (mac.43)

DES officials had increasingly seen advantages in the polytechnics gaining independence from local authorities: 'The institutions were growing bigger and more self-confident, the people who ran them were exercising their powers on a wider stage, we were seeing more of them … in a way, preparing themselves for independence – there were cases where it was manifestly rather silly having an LEA umbrella for something that was larger than the LEA (Kingston Poly was bigger than Kingston LEA more or less and felt like it) … they were spreading their wings and NAB helped with that … I had a sense of a more confident sector – one that was clear that it had great economic relevance both locally and regionally, that had a lot of relevant research as well as relevant teaching, which didn't want to cut its ties with local government but didn't really see why it should be run by local government' (mac.40).

Another suggested it had been a long-term policy of officials which was waiting for a political imprimatur (although one key informant does not share this recollection):

For many years before 1988, DES officials had been in favour of [it]. They persuaded Mark Carlisle to propose it, as indeed he did, but he later withdrew the proposal in the face of opposition from the representatives of local government. Keith Joseph did not revive the proposal but Ken Baker put it into effect with the Department's full support. Our motivation as officials was that operation within local government stood in the way of the management of polytechnics as effective educational institutions. Subsequent experience has shown that we were right. (mac.22)

The decision came at a particular time in the history of central–local government relationships. Ministerial dislike of local government was manifest. Independence was granted, partly out of dislike of local government, partly because there was more general discussion of reducing local government's resource base by taking teachers' salaries out of it. The case for it was reinforced by the accounts of local authority behaviour given by the polytechnic directors to ministers. Some polytechnics got on well with their local authorities, but others complained of political and administrative interference. One senior official quoted several examples of complaints that were put to the Department in the years before 1988. 'One polytechnic claimed that it had to wait for the next meeting of the appropriate subcommittee of the local authority before being able to recruit an extra part-time gardener. Another was astonished to get an audit query about the price paid for a pint of milk: not a lot of milk – one pint. Most serious of all, an ILEA polytechnic director complained that left-wing staff appealed against management decisions to like-minded politicians on the ILEA, thus making it impossible for the director to manage the polytechnic effectively' (mac.22).

Unification

The success of the polytechnics in persuading ministers that they should not only become free of the LEAs but also become universities is all the more remarkable in view of the strict, if somewhat opaque, rules of admission to that status that had been applied in previous years. It was wholly a political and not an academic judgement, and one on which not even the Universities Funding Council, let alone the senior academies or CVCP (mac.108), were consulted. Had there been consultation, some resistance might have been expected. Douglas Hague wrote in *Beyond Universities* (1991): 'One day some politician will be daft enough to let the polytechnics be called universities.' Whilst the moves to university status came more quickly than the polytechnics, or many others, expected, and Shirley Williams had thought the unification must take place ultimately, it was by no means a foregone conclusion. Civil servants may have been in favour of granting the degrees of freedom proposed in the Lindop Report (1985), but found it difficult to persuade ministers; had Joseph remained in office, they would have had to struggle hard to become universities in view of his somewhat canonical view of academic standards (mac.8). Joseph was suspicious of polytechnic standards and of the controls exercised by the CNAA (mac.47). Nor would John Patten have allowed it (mac.108). A prominent junior minister, well after the event, said that he 'would have stopped any move towards polytechnics attempting to get university status in his time'. Higher education institutions 'had a job to do. Now they're all mixed up. We don't have HE any longer, we have longer education in this country and certain places have HE within it ... there should be pecking order all the way through ... the whole system now is a mess and will have to be sorted out again.' With the new names – 'it's a nightmare to the rest of the world now – they think they're going to a first-class university and they finish up at what might have been about the standard of a teacher training college in 1945 and that's a con trick to me, of both the pupils and the parents' (mac.8).

The CVCP had advised ministers against unification over a long period (mac.210) but were not against incorporation – a different matter – 'because they sympathised with them in wanting to get rid of the dead hand of local authorities. They did not anticipate the ultimate outcome of this process' (mac.28). Yet, eventually, they supported both moves. The present distinction was 'now outdated and should be abolished. The government's proposals to legislate to set up unified funding councils, unified quality control mechanisms and to allow institutions teaching at first degree level and above to use the name "university" therefore have the CVCP's support' (CVCP 1991). This may have come about because they saw it as a political inevitability, and also saw they would be by no means the certain victors in any competition for resources with a public sector that had won ministerial approval.

It was an almost casual decision, even if backed by official advice, by Kenneth Clarke – whatever the merits of a unitary system – to follow up incorporation, granted by Kenneth Baker, by full university status. The polytechnics were thought to have earned this, through their positive responses to social and economic needs, and because of what they demonstrated to be inappropriate treatment at the hands of local authorities (mac.1). 'I recall them pressing very hard to be called polytechnic-universities and Kenneth Baker turning them down, and then we had changes of Secretary of State ... It happened very quickly, the change from firm no, beyond the halfway house they'd asked for, to them getting the full loaf they hadn't really been pushing for' (mac.15).

One director recalls a conversation with Kenneth Clarke about possible ideas, modelled on the USA, for institutions, including existing universities, offering their own degrees but having them nationally validated: 'Clarke seemed to think this was just messing about: "Let's take the great plunge and make them all universities, let's get rid of all the arguments."' 'Baker and Clarke in their actions on unification took decisions and gave the appearance of consulting afterwards...they sought change as might Panzer Generals' (mac.105).

The end came quickly. 'There was pressure, mainly from the CDP, to abolish the binary line. The Secretary of State at the time, Kenneth Clarke, indicated that he would want to consider an objective analysis of the proposal by officials before offering a view. For many of the reasons set out in the subsequent White Paper [1991], the analysis favoured a unified sector and bore out much of what the CDP had been saying. Kenneth Clarke decided to endorse the abolition of the binary line. Both the White Paper and legislation [1992] followed quickly without major difficulties. The most difficult areas for policy were quality assurance and research: indeed, the White Paper offered an interim decision on the continuation of dual support arrangements and this was not confirmed until the Science White Paper [1993]. The main interest in the legislation was in the House of Lords, where the focus of attention was the power of the Secretary of the State in setting conditions of grant on the new unified funding council' (mac.108). It is worth noting that the civil servants' analysis was never laid open to external scrutiny, or the issue, one of the most important ever faced in educational policy, put out for public discussion prior to the announcements being made. The issue was decided by the interaction of quite closed interests and politics.

Then it happened. 'One day, the senior chief inspector, Tony Melia, came to a CDP meeting and said, "You have got everything you have ever dreamt of." The directors of polytechnics were astonished to hear that they were all to become universities' (mac.6). According to one civil servant, there was considerable anxiety that the Department might allow only 15 in and that even the most influential ones could not be sure that they were going to be amongst the 15.

The joining together

Some polytechnic directors were uncertain about whether they should join the CVCP and, if so, whether it should change its title. In the end, they accepted they had to join and that there was no bimodal possibility. The CVCP had already had to incorporate a very broad range of universities even before unification. Some of its new members might have imagined that the old CVCP was totally homogeneous. 'It was not homogeneous at all. It was the big civics rather than Oxbridge who had the chairs of the committees in the 1970s' (mac.10).

There was then the esoteric issue of university titles which required scrutiny of the Ecclesiastical Acts of the 1850s. Under those, when the Roman Catholic Church set itself up again with its own dioceses, they were not allowed to use the titles of the Anglican dioceses on the grounds that the use of the same title would lead to 'confusion and offence'. The same principle was now applied to the new universities.

Discussion and conclusions

In unifying higher education, the UK followed the logic of development that seems to apply to other systems. A first step undertaken by many systems has been to consolidate and enhance those parts of post-school education which both depend for their intellectual substance on disciplined enquiry and yet look towards the world of application. For a while, they remain the less 'noble' part of higher education. Increasingly, as concepts of what constitutes advanced learning and enquiry become broader, and the non-university institutions seek to emulate universities in undertaking research, a natural process of convergence sets in. Only where the most determined efforts are made to sustain a viable non-university sector, as in the Californian system, or in German *Fachhochschulen*, supported as it is by the specific requirements of professional entry to employment, is the division sustained. Hence the trends in the creation of single but differentiated patterns in the USA, Australasia and Sweden. The existing binary systems, such as in Finland, Norway and Greece, can be predicted to go the same way within 30 years. The British system was amongst the strongest cases for unification, for it accommodated a smaller proportion of each school-leaving age group than other countries, and assumed from the beginning that most of the higher education student body was capable of reaching degree standard – an assumption not shared by the broader gauge binary systems in some other countries.

In considering the significance of the break, we must distinguish between incorporation and the end of local authority control and the conferment of university status. 'The formal ending was not of great significance because changes among institutions on both sides have been such as to make it an increasingly fuzzy natural phenomenon as opposed to a design phenomenon. Some polys evolved with emphasis on more traditional courses similar to universities and doing quite a lot of research' (mac.16). There was, indeed, an overlap of institutions across the divide. This can be illustrated from the growth in numbers of postgraduate students in each sector (Becher, Henkel and Kogan

1994). But this comment, perhaps, underestimates the market advantages of the university title and the ability to compete over time for resources from which the polytechnics had hitherto been largely excluded.

The out-turn of these changes has yet to be evaluated. The 'old' universities lost the protection accorded to those whose standards were accepted without challenge. Some reshuffling of the order of esteem, particularly at the point of previous overlap, could be expected. The most esteemed institutions would remain secure or, indeed, better secured because comparisons that were difficult to make before could be made. Alongside legal homogeneity went a creed of diversity which continued to accommodate both elite and mass strata of academic existences.

The end of the binary system constitutes a major case study in the post-1970s politics of higher education. Central government responded to those interests whose objectives coincided with theirs. Suspicion of local government and ministers' perceptions of the shortcomings of universities must have persuaded them that these were interests which need not be accommodated. The relationship with the CDP was otherwise. The issue was decided by the interaction of quite closed interests and politics. It was also decided by ministers who lacked the deference to academe of a previous political generation. The Fellows of All Souls were off the educational scene by then, and ministers were the kind of Oxbridge graduate who were *au fait* with university styles but not believers in its culture.

The moves against local authority control were connected with changing assumptions about public institutions. Originally, there had been the parallel theories of the free universities, best able to use their freedom to produce excellent research and scholarship, whilst the polytechnics would be more aligned with public purposes through their connections with local government. Now there was a theory of institutions free to compete with each other but working within far tighter funding and demands for accountability, as largely expressed through quality assurance.

Chapter 6

The Changing State Apparatus

In this chapter we take up in more detail the history of changes to governmental bodies and to relationships between the state and higher education. We examine how far ministers or civil servants were the prime movers behind the 'reforms' and analyse the claim that higher education has been subject to growing centralisation.

I THE HISTORY OF THE CHANGING RELATIONSHIPS

Whilst central-policy makers, but not all former ministers, generally contested the point, higher education has from at least the early 1980s, and in some views before even then, been subjected to more government control. This claim is supported by most with whom we have discussed the matter and many who have written on this topic (e.g. Berdahl 1990, p.179; Jenkins 1996, pp.142–145; Salter and Tapper 1994, p.93; Scott 1995, p.43; Shattock 1994, p.136).

The University Grants Committee (UGC): from creation to 1975

Some government intervention on constitutional arrangements occurred through a succession of Royal Commissions from the nineteenth until the middle of the twentieth century. In the early 1900s, Haldane and others argued for a connected system of education in universities, schools and colleges in which curricula should provide culture and apply scientific and other forms of knowledge to practical life.

The UGC was established in 1919 by a Treasury minute as a committee reporting directly to the Treasury to advise on the distribution of recurrent and capital grants to universities. Throughout the UGC's history (Berdahl 1977; Carswell 1985; Shattock 1994), the relationship between universities and the state was a key issue. The direct link between the UGC and the Treasury was seen as central. The reasons for the Treasury being given responsibility are contested but its impact was important. Only a few other organisations, including national museums and galleries, and later the Arts Council, had a comparable deal: 'The willingness of the Treasury to accept such departures from convention was probably cultural. Universities and the arts were subjects in which Treasury officials had a personal interest. They liked them and knew the people who worked in them. They were thus happy to keep them close' (Jenkins 1996, p.137). The UGC was seen by some as coming out of the New Liberal principles of the actors of the time: 'They knew that the government had got to provide the funds to do this and they damn well knew that the government should have nothing at all to do with the distribution of the funds' (mac.46). The autonomy of the universities and the buffer role of the UGC took a particular form; some interviewed referred to talks in the Athenaeum Club to resolve difficulties (e.g. mac.44). Although others have contested this view, it seems consistent with the opinion that in the 1930s the universities:

> ... were very closely integrated with the state as it then was ... and they formed just as indispensable a part of the framework of national institutions as they do now. The links, however, were personal and social, not bureaucratic or formal. The universities and the machinery of Government in both its political and official aspects formed a kind of continuum, in which only the sketchiest of formality was either expected or required to maintain necessary relationships. (Carswell 1985, p.159)

There was a trustful relationship between the state and the universities so that, even if the universities were closely integrated, the political culture, as described in Chapter 2, was such that control and interference by the state were at a minimum. Such a situation was 'regulation by mutual understanding' (mac.32). The proportion of public funding is no secure indication of the strength of public control, but in 1938 grants were only about one-third of universities' total revenue, although today even such a proportion would be a much higher percentage of GDP.

In wartime, academics were willing to serve the state and in 1946 the Committee of Vice-Chancellors noted:

> Universities entirely accept the view that the government has not only the right but the duty to satisfy itself that every field of study which in the national interest ought to be cultivated in Great Britain is in fact being cultivated in the university system and that the resources which are placed at the disposal of universities are being

used with full regard both to efficiency and economy. (CVCP 1946)

The CVCP also requested greater guidance from the government on how they should 'devise and execute policies calculated to serve the national interest'. However, 'unless there had been fundamental trust that any British government would have a close understanding of what university ideals were, no such request for guidance could or would have been made' (Niblett 1952, p.168, quoted in Salter and Tapper 1994, p.8). This suggests the prewar pattern had been continued. Also: 'At this stage the universities could assume a common ideology to exist between themselves and other sections of the elite' (Tapper and Salter 1978, p.168).

After the war, there were changed attitudes on how the state should be administered, but there was some reversion to prewar thinking in relation to key aspects of administration (Hennessy 1988). In the postwar Labour government, the Minister of Education and the Chancellor of the Exchequer were inclined to put the universities under the control of the Ministry of Education but both ministry mandarins and the Treasury were opposed (Benn and Fieldhouse 1993). Although some moves were made to increase government influence, the importance still attached to university autonomy is reflected in Attlee's recollection: 'When I was in office, I steadily refused to try to increase the influence of the State on the universities... There are matters in which I think it is better to have trust and I think this is one of them' (Parliamentary Debates, 1957, cols 1125–1126, quoted in Benn and Fieldhouse 1993, p.304).

From 1945 to roughly 1975, the UGC was able to promote expansion while maintaining the classic relationship between state and universities. It was regarded by the universities as the guardian of their liberties – the buffer between them and the government as one UGC chairman put it (another called it a septic tank) – and by government as responsible for seeing that increasing sums from the public purse were spent in the national interest. The centre's mode of influence was that of negotiation rather than of control. A proposal for a wide-ranging inquiry into the universities in 1958 was, indeed, headed off by Treasury opposition on the grounds that it would injure their autonomy and call into question the role of the UGC (Walker 1989). The UGC deprecated any attempt to regard research as an activity separate from teaching, 'partly because it might give the impression that useful guidance could be given from the centre on the balance of effort between teaching and research' (UGC 1958).

The central authorities' allocations to the universities had been made on the basis of the judgements of academics working through informal peer review. The judgements of government reflected those of academics co-opted through membership of the central bodies. As we saw in Chapter 3, it has been questioned (Becher and Kogan 1992; Shattock 1996) whether in the period from 1945 to 1980 higher education constituted a system in more than a notional sense: the linkages were relatively loose.

It is not clear how far the UGC was actively taking initiatives. In 1964 the responsibility for the UGC was transferred from the Treasury to the newly amalgamated Department of Education and Science (DES), but the intended connection between higher education and science was never securely made. For the first year of the change, the deputy secretaries for higher education and science never exchanged views. Referring to 1963–79, Shattock claims that 'neither the DES nor the UGC, nor it must be said, for the most part, the universities, were inclined to launch new policy initiatives' (Shattock 1994, p.9). However, in this period the UGC attempted to play a more active role but nevertheless lost power to the government. Between 1952 and 1974, Salter and Tapper suggest that 'the increase in the UGC's power over the universities is matched by a decrease in its power vis-à-vis the central bureaucratic state' (Salter and Tapper 1994, p.124).

An expanding system caused the UGC to become more involved in systematic policy making. University salaries were made uniform. Because in the 1960s many new, and some old, institutions received charters, the UGC was compelled to take, and to express, a view of what universities should be like; vetting bids for new universities inevitably caused the UGC to build up criteria. It became essential that it should be able to review university needs and efficiency, although it stood firm on the quinquennial freedoms of over two decades.

The increase in the number of university institutions from 24 in 1944 to 43 in 1967 required the Committee to exercise a more positive role. It saw the need to take cognisance of what the five research councils, which also reported to the DES, might do. But in the heyday of manpower planning, of the ill-fated National Plan (DEA 1965), the UGC did not itself feel able to translate general expressions of need into particular numbers and types of output, though it would expect to have some say on the introduction of a new block of subjects. For guidance of national and manpower requirements, it looked to the government.

A more directive style over universities is commonly thought to have been initiated in the 1967 quinquennial statement, when UGC preferences on the balance between different subjects and between the numbers of undergraduates and postgraduates were first stated in detail. Although, with hindsight, this guidance was not seen as being strong (mac.48), the UGC commented: '…we are now inescapably involved in making positive judgements, an activity which goes far beyond the capacity of a buffer or a shock absorber' (UGC 1968, quoted in Tapper and Salter 1978, p.170). Committee members saw themselves increasingly 'as becoming more "dirigiste"' (UGC 1968, quoted in Tapper and Salter 1978, p.170).

Although some (for example, Jenkins 1996) suggest the universities ended the 1970s in pretty good shape, many claim a change took place at some point between the 1950s/1960s and the end of the 1970s. For some, the period from 1960 to 1973/74 was the golden age (mac.109). Another interviewee suggests:

> One of the really big changes for a … VC in the 50s and 60s and one in the mid and late 70s was that the quinquennial allocation had gone. We would have assumed in the 60s that first you would have the money you needed (and, of course, then the UGC told the government what funding in its view was necessary, and the first time it gave a penny less there was a total outrage, whereas now it's the other way round) … you had five years' notice for what it was, and you were pretty free to spend it – those were the three things about funding which were true of the 60s. It's not true now … The quinquennium stopped about '73/'74 … An indication that things were changing … was in '69, already somebody like Shirley Williams is saying, 'think about this, that and the other' – that would have been quite inconceivable five or six years earlier. (mac.48)

Shirley Williams's 13 points, referred to by several interviewees, were set out in a memorandum from the CVCP following her meeting with them and the UGC in September 1969 (see Figure 6.1). They consisted of a series of possible ways in which unit costs might be reduced or the number of students engaged on conventional university study limited. They were points for consideration rather than formal proposals but were rejected by the universities. Nevertheless, coming from a minister more likely than most to be sympathetic to universities' values and anxieties, they illustrate the extent to which the impermeability of universities was no longer taken for granted well before the Conservative victory of 1979.

The fact that in 1969 such proposals were made at all suggested things were changing, but that universities were able to dismiss the 13 points indicates the level of autonomy from the state that still existed.

The points are as follows:

i)   a reduction or removal of student grant-aid, coupled with a system of loans;

ii)   a similar policy at the postgraduate level only;

iii)   a more restrictive policy as regards the admission of overseas students;

iv)   the requirement that grant-aided students should enter specified kinds of employment for a period after graduation, which might have the effect of reducing applications;

v)   the greater use of part-time and correspondence courses as alternatives to full-time courses;

vi)   the possibility that the most able should have the opportunity to complete a degree course in two years;

vii)   the possibility of some students not proceeding to the customary three-year course but to a different course lasting only two years and leading to a different qualification;

viii)   the possible insertion of a period between school and university, which would give school-leavers a better opportunity to formulate their views as to whether or not they wished to proceed to some form of higher education;

ix)   the more intensive use of buildings and equipment, including the possibility of reorganisation of the academic year;

x)   more sharing of facilities between adjacent institutions;

xi)   more home-based students;

xii)   the development of student housing associations, and other forms of loan-financed provision for student residences;

xiii)   some further increase in student/staff ratios.

Source: DFEE library

Figure 6.1 Mrs Shirley Williams's thirteen points

However, their rejection also showed (and further exacerbated) a developing rift between the universities and the state. The 1972 quinquennium agreement collapsed within a couple of years in the face of rising inflation and deteriorating public finances.

Developments in the UGC from 1975

Our main period of analysis starts from about 1975, which represents the beginning of the post-quinquennium system. According to one leading participant: 'Modern times begin with the IMF in '76' (mac.46). The Minister for Higher Education, Lord Crowther-Hunt, who was known to be keen on manpower planning, told a conference in 1975: 'It simply will not do to allow universities and polytechnics to produce whatever people they fancy or to relate the number and kind of places they provide to the applications that come forward' (*THES*, 16 May 1975, quoted in Tapper and Salter 1978, p.163). In Chapter 4 we noted that in 1976 the UGC had to report a series of ad hoc decisions related to changing national pressures which was creating a deep and damaging sense of uncertainty. The Select Committee on Science and Technology in 1976 urged the DES to be more directive in its relationship with the UGC and research councils, and asserted that it was 'far too passive' (SCST 1976). By 1979 'the UGC system was in serious disrepair. Its planning mechanisms were in tatters, with the chairman being able to do little more than react to the twists and turns of the Government's counter-inflation policy' (Shattock 1994, p.19). Even before 1979 some were predicting the end of the UGC. Building on their idea that there was no longer a common ideology for higher education, Tapper and Salter claimed in 1978: 'Once fragmentation in the elite ideology occurred the UGC was bound in the long run to succumb to the stronger protagonist, the government. But the process was not a straightforward one, nor is it yet complete' (1978, p.169).

Many interviewees thought that 'the transition was from '79 when Margaret Thatcher arrived' (mac.103). Although elsewhere we suggest the picture is more complex, the main immediate pressures post-1979 were financial (see Chapter 4) and these necessitated organisational responses. Thus, the UGC chairman, Sir Edward Parkes, told the CVCP: 'There is going to be in the future a somewhat greater degree of direct intervention by the UGC in the affairs of individual universities than has been customary or necessary in the past' (UGC 1980, quoted in Shattock 1996, p.14). Student numbers had been gently rising and the Robbins target for 1980/81 was nearly achieved. In approaching the target, there was not 'much serious encroachment on university autonomy' but there was 'the replacement of a social continuum by a bureaucratic system which marks the period. A line came to be drawn between the universities and Government which nobody had felt to be there before' (Carswell 1985, p.166).

The admission of additional students in 1979/80 caused particular problems because the student support budget became overspent and therefore the institutional cuts requested by the Treasury for 1981 were greater than originally planned (mac.108).

How far, at the time of the 1981 cuts, the government encouraged the polytechnics to admit the applicants thus displaced is a contested issue but it was certainly not an explicitly stated policy. The UGC's performance at this time has been strongly criticised (e.g. Kogan and Kogan 1983), either on the grounds that it did not do enough to resist the cuts, or because it imposed them by reducing student numbers rather than reducing the unit of resource. But 'the vigour with which the UGC tackled the task greatly restored its prestige within Whitehall' (Shattock 1994, p.20), although as we have seen (Chapter 4), the UGC, with its determination to defend the unit of resource, came under increasing critical scrutiny from two parliamentary select committees – both chaired by Labour MPs. Joel Barnet chaired the Public Accounts Committee and Christopher Price the Education Science and Arts Select Committee.

By 1985 the UGC was on its way to becoming a full-blooded planning organisation which required universities to respond in the same mode. It called for statements of overall objectives for the planning period, a detailing of research achievements and plans, forecasts of student numbers in various student groups and financial forecasts up to July 1990. This type of request became normal and frequent. The universities were pressed without remission not only for data but also for declarations of their intentions. The May 1985 letter spelled out the UGC's intended method of allocating grants. One of the components was to be a research assessment based partly on the ability to earn research grants and partly on the UGC's judgement of research quality. The letter introduced explicit departmental rankings (UGC 1985).

In 1986 the UGC published ratings of the research standing of all university 'cost centres'; the use of that designation of higher education units was significant in itself. That act of public evaluation was intended to increase resources for those centres deemed excellent, to deflect trade from those deemed to be below par and to assure ministers that academics would respond to their notions of accountability and not simply bask in the informal rules of the Republic of Science. It represented a decisive move towards formula funding. As we saw in Chapter 4, the UGC was under considerable pressure to introduce selectivity because, by now, the research councils, or the ABRC, were campaigning to gain control of at least some of the UGC's research money (mac.22, 45 and 103).

The UGC's 1984 Strategy Document also signalled that attention was going to focus more on the need for institutions to be effectively managed. During the UGC's latter years, its function went beyond the strenuous and detailed determination of funding. At the behest of the DES, it put pressure on the universities to move to models of strong management in both their structures and behaviour. A committee appointed under the auspices of the CVCP produced a report (Jarratt Report 1985) which promulgated a full managerial doctrine. As noted in Chapter 3, this report was part of a series of efficiency studies conducted throughout government departments, but the exceptionalism of higher education was illustrated by the fact that the system was allowed to conduct its own enquiry, albeit with members of the Efficiency Unit, which was conducting reviews throughout other government departments, on the committee. The business approach of Jarratt himself was also thought to be important – it was very much in line with the corporate planning and devolution of implementation that the government professed to support in the public services. The report's implementation was a requirement the UGC placed on universities, a few of which adopted it with avidity. The requirements for universities to respond to increasing UGC enquiries, to meet the demands for selectivity, and to satisfy the Jarratt definition of efficiency, are widely thought to have increased the power of university administration at the expense of senior academics and the academically led committee systems. However, some point out that the few who gained power included academics who served on the committees. These issues are discussed at greater length in Chapter 7.

At every point of control, the centre asserted itself: on the numbers of students to be recruited; on higher education's duty to evaluate its activities; on a selective reapportionment of resources for research; on the development of entrepreneurial activities and attitudes; and by the insistence on efficiency and managerialism in place of the mixture of collegial and hierarchical governance. The central authorities grew certain that their own values, which were assumed to equate with societal values, should be the starting point for higher education's objectives, which would be imposed on both teaching and research through a set of explicit, specifically funded policies. Even the modes of internal management and quality control were no longer to be left to academics to decide for themselves; institutions and their basic units became more accountable to the centre.

The UGC undertook in 1987 to report annually to the Secretary of State on universities' arrangements for drawing up and carrying out plans for the selective distribution of the resources they devoted to research. Universities were enjoined to develop research planning and implement selective distribution of government-funded resources for research. It was taken for granted that research could be planned. In its letter to the Secretary of State, the UGC stated that 'it intended to monitor two aspects of the selective distribution by universities of their resources for research: (i) the machinery for planning and implementing research priorities within the university; and (ii) the distribution of resources among departments, and the extent to which it is correlated with the UGC's research assessments' (UGC 1987). It then went on to give a detailed account of the effects of its 'Strategy Advice'. About a dozen institutions, it reported to its ministerial sponsors, had been unsatisfactory for one or more of three reasons: inadequate detail; lack of clarity; indications of lack of progress in implementing research selectivity. Thus, a predominantly academic committee acted as if it were appropriate to report to a minister on the managerial competence of its fellow academics. It illustrates the growing reach of the central authorities over what had been the terrains of disciplinary groups acting through peer review.

The end of the UGC

The exceptional position of the UGC was seen by some to have been under threat for a long time. To the discerning eye, there could be previous intimations of the UGC's mortality (Moodie 1983; Tapper and Salter 1978). Not only was the creation of the Polytechnics and Colleges Funding Council 'the culmination of a process that began in 1965', but the establishment of the Universities Funding Council 'can be seen as the inevitable result of the public funding of the universities after the Second World War' (Williams 1990, p.262). Williams traces a series of changes since 1948 and suggests the 1988 reforms 'are not much more than another incremental change' (p.263).

For some, the eventual end of the UGC was seen as an inevitable culmination of external and internal factors that had long undermined its position: 'A death long foretold ... rather than a murder committed by Thatcherism' (Scott 1995, p.20).

The timing of the UGC's demise, however, requires analysis because, as we have seen, within Whitehall the UGC was thought to have enhanced its position by the actions it took in the first half of the 1980s and 'there is little evidence that ministers were dissatisfied with the UGC's performance under Sir Peter Swinnerton-Dyer' (Scott 1995, p.19).

Criticisms were made (for example, Kogan and Kogan 1983) of its performance and, however well some may have thought the UGC performed in the 1980s, it seemed to have lost support amongst academics, the universities and the CVCP (mac.44, 46). The evidence collected for the 1984 UGC Strategy Document suggested academics and universities wanted a stronger buffer body with wider academic representation (UGC 1984). It was at this point that the exceptionalism of higher education's position, to which most academics still adhered but which was already weakening, came up against growing forces for reform throughout the public sector, which only served to highlight higher education's anachronistic position. Another participant believed that, given the climate of the times with the government attacking vested interest groups, the UGC had little chance of remaining unreformed. It no longer had the backing of the universities, although it was recovering from the 1981 crisis and could have survived had it not been for this general climate. Its terms of reference were so general as to be unsuitable – it had relied on understandings between gentlemen in the UGC and the Treasury. There was an understanding of how far one could go, rather than having it all written down as in the 1988 or 1992 Act. Criticisms of the UGC for not being a strong enough buffer helped to undermine it and leave it open for changes that went in opposite directions to those wanted by the critics. 'The Secretary of State couldn't issue directives to the UGC and although having the power to do so, had tended not to write letters. The 1982 letter from Joseph was an innovation. Then he got into the habit of writing letters. There was a constitutional untidiness about it all. Ministers and officials wanted to clarify the Secretary of State's right to be involved in the process' (mac.44).

That there was growing pressure from within the government for the UGC to be reformed was indicated in the Green Paper *The Development of Higher Education into the 1990s* (DES 1985), which announced the Department's acceptance of the Jarratt Report recommendation that it should be reviewed. The government invited a former head of the Treasury, Lord Croham, to head a committee which would produce proposals for the reform of existing arrangements. The *Review of the University Grants Committee* (Croham Report 1987) recommended a university grants council with a smaller membership. This would have entailed some reform of the UGC and perhaps served to deal with the untidiness, but the eventual changes went much further. There are various interpretations of why the government ignored Croham's proposals for limited reform in favour of a much more radical solution. One interpretation is that 'for the DES, Croham was simply a holding operation while it prepared for the formal and statutory recognition of its ideological victory ... once it had prepared the necessary legislation Croham became irrelevant' (Salter and Tapper 1994, p.130). Another claim is that whereas the recommendations of the Croham Committee were aimed at strengthening the UGC, the government wanted to 'curtail the UGC's independence ... The UGC increasingly looked like an anachronism in the machinery of government of the 1980s – it was liberal, participative and respectful of university autonomy – while the UFC would be more managerial, more subordinate to government and much less responsive to the universities; it would have more muscle to implement policy and much less to make it' (Shattock 1994, pp.139–140). The system was now much larger and continuing to grow. Therefore, 'older concepts of institutional autonomy became subordinate to arguments about accountability and the right of government to determine policy when substantial government expenditure is involved' (p.141).

The UGC's handling of the growing financial crisis at University College, Cardiff, served further to highlight its unique position and expose it to the forces of radical reform, and made it clear to senior civil servants that they must do something about accountability. It seemed that the UGC was both slow to act and lacked adequate powers to intervene when the Principal was determined to continue without responding to requests to deal with severe financial problems. 'We assumed that because universities have councils with distinguished lay members, the Vice-Chancellor or Principal and his executive supporters would be effectively questioned and called to account. When we looked at Cardiff, we discovered the council had not been properly informed about what was going on. For that reason, it had not been possible for the council to discharge its responsibility to ensure that the college's affairs were being managed responsibly. Cardiff was very influential' (mac.22).

What happened to universities can be seen as part of a much wider movement. Between 1987/88 and 1993/94, there was a major move to reform public services in the UK which, according to Jenkins (1996), amounted to the 'Tory nationalisation of Britain'. In the 1988 Act, the polytechnics and colleges were 'nationalised from local-council ownership as universities had been nationalised from UGC-protected autonomy' (pp.149–150).

The reforms of public sector higher education and the creation of the UFC are widely seen as linked. The incorporation of the polytechnics was thought to be the main explanation of the timing and form of the abolition of the UGC and its replacement by the UFC. This view is held as much by some who defend the changes as by those who criticise them. The UGC was seen as being a casualty of the war in the 1980s between local and central government: 'collateral damage' (Scott 1995, p.19.) According to a Minister for Higher Education, Robert Jackson, the decision to take polytechnics out of LEA control inevitably gave rise to the need to create a national structure to fund them, and that, in turn, required legislation: 'The government couldn't put on a statutory basis the funding of the polytechnics and not put on a statutory basis the funding of the universities. The universities, in my view, failed completely to understand this. They saw it somehow as a sinister conspiracy against the universities – somehow we were trying to undermine the historic role of the UGC. That wasn't the case.' Ministers and officials 'wanted more accountability because one of the problems in the background, and one of the reasons why it was simply unsustainable to continue with the old Treasury minute basis, was the situation at Cardiff [which exposed] a lacuna in the stream of accountability which would have made it inconceivable to argue that we could effectively have a non-statutory-based university funding system and a statutory polytechnic funding system. They both had to be put on the same footing.'

The creation of the Universities Funding Council (UFC) and the Polytechnic and Colleges Funding Council (PCFC)

The 1987 White Paper, *Higher Education: Meeting the Challenge*, set out the government's plans to replace the UGC with the UFC, and the NAB with the PCFC (which would be responsible for funding the polytechnics and colleges which were to be incorporated and taken out of local authority ownership). The reasons for the abolition of the the NAB were set out in Chapter 5, but the story of the UGC's demise is more complex.

Jackson claimed that the only substantial change from the old system was the change in nomenclature from grant to contract. This was overturned in the House of Lords but it was designed to emphasise the idea that the relationship between government and universities in respect of public money 'was a two-sided relationship rather than a unilateral one'. Perhaps one reason for the Cardiff debacle was that the Principal did not feel he was under a service obligation as a consequence of the grant: 'The language of the grant, going back to the establishment of the UGC, had created an attitude of entitlement rather than an attitude of service. It was reasonable for the government to say, "This is not good enough and we're talking about, now, billions of pounds of public money." ... I saw the 1988 Bill as being an attempt to translate the existing constitutional arrangements for universities into a statutory basis and replicate the same model for the polytechnics, with a change of language to contract from grant in order to emphasise the concept of a two-sided obligation.'

The treatment of the two sectors may have been parallel, but the reactions to the White Paper and the 1987 Education Reform Bill were not. The polytechnic directors, in general, welcomed the proposals and had a good relationship with the DES at this time (mac.29, 47). From the perspective of the universities, the battle on the Education Reform Bill was led by the CVCP, and the polytechnics were not seen as contributing (mac.28). The replacement of the word 'grants' by the word 'contract' was the focus of considerable opposition: 'The very mention of the word "contract" in the White Paper was seen as scandalous and everything possible was done to oppose it' (mac.44). Part of the campaign included a debate that was organised by *Nature*, in which the CVCP chairman, Sir Mark Richmond, accused the government of nationalising the universities. This, apparently, caused a reaction from Mrs Thatcher. The campaign against the Education Reform Bill was endorsed in a *Nature* editorial which opened with the words: 'British universities have good cause to fight the provisions of the new education bill, rightly last week called oppressive' (28 January 1988, p.287). The battle was particularly fierce in the House of Lords, with strong objections to the discretionary powers – the so-called Henry VIII clauses – that the government wished to endow on the Secretary of

State to give him the power to direct the funding councils. Section 134 of the eventual 1988 Act stated: 'The Secretary of State may by order confer or impose on either of the funding councils such supplementary functions as he thinks fit.' The Lords inserted an amendment proposed by Lord Jenkins of Hillhead, which stated that university contracts should ensure 'that academic staff have freedom within the law to question and test received wisdom and to put forward new ideas and controversial or unpopular opinions, without placing themselves in jeopardy of losing their jobs or privileges'. It is claimed that the final 1988 Act was considerably different from the original proposals (mac.45).

Membership and operation of the UFC

Nevertheless, there were significant differences between the UGC and the UFC, including membership: of the 18 UGC members, there were 13 academics, three industrialists and two represented local authorities. It was led by a distinguished academic of vice-cancellarial level. The UFC was intended instead to be under the chairmanship of an industrialist. In fact, allegedly following the intervention of Mrs Thatcher, a hybrid personality, Vice-Chancellor of Cranfield Institute of Technology but with industrial connections, was appointed, and the former chairman, an academic, became chief executive. The new body had 15 members comprising nine academics (including for the first time two current vice-chancellors), five industrialists/businessmen and one polytechnic director. The local authority interest disappeared and the professoriat lost out to external enterprise and institutional management. An infrastructure of subject committees was not retained.

It is widely agreed that the UFC did not work well. There were clashes between the chairman, who favoured a market approach, and the chief executive, who favoured the rationalising, planning approach that the UGC had come to adopt. According to one observer, the UFC's 'positioning and rules of engagement were different – the UGC was ... really on the universities' side, the UFC was on the government's side, tempered or moderated by Peter Swinnerton-Dyer's ability, in an internecine way, to weaken the impact of government policy because privately he was on the universities' side' ... 'There was the very odd appointment of the chairman [of the UFC] ... which was generally regarded as very unsatisfactory ... he was a real "one of us", had a narrow political agenda of wanting to introduce market systems in a very crude way, and one of Peter Swinnerton-Dyer's great achievements was to fight it off' (mac.28). It is interesting to observe that it was the rationaliser/ planner Swinnerton-Dyer who was seen, at least by this observer, as being on the universities' side.

Membership and operation of the PCFC

In contrast to the many groups represented on the NAB, the Polytechnics and Colleges Funding Council, like the UFC, had 15 members appointed by the Secretary of State for Education. Between six and nine were to have experience in higher education and the rest, including the chairman, in industry, commerce and finance (Education Reform Act, Chapter II, Section 132). There was no longer any representation from local authorities. There was some initial concern on the part of the institutions to ensure that their newly gained freedom, as they saw it, was not threatened by the PCFC. These fears were initially heightened by the fact that PCFC's chief executive, William Stubbs, had previously been Chief Education Officer for the Inner London Education Authority (ILEA). The PCFC, however, settled down and was seen by many as having functioned effectively. One key participant suggested:

> There was about that organisation ... an *esprit de corps*, a belief that there was an excitement about what they were doing, that they were breaking new ground; and a slight trepidation ... that this vessel we're sailing in could be holed below the water line; it just takes central government to say 'enough's enough – we're not for this animal' and we're away ... On the council there was a chairman who was very astute, and half were industrialists and half academics. The academics, including polytechnic directors, were powerful figures ... This wasn't a body which could be taken for granted ... The institutions didn't want PCFC to be a powerful body, for obvious reasons. So the PCFC had to create its own role, and had set out from the outset not to interfere, not to be a planning body but it would formulate policies, and it did commit itself to being very open – transparent in everything, sharing information, consulting heavily ... and then telling the world what it had done.' (mac.31)

The CDP, despite the fact that some directors were appointed to the PCFC, was not formally represented on it as it had been on the NAB. At the same time, although it exercised some influence through its memberships, the PCFC's practice of direct consultation with institutions over various possible policy options made it difficult for the CDP to say institutions thought other than what was in the institutional responses. As with the UFC, the PCFC was committed to some forms of contract funding and, at initiation, was specific about certain policies, such as rewarding institutions which increased access to different groups of students. A new funding regime and a new planning process were initiated. Institutional strategic plans were submitted to the PCFC, and polytechnics and colleges could no longer simply react to targets for individual academic programme areas. The management style adopted by the PCFC 'suggested that a much more distant, arms-length relationship between the funding body and the institutions could have advantages over the more intimate, hands-on approach of the UFC' (Shattock 1994, p.152).

The 1992 Further and Higher Education Act and Further and Higher Education (Scotland) Act

Under the 1992 Acts, the two funding councils gave way to funding councils for England, Scotland and Wales which incorporated funding for the whole newly unified system. These Acts inaugurated the end of the binary line as described in Chapter 5. But in terms of relations between the state and higher education, the 1988 Act was much more significant. The structure and membership of the new councils, with industrial chairmen and large non-academic representation, did not differ much from that of the preceding ones.

The HEFCE was consulted about individual member appointments. Strong economic representation was considered not to have much impact on academic issues because, unlike with the UGC, academic matters were less important than finance and accountability. In the academic debate, the non-academics contributed mainly on overall patterns within the sector and accountability requirements. Following the Nolan Report, appointments were transferred from the government to be handled by the councils themselves, but with open advertisement for places and with an independent assessor.

Research policy structures

Since 1975, pressures on resources and demands for greater selectivity and planning made an impact on research policies. In 1974/75 the science budget was cut for the first time in the postwar era (Salter and Tapper 1994, p.173). The demands for greater relevance in research, explored in Chapter 4, had an impact on the organisation of research. There was an attempt in the 1970s to put more emphasis on engineering research by creating an Engineering Research Council separate from the Science Research Council (SRC). The issue was resolved by adding 'engineering' to the title of the SRC and by an agreement that the Fellowship of Engineering should have the same right as the Royal Society to appoint a representative to Council. Sir Keith Joseph's attack on the Social Science Research Council (SSRC) has been well documented (Flather 1987) but the Council was allowed to continue, again with a name change to Economic and Social Research Council (ESRC). When he became chairman, Sir Douglas Hague still thought it under threat.

Its attempt to encourage greater relevance in research involved the government and its agencies in increased direction of the activities of researchers (Becher *et al.* 1994). A key organisation was the Advisory Board for the Research Councils which became particularly active after Sir David Phillips became chairman in 1983. In some years, the ABRC would top- (or bottom-) slice the grant of the research councils and ensure it was used for ABRC initiatives (mac.28, 208). In its 1989 corporate plan, the SERC commented critically on this: '...the ABRC Flexibility Fund removes a significant part of the flexibility which SERC formerly possessed and which indeed helped to fund the growth of engineering research between 1975 and 1985' (SERC 1989, summary para. 8.1.6).

There were more determined policy directions from the inner circle of government, led by the Prime Minister's Office, the Cabinet Office and the Advisory Council on Science and Technology (ACOST). As part of the shift away from applied research in the mid-1980s, the ACOST was created by Mrs Thatcher to replace the Advisory Council for Applied Research and Development. Mrs Thatcher also set up a new cabinet subcommittee, 'E' (ST), which she chaired in place of a subcommittee that had been chaired by the industry secretary (Thatcher 1993, p.639). With the encouragement of the DES, the five research councils set corporate plans and applied performance measures to their work. The ABRC encouraged them to sponsor a higher proportion of research which met council-devised objectives rather than proposals put up by the researchers themselves, although, in practice, much of this directed research was still in the responsive mode (mac.117). In 1990 the changes were made to the ABRC to give it a smaller board, and executive powers to improve co-ordination and joint working among research councils which were steps towards the more dirigiste approach long advocated by some scientific advisers: 'This represented an incremental increase in ABRC power but fell short of the views expressed by the Council for Science Policy's Working Group in 1971' (Shattock 1994, p.48).

Appointments to funding and research councils could be used to encourage moves in the direction the government wished. As Douglas Hague put it: 'I'd worked with Keith Joseph for a long time, which is presumably why he made me chairman. Keith knew that if he couldn't trust me then he couldn't trust anybody.' Approval by the DES of the names Hague and the council secretary put forward as council members was almost automatic 'but it wouldn't have been automatic unless we'd have thought hard about who both they and we would be happy about having.' Whilst an MP, but before he was made Minister for Higher Education, Nigel Forman was appointed to the ESRC. (The Medical Research Council (MRC) had long had an MP member.) Members of the research councils such as himself were 'introduced into the mix in order to make sure that this more utilitarian point of view was adequately reflected in the funding'. Others, however, questioned how far there had been a change (mac.39, 114).

Although there was no mention of it in the Conservatives' election manifesto in 1992, pressure had been growing for responsibility for science to be transferred from the DES to a separate department. Partly, this pressure came from the science community, one of whose members, Brian Flowers, explained: 'Two weeks after John Major came to power, he invited about a dozen people, led by Sir Ian Lloyd MP whose idea it was ... and we met him in the Cabinet Room.' It included Sir Robin Butler, Sir Peter Swinnerton-Dyer, Sir William Stewart, Sir Michael Atiyah (and Lord Flowers himself): 'A small group of very senior figures in the science policy/parliamentary field.' He asked what their problems were and listened. The main thing they urged on him was the need for a Science Minister. 'John Major did what we asked.'

The move was seen as a coup for the then Chief Scientist, Sir William Stewart (mac.204). Pressure came from the House of Lords Science and Technology Committee, and had built up from Mrs Thatcher's centralising tendencies. For Nigel Forman, the move 'was very much a function of the point of view which first became fashionable when Mrs Thatcher was Prime Minister because ... she liked to take a grip on science policy ... keen to pull some of the levers of power and influence and policy into Number 10 away from the

DES ... she had rather bitter memories of her time there ... On the whole, the transfer was well received because the science community, broadly defined, realised that it had a greater possibility of punching its weight in financial and policy terms ... if it was drawn into the centre of government ... rather than in a conventional department where it is often the poor relation ... particularly bearing in mind the ethos of the civil servants running the DES.' It wasn't in the 1992 manifesto but 'it had certainly been mulled over'. The research councils and community were pushing for it. They hoped they'd do better financially having their own department in Whitehall than 'being a fifth wheel on a wagon headed Education'.

The DES put up quite a bit of resistance but it lost science and was renamed the Department for Education. According to another participant, prior to the 1992 general election there was a general understanding that science needed to be in a central place accessible to all kinds of user groups in all departments. He thought Labour would win the 1992 election and implement such a policy, and was surprised when the Tories won and introduced these changes (mac.115). William Waldegrave explained that it was not part of the original Cabinet Office portfolio offered to him by John Major. However, within hours various people at the top of the political and bureaucratic machine had realised that it might be appropriate to make him Minister for Science in the Cabinet Office and so the long-wished-for policy decision was reached. Once again, the dynamics of a highly individualised decision-making process were interacting with longstanding pressures from the environment.

It had been 20 years since the previous major review of science policy (Rothschild Report 1971). The new minister and the OST undertook a major consultation exercise. Our interviews reveal a mutual respect between Waldegrave and leading members of the academic elite. As discussed in Chapter 3, science policy is an area where a wide range of ideological positions clash and overlap. Ministers such as Michael Heseltine, influenced by the writings of Correlli Barnett, were keen for the state to be more interventionist in requiring publicly funded research to meet the requirements of the economy. On the part of others, there was support for the traditional liberal ideology of non-intervention and a belief in the funding of excellence. With its wide level of consultation, the White Paper engendered a degree of consensus. Nevertheless, the 1993 White Paper, *Realising Our Potential*, proposed radical changes in the organisation of research councils. Areas of responsibility were reallocated; the SERC divided into the Engineering and Physical Sciences Research Council (EPSRC) and the Particle Physics and Astronomy Research Council (PPARC). Each research council was now chaired by an industrialist with an academic as chief executive. The intention, according to the White Paper, was 'to build on the advances made in recent years under Sir David Phillips, the Chairman of the Advisory Board for the Research Councils, to give more central co-ordination and strategic direction to the Councils' activities' (OST 1993, para 3.24). According to one interviewee, the managerial set-up in the OST was far more centralised than it used to be. The bidding was submitted to a director-general instead of the ABRC, upon which the heads of research councils had been represented. That was a more collegial structure. The letter to the chairs of the new research councils spelt out the enhanced role to be played by the Director-General of the Research Councils. It included:

> (b) helping the Council to set their policies within the wider framework of Government support for S & T as set out in the Annual Forward Look, and in the light of the findings from the Technology Foresight Programme; ... Sir John has my full authority to take whatever steps he considers necessary, working with you and your fellow Council Chairmen, Chief Executives and the other members and staff of Councils, in discharging these responsibilities. (Quoted in Waldegrave 1994, pp.v and vi)

Before the 1993 White Paper, there had never been a spelling out of objectives of science in that way. The themes were accountability, more selectivity and responsiveness to business and industry. Concepts of the users and beneficiaries were introduced. Previously, the research councils would have talked of dissemination. The White Paper spoke of different stakeholders. It also announced the introduction of the Technology Foresight Programme. It was strongly directed to the theme of realising the potential of British science in global markets.

The 1995 reshuffle

Increasingly, the education department became influenced by the policies of other departments. Eventually, in 1995 it was merged with the Department of Employment from which the deputy secretary responsible for higher education had come. Again, this was seen as likely to increase the emphasis given to employment concerns and to result in greater attention being paid to the relationship between further and higher education. The education department had earlier lost the fight for control over the MSC-style programmes and resources (Kogan 1987), and in the early 1990s the DES permanent secretary, Sir Geoffrey Holland, had come from the Department of Employment and, earlier, the MSC. Apparently, the merger had long been discussed (Holland 1995).

In 1995 changes were also made in departmental responsibility for research policies. The OST was transferred into the Department of Trade and Industry (DTI), a move widely regarded as symbolising its increasing subordination to economic concerns (House of Lords Debate, 6 March 1996). According to one commentator, it probably moved because 'Heseltine thought science should be underpinning industry. The DTI got upset at the Cabinet Office when it started talking about networking and interacting basic science with industry because the DTI had stripped out all its applied work – under a market system it wasn't any longer able to invest in companies and take initiatives, so its only role was also beginning to be networking. It had a huge staff and here was OST talking about using basic science for networking when the DTI considered that the OST didn't know anything about industry. So Heseltine felt it should be transferred and won the argument; but on the day it went to him, he went in the opposite direction' (mac.115). This policy decision reflected the views of Heseltine described earlier and seems to have been taken with no prior consultation in the science community.

II CHANGING NATURE OF THE POLICY MACHINERY: THE ROLE OF OFFICIALS AND MINISTERS

The central bureaucracy

We begin with the thesis, advanced by Salter and Tapper (1994), that, armed with an economic ideology of education, a centralising bureaucracy in the education department was able to gain considerable control over higher education. Salter and Tapper's centralisation notion was first developed in relation to school education when they argued that the education department was responsible for society's certification processes which inevitably lent it a centralising propensity (Salter and Tapper 1981). The economic ideology first emerged 'as a set of state-sponsored values in the post-war years' (1994, p.118). It challenged the traditional liberal university ideal, but 'during the 1950s the conflict between the two ideologies of higher education remained latent with the universities and the UGC protected by the Treasury from the main force of the rising ideology' (1994, p.118). Although Salter and Tapper claimed the economic ideology was 'internally generated' (1994, p.81), they suggested the Department's attempt at a more positive posture towards higher education was partly caused by external pressures, 'from other departments, government, Parliament and the political parties ... and some of these pressures were ahead of the Department' (1994, p.81). More so than in their earlier writings, therefore, Salter and Tapper discuss the political dynamic, but the central thrust of their argument remains the bureaucratic dynamic.

We have already noted widespread agreement that there was centralisation; the rebuttals made by those in funding councils are examined in more detail later. But interviews with DES officials show they generally reject both the charges of centralisation and, in particular, that changes in the relationship between the state and higher education were driven by civil servants. Although it does not entirely tackle the intentionality issue, many point to the lack of capacity or planning mechanisms within the DES to enable them to centralise the higher education system – at least before the mid-1980s (see Kogan 1987). There is no evidence that the DES had the capacity for, or saw its role as, assisting the UGC to interpret national need (Shattock 1994, p.8). 'The DES had little capacity to generate policy in this area and its interference in UGC policy was almost entirely in administration and budgetary matters until the late 1970s' (1994, p.132). Even in the 1980s, one official maintained that 'the Department really left the UGC to get on with things to an extraordinary degree ... In purely mathematical terms, the staffing of the department that dealt solely with the universities and the UGC consisted of one assistant secretary, one or two principals, and three or four other people – there was no way the department could nanny the UGC along in any detail' (mac.47). Sir Alex Jarratt suggested that in relation to his enquiry, 'the officials kept an incredibly low profile in all this. Peter Swinnerton-Dyer was extremely helpful ... but I got no background briefing from any official.' The view that civil servants had long-term views was also dismissed by Richard Bird: 'Another belief which some many hold, even assert, is that officialdom maintained some kind of pervasive intention which was and is progressively being realized. But the truths about power and influence within the workings of Government deny this possibility' (Bird 1994, p.84).

Yet there is evidence that officials began to play a stronger role following the election of the Conservative government in 1979. This can be seen in the DES evidence to the Education Select Committee. The need for manpower planning and for the DES to play a major role in the co-ordination of higher education was being aired. From the perspective of the UGC, the change was noticeable after the 1979 election with the 'deputy secretary for higher education ... coming to meetings and in the nicest possible way trying to achieve an input into policy making of an academic kind which was regarded as fairly heretical. It was not really for government to utter on this front but he began to utter things about a broad steer. The message was clear that the government wanted relevance ... to be coming through the system ... in my memory it had never appeared before ... there's no doubt ... when this change began' (mac.41).

The evidence points in several directions about the extent to which there was a bureaucratic dynamic to create centralisation. Different individuals have played different roles. It could be claimed that had the Department really been concerned to reduce the independence of the UGC, and the autonomy of universities, then two officials such as Geoffrey Cockerill and Norman Hardyman, who shared the Department's traditional ethos, would not have been appointed as the last two secretaries to the UGC. The number of permanent secretaries to the education Department appointed from outside the Department 'indicates the constant itch to make the education system more "responsive"' (Carswell 1985, p.69). Sir Antony Part's autobiography reveals how disappointed he was at not being promoted from deputy to permanent secretary within the education Department (Part 1990), even though he was of the calibre to become permanent secretary – as he did in other departments. More recent senior appointments from outside the department have included officials, such as John Vereker, who were seen by some of our inter-viewees within the university system as keen on increasing the powers of the Department. Transfer at senior levels was in fact common civil service practice but one from which the DES was for a long time somewhat immune, a separate vice-royalty (Kogan 1975).

Moreover, many of even those who believe that there has been centralisation do not sponsor the thesis of a bureaucratic intent-ionality related to an economic ideology (mac.213). Other influences were at work: for example, the determination of officials, as well as ministers, that universities should avoid the kind of crisis created at University College, Cardiff, when accountability was shown to be a low point. Others suggest the centralising pressure from civil servants arose more from a natural desire for power than from the desire to promote an economic ideology (mac.102). One official developed an alternative scenario to that of Salter and Tapper and suggested officials 'were the custodians of the local authorities ... were often the ones who were pointing out to ministers, "Well, I'm sorry, that's the way it is and you've got to recognise that you act in concert with the local authorities." I never heard them saying, "Of course, like you I wish to hell they weren't there and we could do away with them, Minister." [Salter and Tapper] are probably correct in the sense that these feelings are more associated with the 60s and 70s than they are with the 80s – you may have seen a more managerialist, inter-ventionist view coming through the Department as the 80s progressed ... and that was at least, in part, a recognition that that was the way the political land was lying – there was Mrs Thatcher and the things she was doing ... I'm not a great one for these bureaucratic conspiracy theories but bureaucrats are as opportunist as anybody else and you borrow the political imperatives of the day and you rationalise them in the ways that you feel are appropriate. You're traditionally so forced to be relatively pragmatic in the positions that you adopt that you could severely limit your effectiveness as a civil servant by trying to pursue some constant thread of a position, irrespective of the things that are going on around you.' (mac.106)

Officials might have had more of a centralising agenda for some parts of higher education than others. We noted earlier the claims that officials had for some time favoured the idea of a national PCFC-type body for public sector higher education. It is possible that some officials supported an economic ideology in relation to public sector higher education but also favoured the traditional liberal ideology in relation to universities. This could, indeed, be seen as the rationale behind the binary system promoted so strongly by Toby Weaver. Even in this policy area, however, a paper by one of the officials most closely involved traces in great detail how the officials were following lines determined by the shifts in attitudes of ministers in the early 1980s. Following the decision by the new ministers, Sir Keith Joseph and William Waldegrave, not to go ahead with the previous ministers' support for a policy of 'limited centralism', Jones comments: 'Once again the task for DES officials was to find a rationalisation for the new policy direction' (Jones 1983, p.22).

The key role of ministers

Many interviewees thought policies were driven by ministers; most post-1979 Tory ministers can be regarded as wanting to create change. In the period of greatest change – from 1981 onwards – a type of 'reforming' politician, wholly alien to the gradualist and consensual political tradition evinced by previous Conservative administrations, emerged. They believed that the market would free universities of state dominance and dependence; Sir Keith Joseph was at one time contemplating making over a once-and-for-all capital sum to universities so that they could make their own way in the market. They led the radical changes, mainly out of deep distrust of professional dominance and autonomy. They backed selectivity, partly because of its assumed intrinsic merits, but also because they believed it was the best way to use the money. They certainly believed that the primary justification of higher education was economic advancement. Joseph was, however, exceptional in his attempts to challenge higher education on its own ground, as when he launched an enquiry into the alleged Marxist bias of teaching at the Open University and North London Polytechnic, and into the place of the social sciences as represented by the Social Science Research Council. A prime example of individual power at work through personal preferences was the importance attributed by more than one witness to the personal connections between Young and Joseph in creating enterprise and other policies. In fact, it is widely believed that Joseph's key concern was to contain public expenditure and that his belief in the value of local democracy meant that in practice the radical changes came after his departure. As noted above, he did not initially move against local authority control of PSHE.

The change of minister from Joseph to Baker influenced many policies, including on expansion. According to one interviewee:

> Keith Joseph came in with a very clear agenda about what he wanted to do and how he wanted to do it, but of course his own temperament and Whiggish principles made it very difficult for him to do anything about it. He saw clearly but was shackled, principally by himself. Then in came Baker, who was the very model of a modern minister, and I believe that he determined to bring to an end that long history of the universities in which they'd inhabited, people might say a grey area, but it was really the sunny area between government and HE. He pushed to the limit what was central to Thatcherism, which was that you restricted the range of government but where you were inside the range there was no doubt about who directed ... The universities for a long time had virtually been outside the range of government, but in the 80s that question was decided. When Joseph was Secretary of State, there were a number of questions lying about and they really stemmed

from Keith Joseph's preoccupations: the failing the nation bit, the lack of managerial skills and inefficiencies in universities, the failure to monitor and assess, the failure, as Joseph saw it, to ensure proper free speech and the sheltering of some things that we ought not to be allowing in universities ... the CVCP took the lead in setting up all these committees like Jarratt and Reynolds and so on which were designed to ensure that these areas of competence were filled (and they could only be filled by the CVCP given the conditions of the time) before the government laid hands on them. So when Croham began to sit all those rather secondary issues which involve policy questions in which the state and the universities have active business together, as far as the current agenda was concerned, were settled. Keith was happy about Jarratt; the Department thought that Reynolds didn't go far enough but were willing to settle for it ... By the Baker period, a good deal ... was simply overcome by much greater forces which the universities found very difficult to resist. (mac.46)

When Baker replaced Joseph: 'The change was total, from what Joseph described as exhortation to what Baker denied was centralist rule' (Jenkins 1996, p.42). The policies adopted by Baker have been seen by some as part of a wider movement by the Thatcher government from 1987. Kenneth Clarke had been radical as Secretary of State for Health, and when he became Secretary of State for Education, the abolition of the binary line was seen, as discussed in Chapter 5, as very much his decision, albeit in line with official advice. This wider movement following the 1987 election was a deliberate attempt by the Thatcher government not to lose the momentum of reform in the way that it had been alleged occurred following the 1983 election victory.

Various interviewees saw the Treasury as an important source of the policies that impinged on higher education. To some extent, this could be seen as standard practice by the Treasury through its usual operations, as described in Heclo and Wildavsky (1974), but there were some special factors. As noted earlier, the Treasury had defended the autonomy of universities and the independence of the UGC when it was responsible for it. In the 1980s the position was thought to be different and the Treasury 'began to push like heck' (mac.201). Some claim the Treasury had been more responsible for intrusive policies than the DES officials (mac. 213) and that the decision to not allow the UFC to proffer advice was taken at their insistence. In his autobiography, the Chancellor of the Exchequer, Nigel Lawson, whilst not directly referring to this, makes clear his disapproval of the DES: '...its ethos was wholly opposed to that of the government' (Lawson 1992, p.600). He also claims to have been making an input into the discussions about education reforms in general.

III RELATIONS BETWEEN GOVERNMENT AND FUNDING COUNCILS

From the establishment of the Oakes Committee in 1978 to the passing of the 1992 Further and Higher Education Act, the government wrestled with the issue of how to govern higher education through its intermediary bodies. No government, since it abandoned the direct controls that it had exercised over the non-LEA teacher training colleges and, for a brief time, the colleges of advanced technology and a few other direct grant institutions, had thought it appropriate to govern higher education other than through intermediaries. But the political composition and powers of those bodies changed throughout the period. The powers that the Secretary of State had over the new bodies, the UFC and the PCFC, were considerable: 'The government was taking a different degree of grip in setting up PCFC and the UFC than either the NAB or the UGC' (mac.43). In practice, the two funding councils appeared different because of the way they differed from what preceded them and because of the way they each operated, as described earlier.

From the UGC to the UFC

Many saw the move from the University Grants Committee to the Universities Funding Council as a bigger change than the subsequent move from the Universities Funding Council to the Higher Education Funding Councils. It marked a significant break with the past:

> Given the strength of the economic ideology of education there is little possibility that academic values will again dominate the university–state relationship ... the central state created a new organisation, the UFC, with the express intention of making its power felt. (Salter and Tapper 1994, p.130)

We noted earlier that the UFC did not work well because of a clash between the chairman and the chief executive. Some have suggested that this created something of a vacuum in which the DES assessor was able to, or almost forced to, play a bigger role than otherwise might have been the case. But even without these developments, the move from the UGC to the UFC was seen by most actors outside government as increasing the position of the government/DES officials. One pointed out that irrespective of any formal provisions, 'a new body doesn't inherit the traditions and practical advantages of the old one', and he believed civil servants 'wanted a greater deal of ultimate control' (mac.45). Shirley Williams strongly opposed 'the way the 1988 Education Act established the state in a controlling role vis-à-vis the universities'. A leading academic claimed that the upshot of the 1988 Act 'was that the funding council became an agent of government policy [as part of the general trend] really in pursuit of the Thatcherite doctrines ... the intermediate bodies were being transformed – against their will very frequently – into agents of government policy rather than buffers' (mac.28).Yet we repeat that some central officials believed that central control had been diminished rather than increased.

From the NAB to the PCFC

Whilst the NAB, as a body created in the 1980s, did not have the UGC's traditions, and the status that went with them as a buffer body, its membership consisted of representatives of elected local authorities and interest groups. It thus had an authority that the PCFC's appointees could probably never match. Although it might, as a result, have been less independent of government, we have already noted the claims, widely supported, that the PCFC worked well as a body. Its chairman, Lord (then Sir Ron) Dearing, later also chaired the UFC and was first chairman of the HEFCE. He claimed: 'I don't remember any occasion when the council, or the chief executive, or I felt we'd been pushed by the government to do a thing we didn't want to do ... I don't recall the government, I may be wrong, using its powers against an unwilling council. I rather thought the council was making the policies and the government was very pleased by the way it was going.'

The HEFCE

A former junior minister did not think the autonomy of institutions was ever seriously in doubt but that ministers felt able to guide the funding councils – the UFC in his time and subsequently the HEFCE: 'The HEFCE as a buffer, an allocative channel for public funds, developed its own methodology but, ultimately, it was working within the guidance of annual letters or circulars sent out by the

Secretary of State of the day to the chairman of the council and then implemented accordingly, and that, in its turn, would reflect the constraints of government policy – both financial constraints and political constraints. So there's no question but that the HEFCE, and the Further Education Funding Council too now, essentially were doing the government's job and that's normal because that's the way allocative quangos of that sort normally operate.'

The HEFCE's degree of independence 'was less than it had been for the UGC because the UGC used to frustrate and even annoy successive secretaries of state, particularly when it behaved in a rather baronial way. There was a time in the late 70s and early 80s when a lot of these great intermediate organisations behaved in a very baronial way as if they had a fiefdom and everybody else was to steer clear, including ministers, regardless of the fact that they were spending taxpayers' money. Therefore, we had, as it were, to bring them to heel ... we did expect to set the objectives and to some extent set the priorities ... but then we would leave it to them, quite properly, to implement that policy in a cost-effective and sensible way – because they were necessarily in closer, almost day-to-day, touch with their clientele ... than any departmental minister or officials could possibly be.' 'The Department's assessor was on council to act as a continuous adviser' (mac.17).

The role played by the assessor was seen by others as varying with the individual. We have noted a change in approach by the assessor when the UGC became the UFC. Another appeared to have been very active but yet another only to intervene when the Department's view was sought. According to one former official, 'the reality is that the Higher Education Funding Councils do exactly what the ministers ask them to do. There is no way that they can say that we are not doing "x". And what appalled me ... was that these quangos had no involvement in ministerial policy making ... They were seen out there as bodies to whom ministers thought we will write ... and tell them what to do and what their priorities should be' (mac.23).

Those working in a funding council, however, found the relationship with government to be multiple and to vary over time. There was more interchange than in the early years over the key Public Expenditure Survey process. Interviewed in 1995, one official described the relationship: 'On the total money we have available and the number of students, the government decides. They might follow our advice but it's a government decision. Then there are grey policies, where the Department does not dictate but we are pretty aware of what they think. By and large we agree with them; for example, selectivity ... The Department is never sure of its relationship with us. Should it treat us as special partners or something different? We knew nothing of the Department's review of higher education or were accorded any particular status in the consultation of it. We were one of the list of fifteen or twenty bodies who were consulted. We thought that odd ... On quality assurance, there is a three-way dialogue. CVCP, funding council and the Department. In that, the Department is the third partner. They are not dictating it by any means. They are standing back and watching the other two slug it out ... There are some cases where we develop a policy about which the Department is not happy. They had a bee in their bonnet about degree courses becoming too long. We have resisted penalising longer courses. On many issues, the Department have no particular interest or knowledge. We may be at odds with the government on accountability for research funds. The Department would have liked us to be very much more prescriptive and interventionist with universities' (mac.3).

This account of the funding council's role over quality policy fits with our discussion in Chapter 4, as do these remarks on government's reluctance to direct.

> Under the Act, the government can direct. But it is a very public and political thing to do. One issue on which there had been ministerial pressure but no actual direction was on linking the assessment of teaching to funding ... they keep on coming back to that and we keep on saying no ... The council is independent and will tell the government that it won't do something. (mac.3)

This issue was also referred to by a former chief executive who stated: 'They have the power to direct, but in all the time I have been here they have only once given direction, on a technicality concerning an accounting matter. The direction was about publishing salaries in annual accounts. There was never direction on policy. When we were setting up quality assessment, the Department was refashioning HMI and I was under great pressure to take on a lot of ex-HMIs. I indicated that I didn't wish to do that because the process we were evolving would need to be peer dominated. While we could do with five or six HMIs who knew about organising visits and the like, we certainly didn't need many. The Department indicated its intention to write a letter to me proposing that, notwithstanding, I should take on a number. I responded by asking, "Are you going to direct me?" In due course, the letter arrived and there was no reference to HMIs. Here it should be noted that if a direction is given and the outcome is unsuccessful, then the Department would be responsible. If we are given guidance and matters go wrong, we take the blame.'

A former departmental official considered that when resources were tight, ministers liked to push things away for the HEFCE to decide (mac.206). The relationship with government, as described by the former chief executive, could be quite good: 'They have been most arms-length about funding methodology; the centre has not intruded in such matters. The relationship was quite positive. We have a series of think-tank days where for half a day their senior officers and ours get together to exchange ideas. They expose their thinking and we can expose to them where we think are pressures ... where we think it will be helpful for them to go further'.

Many commentators and academics, however, see the government as occupying the dominant position: 'The new funding councils are agents of government not buffer bodies ... The job of HEFCE, and other councils, is to implement the government's predetermined objectives through second-order policies' (Scott 1995, p.27). Some commentators, however, suggest the councils might go further than the government had considered and expected.

IV THE RELATIONSHIP BETWEEN BUFFER ORGANISATIONS (QUANGOS) AND INSTITUTIONS

One problem faced in our analysis is that when comparing the new funding councils with the UGC, some make a comparison with the UGC as it became in the 1980s and some with as it was before the end of the quinquennial system. In our interviews, two versions of the changing relationships emerged. Almost all at the working base of the system, particularly academics within their departments, but some vice-chancellors, too, believed the funding councils had become more intrusive. At the same time, policy makers in the centre maintained that institutions were now more free of the detailed controls exercised by the former University Grants Committee.

To analyse the contradiction, we need to consider a range of overlapping factors, including: the perspective of different actors; the changing membership of the intermediary body; the increasing transparency and formulae funding; the growth of accountability; the clash between intentions/rhetoric and context/reality. Each is overlapping but considered in turn; much of the discussion here illustrates points made in the theoretical analysis made in Chapter 2.

The perspective of different actors

The different perspectives arise from both historical traditions of the two sectors of higher education and the individual backgrounds of key actors. The perspectives of the pre-1992 universities are quite different from those of the former polytechnics which have gained greatly in freedom. The universities, who were never quality assessed by a body such as the CNAA and who had enjoyed the unparalleled freedom of the quinquennial grant, lost those freedoms in the latter 1980s and 1990s. Sir Ron Dearing observed that having come from being chairman of the Post Office it appeared to him that the PCFC was operating a light touch over the polytechnics when compared with the touch of government over the Post Office. In relation to the enormous increase in circulars etc. emanating from the HEFCE, several interviewees suggested that if one was on the receiving end of these documents, the funding council certainly did seem intrusive.

The membership of the HEFCE

We have noted the changing nature of the membership of the funding body; this is also subject to alternative interpretations. For some, the UGC, with its predominantly academic membership, was a guarantor of academic autonomy. For others, the introduction of more non-academic members was not thought to affect the nature of decision making. 'There has been shift from academic to lay control, as a result of deliberate government policy ... But the most influential members of our council are the academics because they know the subject intimately ... It was not the industrial members of the council who pressed for more emphasis on funding of applied research. It was a low-key political response to government and the CBI' (mac.3).

Unlike the UGC, the HEFCE did not depend upon the expertise of its subject committees. The subject committees not only made judgements about who was doing well (a weak version of RAE judgement making); they also contributed, albeit indirectly through chairs who were all on the main committee, to the UGC's planning of provision. The new system does not have the academic base on which the judgements were made: 'There might be a circularity here. It doesn't have the members who can do so and so doesn't act that way. It was a deliberate decision to structure it that way. It comes back to the question of autonomy. We don't tell universities how to behave academically. We give them the money to do so. We do not take academic decisions and are not able to do so' (mac.3).

Increasing transparency and formulae funding

There has been increased centralisation on the main framework policies. Nevertheless, there is evidence from HEFCE officers to the effect that controls are less detailed than were those of the UGC and that it has created transparency in its decision making and has thus replaced the 'black box' approach of the UGC: 'You could understand many of its decisions, but a lot of them were shrouded in the confines of committee deliberations ... The UGC may have seemed more consultative because its membership was so heavily drawn from the academic world. There were visits to institutions and "one could get members of subject committees into a corner" ... we don't penetrate down in the way the UGC did ... One management and business visitation got down to the level of looking at the way a university described its courses. If it were not taken out of the UCCA form, "we will behave very unkindly to you"' (mac.19). This example was presented as a way in which the UGC visits could be more intrusive than the approach adopted by the HEFCE.

Now 'changes in interpretation of administrative law make it a duty to tell people how we arrive at our decisions and what is behind them' (mac.19). Certainly, the use of judicial review as in the major precedent case of the Institute of Dentistry challenging a grading given by an RAE panel, while unsuccessful, would never have occurred in previous decades, largely because there would have been no such decision to challenge. 'We have also tried hard to cause information to penetrate down into the institutions. We put out multiple copies of everything and put all documents onto the Internet' (mac.19).

It is widely agreed that the funding councils have been more transparent than previous bodies. Part of the transparency is that the funding is now driven by a clear formula. The debate surrounds the impact these developments make in comparison with the previous systems. The HEFCE has not attempted anything like the rationalisations of the UGC in the 1980s. It does not have the subject committee structure to analyse the provision of different academic areas in the manner of the UGC. The exact nature of the former UGC approach is somewhat contested, but some not only argue the subject committees were intrusive but also claim they were 'not properly controlled – there were no accountability mechanisms within the UGC' (mac.103).

Others take the view that the old UGC 'formed a broad-brush opinion of institutions' (mac.42) and the controls exercised by the

UGC were essentially suggestions made by visiting subject subcommittees on future academic development. Once the grants were offered, no detailed controls were attempted. It is the existence of the block grant, but now determined according to a formula, that can lead defenders of the reforms to argue:

> In many important respects, university autonomy has increased. That's partly a result of the move from the UGC to the funding councils. UGC was a very interventionist, hands-on body, and did not hesitate to tell the universities how to organise themselves ... particularly at the subject level. The HEFC does not engage in that kind of detailed control. The block grant remains although it is being eroded. It is not as integral as it was. But once they get the block grant, we do not interfere in how the universities organise themselves. (mac.3)

There is a strong feeling from within the higher education system that the current transparency and formula-driven system does not provide the degree of autonomy that the old, more political model might. Under the old, more political model, there was scope for the vice-chancellor or registrar to have private talks with the chairman or secretary of the UGC but now, according to one insider, you may as well go and talk to your grandmother (mac.213). Yet whilst the formula is public, it was also thought to be so complex and opaque that, at least in its early years, great benefit was gained by those institutions whose administrations knew how to interpret the regulations to their best advantage. The financial memorandum attracts particular discontent (mac.102) for the way it 'ties you down hand and foot' (mac.213) and is probably a good example of over-zealous prescription in operational matters.

Accountability

The key point raised by those inside the system who believe the formulae are intrusive is that the accompanying accountability mechanisms reduce autonomy. This is illustrated by comments from two leading members of the university system:

> Today, one of our departments is being turned over by TQA ... against a series of formulae. Last night, the chair of the assessors said we don't issue a handbook for second-year students. No, we replied, we put things on notice boards. In no way is that not a loss of autonomy. (mac.213)

The formula that determines the allocation of resources to universities is much more public/open than it used to be; however, the formula is itself based on mechanisms of centralised evaluation which are far more intrusive than anything that universities underwent in the 60s and 70s, and the fact that the process is transparent doesn't mean that what you're seeing through this transparent piece of glass is not a system of much greater control. The answer's so obvious it barely needs spelling out – universities were not subject to frequent, periodic inspections in their classrooms of the so-called quality of teaching in the 60s, 70s and 80s, their departments were not assessed by funding council panels. (mac.113)

There are differing views of the impacts of increased accountability. Those reforming the public services claim accountability is inherently linked to devolving responsibility to the rim. Even here, some note that whilst institutional autonomy has increased, that for the individual academic has not (e.g. mac.3; Tapper and Salter 1995):

Accountability is the reverse side of the considerable autonomy that universities have. There was an OECD study of autonomy of higher education in the 1980s in which the UK system came top. If that were done now, we should still come up high on autonomy. (mac.3)

… institutional autonomy has increased but this may mean less autonomy for individual academics … some vice-chancellors certainly feel that they have more autonomy than under the UGC, and they have said so to me. But academics may not share that perception. With worsening staff–student ratios, they have less freedom to do their research etc. With the research assessment exercise, they are more accountable. They are more managed by the universities. There are the makings there of a paradox. (mac.3)

There is considerable rhetoric surrounding the approach adopted by the Conservatives to reforms in public services. An important element is that responsibility and decision making should be, as far as possible, passed from hub to rim. The stated intention was that the funding councils should not be planning bodies and should enhance institutional autonomy. Various reasons are advanced for why this has not happened. First, autonomy is more likely to be interpreted in terms of institutional leaders' right to manage than in the traditional context of the academic freedom enjoyed by teachers and researchers. Second, there is a tension between the three administrative cultures of planning derived from the UGC, mass markets inherited from the the NAB and the PCFC, and external evaluation used to decide award of course approvals taken from HMI. Third, control systems have not been relaxed; they have simply been repositioned – the emphasis has shifted from planning inputs to auditing outcomes. Fourth, it is the government, not the institutions, which has filled the strategy 'gap' created by the funding councils' retreat from planning. The effect of these developments 'has been to replace the kind of strategic overview generated by the UGC that, at its best, was sophisticated, long-haul and reflected the inner values of higher education, with a strategic overview generated within government which is likely to be crude, short-term and more heavily influenced by external considerations, leaving the funding councils responsible for attenuated business plans' (Scott 1995, pp.29–30).

Intentions/rhetoric versus context/reality

There is such a strong contrast between stated intentions and reality, as perceived by those in the system, because of the nature of the intentions espoused by ministers. Thus, the Minister for Higher Education told the Conference of European Rectors:

> In my view, it is a fundamental error for governments to see the universities as a branch of the public service or a kind of nationalized industry, to be progressively integrated into the bureaucratic machinery of the State, and to be directed towards government-determined goals – however worthy these goals may be. To use Hegelian terminology – universities are properly an element in civil society, not a function of the State. In Britain, this line of thought is leading the government here to a new emphasis on the autonomy, independence, and self-responsibility of our universities and polytechnics. We are seeking to redefine our relationship with the institutions of higher education, so as to get away from the post-war idea of government as guarantor – and therefore provider, and therefore manager – and to move towards the idea of government as a 'customer' for services from higher education institutions, and as an enabler of others, notably students, to act as customers for higher education. This is a difficult and complex process sometimes involving the paradox of 'forcing to be free'. But no one should mistake the direction in which we are moving. (Jackson 1989, p.75)

In practice, however, many would claim that the government was attempting to apply a series of general ideas about how public services should be run to higher education. As we discussed in Chapter 2, this bundle of ideas has become known as New Public Management

(Pollitt 1995), but perhaps the major difficulty facing those who are claiming the Conservative government's reforms were aimed at increasing autonomy is that the starting point for higher education – or at least for traditional universities – was not the same as for some other public services or the same as the position of universities in most other European countries.

CONCLUSIONS

In this chapter we have described the major changes that occurred in the state apparatus for funding higher education. The UGC, with its exceptional position as a buffer organisation, was replaced by more standard organisations. There were long-term pressures, including the growth of the system, behind these changes, but their exact form was viewed by many of those within the system as reducing the traditional autonomy of universities and academics.

The changes in governmental machinery for higher education derived from some of the principal policy imperatives. Thus creating a single funding council for each country was an obvious consequence of the end of the binary system. But, for the most part, the changes represented a shift in the modes of control and co-ordination, from the professional-academic dominance in the University Grants Committee to the deliberate advancement of lay and private sector power and influence, and the increased power of the central departments. The changes accorded to no discernible dynamic derived from academic needs and considerations, apart, perhaps, from those related to the end of the binary line. Within the contextual and long-term pressures, ministers played a key role whilst civil servants generally responded to, rather than dictated, political imperatives.

Chapter 7

The Impact of Policy Changes on Institutional Government

Many of our interviewees referred to the extent to which there had been a greater emphasis on management, often at the expense of professional power at the base of the system, and a strengthening of the role of the institution as a part of policy change.

In this chapter we therefore consider the impact of policy changes on institutional government. We offer contrasting conceptual constructions of the role of institutions before noting changing perceptions of their functions from the perspectives of the national authorities. We note the requirements placed on them by the increased legalisation of higher education and by the prescriptions of the Jarratt Report (1985) and of quality assurance. These external forces had effects on internal structures and processes and on the powers and responsibilities of governing bodies, vice-chancellors and administrators. And both the external and the infrastructural changes themselves had impacts on individual academics working within the basic units.

Many of the government-led reforms of higher education were, indeed, intended to affect the behaviour of individual academics. Such initiatives as Enterprise and Foresight (see Chapter 4) were intended to shift the priorities and targets of academic activity. Teaching and research were now to be assessed through a public process, including student evaluation. The assumptions of autonomy entailed by tenure were removed for future faculty appointments, presumably to ensure greater accountability. Mary Henkel's *Academic Identities and Policy Change in Higher Education* (Henkel forthcoming) considers the impact of these in detail. If, however, all the reform policies must have been intended to ultimately affect academic behaviour and performance, some were mediated through institutional arrangements that ultimately, too, would affect individuals. We are concerned here, therefore, primarily with the impact of government on institutions.

I HISTORY AND CONCEPTS

We have seen (Chapter 6) that institutions have never been free from the influence of the centre. Even in the nineteenth century, before the state provided resources for them, Oxford and Cambridge were subjected to the scrutiny of Royal Commissions. The very status of all but the ancient foundations relied upon the award of Royal Charters granted at the instance of ministers via the Privy Council. The modes of internal government were the subject of approval by the Privy Council, which provided model constitutions and articles, again acting on the instance and advice of the competent ministry. Public sector institutions were required to follow the articles and instruments of government provided by the ministry of the time.

It has been assumed that even in the golden age the UGC 'exercised a profound influence on the internal organisation of British universities' (Shattock 1994, p.146). This was, Shattock argued, because the UGC was primarily made up of senior academics chosen to represent their disciplines and not their institutions and it related most easily to the academic community. Relationships developed out of the network of academic contacts, and informal lines of communication supplemented UGC circulars and visitations: 'The effect of this was to reinforce the reduction in the role of university councils and the lay officers ... and elevate the role of senates in the management of universities. Knowledge of the external world became much less important than expertise in UGC procedures in institutions which received 90 per cent of their income from the UGC' (Shattock 1994, p.147). Furthermore, because the UGC's resource allocation system was subject-based, 'it shaped the way disciplines were taught and managed in institutions. Thus it favoured coherent subject-based degrees where student "loads" could be apportioned relatively simply to mono-disciplinary departments' (Shattock 1994, p.153). Although this approach reached its apotheosis in the subject reviews of the 1980s, it had the effect much earlier of emphasising 'the primacy of the discipline, or the subject, in academic organizations and in university planning' (Shattock 1994, p.153).

This account illustrates the duality of influences on institutions. Central government always had powers, even if exercised in the background, but the invisible colleges of academics also affected the way in which universities acted. Yet Shattock's account can be criticised on two counts. First, academic working in universities is always conditioned by the powerful operation of the 'invisible colleges' of other academics outside the institution which affect curriculum content and research criteria. It would be logical to assume that the UGC subject-centrism followed, rather than led, this propensity. Second, it assumes for senates a role in the management of universities that must have been highly variable. In an earlier study of the impact of employment considerations on the curriculum (Boys *et al.* 1988), we did not find that either of the university-level bodies – council or senate – had any influence on educational or research substantives, but only on regularising procedures. That would be an abiding feature of higher education governance.

Some conceptual constructions

The conceptual constructions of higher education institutions have almost always been based on the example of the classic research university, and particularly that which led the status hierarchy in the USA, where, as we saw in Chapter 2, most of the formative writing on the subject originated. This remains the best reference point for what we have to say because if change has affected them, they will have been the institutions with most room for change.

Two potentially conflicting versions might be applied to the *status quo ante*. In Becher and Kogan's (1980, 1992) conceptualisation, the state, the institution and the basic unit (departments, or research units) are connected in the normative mode, through which each level evaluates the next, and the operational mode, through which the higher level determines allocations of resources and status to the next. A property of an institutional level is its capacity to sustain its own value positions. They ask whether the institution is a true level of the system. Can it generate its own values which it can pursue with the requisite authority? In an earlier edition (1980), Becher and Kogan had concluded that it could just about establish its case as a values generator. But they were not entirely satisfied that the university was other than a holding company for the real contenders in the basic units. This picture had, however, changed by the time of their second edition (1992).

If they, as other authorities before them, tended to marginalise the importance of the institutional level, others, whilst sharing their view of the dominant role of the individual academic and the basic unit, gave a strong version of the place occupied by the institution. The most important alternative picture is the empirically based, but also normative, ascription, produced by Burton Clark, of the *Distinctive College* (1970, 1992) and, more recently, the *Entrepreneurial University* (1998). In these accounts the institution is, or can be, a potent cultural entity capable of creating its own organisational saga, or story that it tells about itself.

In the UK there is no doubt about universities possessing, or seeking to create, their sagas. Not only Oxbridge, as in the self-praise bestowed by the novels of C.P. Snow or in the recent history written by Halsey (1992), but also the great science colleges of London found their place in literature. The somewhat louche style and cultures of universities in the novels of David Lodge and Malcolm Bradbury were perhaps more stories told against them than sagas. So we can grant the institution status as a powerful cultural personality even before the recent reforms caused shifts of power from the working base of the system.

II THE PERSPECTIVE OF THE NATIONAL AUTHORITIES

As part, and as a result, of the reforms created by government action, we can identify changed perspectives on the part of the national authorities of the role of the institution. The starting points differed for different types of institutions. Some non-university institutions offering what would now be construed as higher education depended strongly on national decisions, e.g. on the approval of the staffing establishments of voluntary teacher training colleges and the range of advanced further education courses in local education authority colleges. The polytechnics were made increasingly free in their educational programmes but, as we have seen, increasingly became subject to the national planning structures created by the NAB. The 'old' universities were, however, virtually autonomous within the broad boundaries set largely by resourcing conditions and the freedoms entailed by charter status. In Chapter 2 we have noted how this range of institutions fitted in to the wide range of relationships that public institutions have enjoyed with the state in the UK.

Yet it is by no means clear that the central departments had an explicit policy on institutional consequences of their activities. In the view of one former official (mac.36):

> The thinking about institutional governance was pretty confused. On the whole, the DFE thought that institutional governance was not their concern, and they were not really aware of the general

feeling that government and the funding councils were on the one side and the academic community was on the other.

The sources of influence on institutions include legislation and the use of the royal prerogative, government instructions to the funding and research councils, the conditions which they lay down making funds available for distribution to universities, the operation of quality assurance and government auditors. Whilst it was true that there was no substantial body of law specifically applicable to higher education before the legislation of the 1980s, except for the award of fees and grants to students, higher education institutions were subject to the same laws as any other public or private body. But government could always find ways of acting so that national policies were implemented. 'In several instances in the period 1980–88, the government acted through various agencies to force institutions into taking action which they may not have initiated themselves. Thus the new University of Ulster established formally only in 1970 had to surrender its charter … in a merger with the larger Ulster polytechnic. Two constituent colleges of the University of Wales were merged … a number of universities were forced into academic "restructuring" by the actions of the University Grants Committee in 1981' (Farrington 1994).

From 1989, when all institutions not already chartered became incorporated, we can think of them all beginning to enjoy similar relationships with the state. Differences may have resided in custom and convention, and in the relative freedom enjoyed by those possessing major resources. But, in general, the relationships were made the same. We can identify changes from the earlier conditions enjoyed by the 'old' universities by considering, first, the legal requirements imposed from the 1980s onwards. Second, we can read the assumptions of the Jarratt Report which had no direct prescriptive import but became influential and, third, we can make a judgement on the growing prescriptive content of circulars from the national authorities, by noting the requirements imposed by quality assurance.

Legal requirements

Generally, government had not used legislation as a means of exerting control over the universities. In the 1980s the relationship between the state and its agencies and the universities became increasingly legalised. Attempts were made in the original drafts of the Education Reform Act of 1988 and the Further and Higher Education Act 1992 to permit the Secretary of State to intervene directly in institutions over a wide variety of activity. The 1988 Education Reform Act allowed for the appointment of University Commissioners to amend the university statutes so as to bring academic staff of the universities within the operation of the general law relating to employment, with some continuing protection for academic freedoms. The University Commissioners insisted that all new and supplemental charters, which had to have their approval, should contain explicit provision for dismissal on grounds of redundancy, although the procedural safeguards were greater than the general law requires. The 1992 Further and Higher Education Act gave the Secretaries of State for the three countries powers of approval of courses in relation to specific academic and vocational disciplines, including teaching. It also laid down strong powers over the funding councils, including the power to give them general directions and to require information and advice from them, to confer or impose supplementary function, to dissolve higher education corporations, and to direct them to provide for the assessment of arrangements for maintaining academic standards.

In their turn, the funding councils, as do the research councils, produce corporate plans, for approval by the government, an annual report and accounts, and issue financial memoranda which lay down in some detail the way in which money should be spent. They also have powers to mount economy, efficiency and effectiveness studies by virtue of the 1992 Act. If universities are now more explicitly regulated by the law, it should be emphasised that on substantive issues of the curriculum, and of research objective and methods, no legal prescriptions are laid down. These are affected by funding or by governmental influence, but they remain almost wholly within the domain of academic discretion.

The Jarratt Report

The Jarratt Report (1985), the setting up of which was made a condition for some restoration of university funding, had long-term effects on the internal management of institutions. According to the report, vice-chancellors were to adopt the role of chief executives to whom deans and heads of departments would report as line managers. The universities would create and work under a corporate plan that would be formulated by a small group drawn from the lay council and the senior academic management. The report was explicitly hostile to the power of departments. It urged the use of performance indicators, but failed to mention the functions of teachers, researchers or students – an omission not repeated in the less-publicised equivalent NAB Report (NAB 1987). Many vice-chancellors have taken on the style and assumed the functions of a chief executive. Internal management is led by a resources and policy committee in virtually all institutions. The transfer of power from departments to the central institution and, to a lesser extent, to faculties may well have occurred anyway, in part, as a response to the pressures caused by reduced funding and increased institutional responsibilities, but was given its clearest mandate by Jarratt.

Managerialism, that is, the shift in power from senior academics and their departments to the central institution and the dominance of systems over academic values, resulted, in part, from institutions' need to meet new demands with fewer resources. The importance of institutional leadership was illustrated at the time of the first major cuts in 1981 (Sizer 1988). But it was Jarratt (1985), the government-inspired report, which promoted the statement of objectives, the creation of new management structures, with chief executives in place of the *primus inter pares* roles of vice-chancellors, the introduction of management terminology and of performance indicators. Of these, 'it was the shift from senate to council and vice-chancellors of institutional power that was most significant and the emphasis on treating universities as managed organisations' (mac.104).

The shift towards greater accountability and corporate mechanisms were all part of the general shift in public services. In the mid-1980s, as part of UGC visitations, small groups and members would report back to the chairman on the management of the institution being visited. Discussion increasingly was directed towards the financial health and overall management. There was also the concept, developed at the time of the ministries of Mark Carlisle and Rhodes Boyson and later reinforced by Jarratt, of 'delivery' which would mean 'the management of an efficient and effective system from a national point of view' (mac.106). Among the aftermath of Jarratt was the encouragement by the DES of Audit Committees in universities, a change also encouraged by the Cardiff episode.

When we suggested to him that his report promoted the corporate enterprise but that academic researchers need to pay more attention to the discipline at the invisible college, Jarratt replied that 'if you are not paying attention to the invisible college then you won't succeed because you would ignore the very thing you are there to do. However, you will only be able to stay there and do it if you are doing it within the resources and confines placed upon you within the establishment.

You can't do it in a vacuum. You have to shape your affairs such that you can do it efficiently and sensibly.'

The Jarratt Committee had included leading academics from strong universities as well as more publicly committed managerialists, and could be assumed to follow current thinking among some institutional leaders if not among the whole range of academic opinion. Although Jarratt himself noted a mixed reaction (some institutions were favourable whilst others said it wouldn't work), 'The impression I have got is that it was taken on board pretty extensively.' At one major university the recommendations of Jarratt for institutional planning and devolved budgets 'caused strains but these were now recognised as part of the way of making the system happen'.

The changes were, in part, common-sense moves towards rational management; for example, delegation of funding to cost centres: 'Don't hold it centrally, so if you save money over this year ... it's down to your account' (mac.104). The 'marketisation' of higher education was encouraging market behaviour in the basic units, for it was they who had most to sell. 'Some institutions have expanded enormously with franchises etc. and a great network. So the setting up of universities by Act of Parliament in the way they were set up has allowed enormous changes which really mirror the best of the American system' (mac.105).

Impact of quality assurance

The financial memoranda and other forms of circular from the national authorities provide strong prescriptive boundaries within which institutions work. They have, since 1967, regulated the numbers of students and the levels for which they are recruited, but, as noted in Chapter 6, the increasing number and changing nature of the circulars is thought to have had a particularly strong impact on institutions in the 1990s. The financial provision for each student constitutes government influence on the range of courses to be provided. The requirements for quality assurance, to some extent at least, affect the planning of the curriculum and its delivery (see Chapter 4), as did institutional initiatives in modularisation. The research assessment exercises affect departments' planning of research, the choice of subjects pursued, the choice of staff for teaching as well as for research and the use of time allowed to different members of a department.

Our evidence is that research selectivity lent more power to central institutional managers, that it made academics more visible and their performance to be assessed publicly. The quality assessment system changed the balance between managerial accountability and the power of the academic community. Academics began to prepare accounts of their work to be monitored by those at the centre, both institutional administrators and academics. Evaluations were in the public domain, and more easily informed institutional decisions about financial and staffing allocations, salary awards and the like.

Work on professional organisations other than universities (e.g. the British National Health Service) has led some of us (Joss and Kogan 1995) to conclude that institutions depending on the use and generation of knowledge engage in three kinds of quality assurance. They are quoted here, with some adaptation to academic life, because they denote the different value positions that can be found in both parallel and contingent relations with each other:

- 'technical quality', concerned with the specialist quality applied by individual providers in their work;

- 'generic quality', concerned with the common aspects of quality, in the way that work is organised and managed, and its results and relationships, as applied by departments, services or management units (includes behaving with a respect for agreed procedures, punctuality, relationships with colleagues and customers and respect for the delivery of the service). In the case of universities, it would include equitable admission and assessment procedures; and

- 'systemic quality', concerned with the quality of an accountable and well-managed comprehensive and integrated set of services, as applied by departments, services or management units.

In academic institutions, the technical values have predominated. The creation and certification of knowledge and its transmission according to academics' epistemic assumptions are the ultimate ends of administration. Such values continue to dominate the RAE, although even here the preparation of submissions and the importance attached to achieving good grades have increased the part played by institutional management. Teaching quality assessment and, in particular, the quality audit bring in, also, concern for generic and systemic quality and can involve a considerable amount of administration at the institutional level. As we move, however, into the market and state corners of Clark's triangle (Clark 1983), discussed in Chapter 2, so institutions move towards more corporate concerns. They become more concerned that clients will receive services and enjoy relationships with the institution and its parts that will guarantee continuing market shares. Other forms of generic behaviour which convert into systemic patterns derive from the requirement to conform to external legislation and expectations of institutional behaviour in appointments and the like. They are required by outside forces and the pressures of resource constraints to think and behave systemically in terms of planning, portfolio building and resource use. The broadening of concepts of quality thus reinforces the changes in internal distributions of power.

III IMPACTS ON INTERNAL STRUCTURES AND PROCESSES

Institutions respond to external changes (Gumport and Sporn 1998; Kogan 1999) and their responses become structured in terms of organisational and power structures. Many of the more important changes have been described as bureaucratisation (e.g. Gornitzka, Kyvik and Larsen 1998). This word is currently being used to mean two quite separate things. The first is the move from individual and academic power within the sometimes mythic collegium to the system or institution, and a resulting new structuration of decision making. The second is the growth of power of non-academic administrators. The first is the major phenomenon and the second a possible, but not invariant, consequence of it. Indeed, as we will note later, the opposite may happen: the shift of power from the professoriate to the university may lead to an increase in some forms of academic power.

Some of the established literature represents academic org- anisation in a bureaucracy-free and romantic light: 'The community of scholars remains as a myth of considerable strength and value in the academic world' (Harman 1990). Middlehurst (1993) comments that, although weakened by the requirement to compete, collegial behaviour can be seen in the sharing of information, ideas and tasks, and in the professional critique of each other's work before it enters the public domain. These ascriptions are, however, mainly modal and stylistic, but can also be used to describe behaviour in enlightened hierarchies. The nub point is where authority is exercised. Here, we need a more parsimonious description than that provided by Middlehurst of the collegium. We define it as a group of academics of equal decision-making power acting together to determine standards of entry and accreditation, to share collective resources, and to determine divisions of labour and reward systems. This is minimalist, but to say much more includes categories of power which could be equally found in other forms of organisation.

The collegium has hardly ever existed except in mixed or diluted form. A group of academics within a university department may act collegially when they meet as a course committee or as a board of examiners where all voices may be equal, at least in formal terms. But universities, even when a collection of collegia, are also hierarchies in which resources are allocated, policies and promotions made. It has been assumed (Scott 1995) that universities have become more bureaucratic and less collegial as they grow larger. This generalisation cannot easily be applied, for example, to US universities where some of the largest are also among the most academically strong, and where the professoriate sustain a major voice in the creation of policy and in managerial decisions such as the awards of salary differentials. Bureaucratisation has, however, resulted from the increased need for holistic institutional planning to meet reduced resources, the requirements of quality assurance and many other prescriptions placed upon academic work by central government policies, as expressed by the funding councils.

The effects of the changing role of the institutions on internal structure can be enumerated as follows:

- the changing relationship of council or governing body to senate and vice-chancellor;

- the changing nature of vice-chancellorships;

- the changing nature of internal structure: relationships between academics and non-academic administrators;

- the impact on individual academics and the basic unit.

The changing relationship of council or governing body to senate and vice-chancellor

The balance of power shifted at the top levels of institutions. In the public sector 'the role of academic board is much less than it was, and the role of the executive working with the governing body, as a collective, is much stronger than it was ... [There is now] a small very supportive governing body, whereas in my day you had to convince the academic board, in the face of quite strong traditional/progressive differences of opinion ... and you certainly had to convince the governing body with the same balance of progressive and traditional interests. Now that second source of conservatism has already gone ... The professoriate's role in forming institutional policy and arguing that through the governing body level is certainly reduced' (mac.49).

In the view of one vice-chancellor of an old university, the new universities never developed effective organisation for the academic community to operate. 'They did not have the same structure as the older universities with a community of scholars acting through senates and boards. As far as universities were concerned 20 or 30 years ago, councils were much less important because there was plenty of money. There is now a mechanism where a vice-chancellor might propose a budget to council and council either accepts it or modifies it. It is then handed to the vice-chancellor who is responsible for controlling and implementing the budget and delivering the final result. But before the period of expansion, 50 or 60 years ago, many of the civic universities had important local businessmen on powerful councils. Often at this time, universities were very hard up, there were real financial discussions going on in the councils and the VC was told the University can't afford to do this' (mac.102). Yet another vice-chancellor, however, believed that academic policy at the university was still set by senate and had to be approved by it, but the vice-chancellor then acted as chairman of senate and not as a chief executive (mac.113).

The changing nature of vice-chancellorships

The Jarratt recommendation that vice-chancellors should be chief executives and thus in charge of a hierarchy of academics, rather than leading a collegium, is thought by some of our interviewees to have had an influence on vice-cancellarial appointments. One informant thought: 'The big universities are risking something if they don't have a scientist or engineer as VC ... There is a tendency, more than hitherto, to bring in former permanent secretaries', a tendency long followed by Oxford, but not Cambridge, colleges. 'There are some who have figured in both academic and industrialist life, e.g. Wallace at Loughborough and Roberts at UCL' (mac.28). In recent years, a group of vice-chancellors, or their equivalents, with expertise in education have also been appointed. But these assumptions are to be modified by recent findings (Smith *et al.* 1999) on the educational career paths of UK university vice-chancellors between 1960 and 1996. This provides 'little support for the hypothesis that the shift from academic and administrative, towards executive and managerial, interpretations of university leadership has produced major changes in the career preparation and professional profiles of those occupying the top institutional post. The senior academic hierarchy remains the overwhelming source of recruitment.' (p.113) 'In total, almost 80 per cent of vice-chancellors have been promoted from the ranks of professors or higher managerial posts, and over half come in from positions as head or deputy (or their equivalents) in higher education institutions.' Just over one-third of UK vice-chancellors (p.118) had attended either Cambridge or Oxford. A constant proportion between the pre- and post-1981 eras, 16 per cent, had a first-class honours degree. Those with science backgrounds account for nearly a half of all vice-chancellors in this period (1960–96). The remaining half are split fairly evenly between those with arts (22%), technological (17%) and social science (14%) degrees. In the 'new universities', those with arts degrees were in the minority whilst those with science backgrounds constituted the largest group. Those with social science backgrounds were nearly equal to those qualified in a technological discipline. Academic backgrounds of vice- chancellors, therefore, summarise quite neatly the diverse origins and academic missions of the former polytechnics and old universities.

Jarratt himself thought the change to the chief executive role had had an impact on vice-chancellor appointments but stressed that his report argued that if a vice-chancellor did not have academic credibility, he would not succeed. Irrespective of Jarratt, universities would be obliged to think of vice-chancellors as chief executives: 'And now with the old polys as universities they were more accustomed to think this way – so that all raises the profile of this sort of thing.' He referred to a report from a Vice-Chancellor of Birmingham: 'He's saying all the things you expect a chief executive to say about the market place – it's that sort of report and he's a very distinguished academic, very academically inclined.' An appointments board today would have to be concerned about management ability: 'They couldn't say we want a distinguished academic and who cares about the rest, which 30 years ago they could have done.'

Our interviews give no conclusive evidence on whether there was a predisposition on the part of some vice-chancellors to encourage the onset of managerial approaches, and whether this can be related to their educational or other origins. A key informant (mac.11) thought that would make little difference either way, because 'many talk about administration and know nothing about it … They have little concept of what senior administrators in universities do and many of them do not have political nous. They live in small university towns away from London and come down once a month.'

As to their changing functions and styles, observation of systems both western and further east suggests that wherever systems either centralise or decentralise, authority at the head of institutions is strengthened. It occupies whatever space central government or the collegium yields. One vice-chancellor put it as follows: 'The role and status of institutional leaders have changed. Government and funding councils put more emphasis on an institution being able to demonstrate that it's tightly managed, with decisions made as part of a coherent plan, and there is control over resources. Institutions realised, at a time of declining resources, they have got to be quick on their feet and have tighter management systems. Some of the cumbersome multi-layered committee systems been replaced by networks – task forces, working parties, rapid consultation.' 'This has led to professors being seen as middle managers as well as, not rather than, being academic leaders. They often have to discuss quickly in departments' (mac.16).

One former vice-chancellor noted the changes in the role as follows: 'In the 50s and 60s a VC saw himself as a fellow academic ... institutions were so much smaller and you still felt as VC that you were a fellow academic, a member of a community of scholars. We didn't use the word "manage". The change started in the early 70s. Because of the sudden and drastic cuts in the grants to universities, decisions were more urgent and tougher. The VC has somehow to reconcile the decisiveness of a chief executive and his membership of an academic community. It was a change from a VC who went to his senate, listened to the different views on the subject in question, and at the end of the discussion found a consensus, and a VC who at the outset made clear what the decision should be. He had, of course, still to persuade a majority of his colleagues. Today, things appear to be very different. Posts of VC are advertised, they may or may not be academics, they are paid three or four times what most professors are paid. My generation of VCs had to take tough decisions – winding up a department, selective funding cuts – but being another member of a community was very important' (mac.48).

Vice-chancellors have become more managerial: 'They've become more like the poly director than the old VC ... The professoriate felt their role and status had diminished and they were now part of a corporate enterprise: there are a lot more of them than there were ... If you had a VC who's more like a poly director then it's less of a collegiate management system ... The professors in the old days could rule the roost more and the VCs can't afford to let them do that any more ... The institutions themselves have become less baronial – that's even true of Oxford and Cambridge with their collegiate system

– the influence of heads of houses is no longer as great and they don't have as much independence vis-à-vis the VC and his bureaucracy ... The bureaucrats have to manage what are effectively very large businesses now. In some of Britain's cities, HEIs are ... the largest employer as the Goddard Report showed' (mac.111).

There have always been examples of authoritarian behaviour at the top. A current example, and not from a 'new university', is described as follows:

> The director [not the actual title] has some cronies called something like pro-directors. Only they have policy input. There is no way in which a modest worker in the institution can influence policy. He is doing a good job of doing well for the institution, in the light of the constraints. The academic board, the professoriate, used to have huge influence on what happened. In the past, one could argue one's case before the academic board. The director could then do nothing about it. Now he even makes appointments, and has suspended some appointments boards. Most meetings are the director reporting on what he has done or what he has heard. Many things have happened where no one has had the opportunity of making an input. (mac.203)

Another former vice-chancellor advised caution to those indulging in authoritarianism. 'Vice-chancellors may be more powerful, but more power may mean less influence – the powers of resistance in a university ... inherent in every such organisation ... are very large.' More managerial powers to look after the money 'won't actually allow you, it will probably cut you off from people able to influence the real life of the university which is what makes it perform and be the kind of place that people really do want to work a 55-hour week in and don't look upon it as something they've been driven towards ... People have got to feel that they're part of it and participate – that they can go and talk at any time ... but it's too early to judge – a new system is evolving which is bound to be unlike the old system and some parts of it will be better and some parts will be worse' (mac.46).

A further possible effect of growing management concerns is that vice-chancellors have moved from the role of academic leadership to that of institutional management. 'Within the universities, the power that was once in the hands of registrars is now being shared between registrars and pro-vice-chancellors' (mac.3). Their power is, in any case, being shared with pro-vice-chancellors recruited from academics (Kogan 1999; Lockwood 1996).

The effects of these changes were felt less in the new universities which, already managerial in style, on incorporation had already allowed for more power to the management role of directors. The academic board became weaker and an executive working with the governing body stronger. The academic board had been quite strong in the past (mac.47): 'Under the Act, setting up the new universities ... the VCs have virtually become chief executives of firms, and the change in the governing bodies with far more people from industry and accountancy etc. has reinforced the idea that the ex-polys can be better managed, whereas the universities individually have got to take steps if they want to be better managed and introduce these things' (mac.105). Incorporation enhanced the role and status of directors. 'They were quite comfortable with the term chief executives ... where they were already the main shakers and movers that confirmed their position, where that wasn't already the case it gave them a formal opportunity to become so ... One of the genuine challenges for any head of institution is to ensure there is a balance between managerial accountability and giving a say to the academic community. But this has been less difficult for the old universities because they have senates. It's difficult to bulldoze senates. They are largely consensual bodies. The absence of senates and academic boards in new institutions has many long-term disadvantages' (mac.43).

The changing nature of internal structure: relationships between academics and non-academic administrators

Within institutions, cross-cutting administrative sections concerned with external relations, market operations, quality assurance, research policy, personnel policies – now much more pressing than in previous decades – were established, and these took power away from the academic and specialist base and rendered decision making subject to institutional rather than academic definitions (Kogan 1996).

Scott notes that structural factors behind managerialism were reflected in the growing professionalisation of university administration through the medium of the Conference of University Administration and more specialist organisations. 'Much of the impetus for, as well as expertise on, corporate planning originally came from administrators rather than academics' (Scott 1995, p.64). At the same time, it has been noted in Scandinavian systems (Karlsson 1996), in the USA (Dill and Helm 1988) and in our own evidence that the growth of central management functions has often been achieved by the placing of senior academics into administrative roles. An important distinction between polytechnics and the universities was thought to be that deputy directors in polytechnics would have left behind their academic posts for management responsibilities permanently, whereas pro-vice-chancellors often regarded themselves still as academics undertaking a temporary task.

At the same time, faculties became more powerful in relationship to departments, as the needs for priority setting and demonstration of worth became pressing (Boys *et al.* 1988).

The thrust towards central institutional power has been reinforced by the imposed requirements to produce corporate plans and mission statements (see Mackay, Scott and Smith 1995). An increasing amount of information and requests come from the funding councils, and these need an administrative capacity for their treatment.

The results of these movements have been changes in management structures:

- creation of pro-vice-chancellor roles for the development and implementation of policies cutting across the faculty and departmental lines of authority;

- growth in total managerial and administrative work at institutional and infra-institutional level, resulting, in large part, from the more dominant policy frame within which the institutions must now work;

- changes in the tasks and relative power of academics and administrators within universities;

- increased range of tasks for non-academic administrators as well as increase in their numbers;

- part takeover by academics of university administration.

An example (see also Henkel forthcoming) of the growth of power at the centre and its newly gained capacity to work across traditional academic divisions can be taken from one UK university, and something similar can be found in others, where an academically trained administrator is responsible for research strategy and for a management group for departmental support. The aim of his group is to keep in a good interaction with the departments, with good knowledge of their aims and objectives, and, at the same time, to keep departments informed of administrative policy issues. Where there is need for improved networking, they identify and address that. They support the Academic Development Committee, where most of the policy development takes place. They work with faculties and departments to develop models for their costs. They monitor the relationship between departments' incomes and expenditure. They aim to enable the university to make decisions about how to handle inequalities of performance between departments and determine what to do about them. They secure focusing on priority research funding areas and on options: they pay attention to a declining area due for restructuring or an area that needs refocusing. The administrator, in this case, has developed views critical of traditional academic organisation in favour of cross-cutting structures related to student and other client needs rather than to traditional disciplinary-based organisation.

These changes cannot be typified as simple transfers of functions and power. Thus the remark of one UK administrator in 1981 after big cuts: 'there is now no academic veto' is an example of what Tomas Kozma (unpublished) has typified as being a statement that is both true and untrue.

The earlier simple diarchical assumptions of how institutional tasks are performed, however, no longer hold. Academics move into systems management, and administrators increasingly help create the policy and procedural frames for academic work. The structural consequences are:

- in virtually all higher education institutions there are mixtures of collegial, academic-based decision making, and bureaucratic/hierarchical working. Those operating the bureaucratic lines can be, however, either academics or professional administrators;

- collegial working is not simply a coming together of peers, but is itself structured into hierarchical and bureaucratic formats;

- for institutions to work effectively, there are hinge or interfacial mechanisms which enable collegial decision making to be authorised, legitimated and resourced by the institution. These are put into effect, at least in part, through the activities of the administrators or bureaucracies;

- as institutions become more complex so they elaborate staff or regulatory or developmental roles cutting through traditional academic organisations.

The impact on individual academics and the basic unit

The impact of these changes has been felt within the basic units, although it must be recognised that the reforms in governance and management have been under way for a decade and a half now and there will be many younger academics who have known no other ways of working.

Mary Henkel's study (Henkel forthcoming) of the impact of reforms of academic identities will confirm in much more detail what we have to say here. One of her more important findings is that academics began to feel more part of the corporate enterprise not only because of the coercion implicit in managerialism but because the new conditions of resource seeking and quality grading made them more dependent on the university for support. Academics are managed not only by management but by peer group pressure because they are part of the corporate activity. For example, universities may refuse to give sabbatical leave from university funds and that creates a strain within departments. 'Occasionally when a reference ... has arrived late, it is accompanied by a xeroxed list of reasons stating all the duties academics now have' (mac.107). 'Academics' role in forming institutional policy and in arguing that through in governing body level, if not in academic board and senate level, is certainly reduced. Their influence in the management ... of institutions has diminished ... and that's unfortunate ... The professors are not knocking on the VC's door in quite the way they used to ... it's a much more structured management system' (mac.49).

'Heads of department have to work much harder – being a head of department is much bigger than it was ... In laboratory-based subjects where research is increasingly group research, professors lead groups and so there may be an enhanced role, but that's not so much because of the political developments you're thinking about as the developments in the way science is done.' 'Professors were much more autonomous. Remember, it used to be the convention that you had one professor per department and he was head of department and dictator and that's much diminished because there are now many more professors ... you're now the head of your research group – it's only in medicine that you're the head of your department ... The professor who wasn't head of department wouldn't expect to have the same role and status, and with the diminishing role of the senate there is less of a role there for professors to play' (mac.42).

'The professoriate have come under pressure. There were pressures coming from various directions, including: shortages of resources; the need for management within departments and for the head to carry the department with them; and the pressure from research committees, established now in most institutions, which mimic the RAE and assess and allocate resources' (mac.107). Asked whether the professoriate is changing to become more part of a managerial structure, possibly middle managers, in a system with enhanced positions for vice-chancellors and administration, one respondent noted: 'Inevitably, when it comes to the allocation of resources that is true – but if you say that's the whole story you'd be very misleading because the professors remain influential on the nature of teaching and the nature of the research that is done' (mac.22).

The impact of changes varies according to the type of institution and of academics affected by them. Study of a further three institutions (Bauer and Henkel 1997) shows that in the most prestigious the non-scientists were concerned about the new emphasis on institutional administration, whilst the scientists were more concerned about the power of external institutions. In another leading university, structures for quality assurance had become powerful but significantly were mainly in the hands of senior academics. At the same time, more authority had been taken by administrators. In a technological university, administrators had gained power, as had students, but these shifts were led by an assertive vice-chancellor and his administrative team. In other universities, cross-cutting mechanisms took on this role.

CONCLUSIONS

One commentator (mac.112) has noted that there is a perception that universities have become more managerial but that 'paradoxically most universities are still struggling ... to be collegial in their values but are forced in their practices to be increasingly managerial'. This raises the issue of the extent to which the essentials of higher education work make it difficult to yield to managerialist values, a point to which we will return in Chapter 9. Our evidence makes us uncertain about Scott's identification (Scott 1995) of four phases of the internal government and management of the old universities outside Oxbridge: the civic phase in which lay people wielded considerable power, at the turn of the century; the donnish phase until the 1960s; the democratic university until the late 1960s and

1970s. The fourth and current phase is that of the managerial university. For within the managerial and the entrepreneurial university remain powerful counter-forces which still place more credence on individual discretion and the culture of collegiality than on management power.

Whilst the impacts have been strong, it is difficult to form a clear view of the degree of support for them. We interviewed many systems and institutional leaders who recognised the need for change towards better management but were equivocal about the managerialism that had seemed to come with it. 'People running universities have become more and more managers who are judged by almost entirely economic or financial criteria, which should not have been the object of the operation' (mac.49). The result of these changes, as perceived by one systems leader (mac.42), was that 'scholarly values are being to some extent suppressed in favour of business attitudes and criteria and ... if we're not careful, that will mean the downfall of something that is rather precious'.

Yet throughout our interviews with vice-chancellors and pro-vice-chancellors in this project and in our associated projects (Henkel forthcoming; Henkel *et al.* forthcoming), many statements were made about the importance of recognising, and indeed compulsion to recognise, that academic autonomy and intrinsic motivation are sustained because they are the motive power of institutions. Many believe that academic management must incorporate these assumptions. At the same time, there is more monitoring of individual behaviour and more collective action, particularly in response to external assessments.

Change was certainly clear in terms of the status of universities within the state. Hitherto, they had been regarded as private institutions enjoying public status by virtue of their charters. They had now become unequivocally public institutions, still enjoying a great deal of freedom but, without any doubt, subject to roughly the same degree of control over framework policies and modes of quality assurance as local or health authorities. In Scott's term (Scott 1995), they had been 'nationalised'. Our account of the impact on academic values and working (Henkel forthcoming) will address the question of how far that has affected higher education's essentialism and academics' academic and epistemic identities.

PART III

Theoretical Perspectives, the Exercise of Influence and the Role of the State

Chapter 8

The Exercise of Influence

In this chapter the focus moves from the nature of the policies and the machinery for their creation and implementation to a discussion of the nature of the policy processes in higher education and the connection between the policy machine and the groups who influence it. We start by describing the dual policy processes in higher education before examining the role of Parliament, parties and the various groups which attempt to exert influence. The range of theoretical perspectives on the nature of the state and on policy making have been considered in Chapter 2. Here our data are applied to them.

I THE POLICY PROCESSES IN HIGHER EDUCATION

We noted in Chapter 2 that UK higher education is regulated by more than one system. Governmental regulation takes place through the central policy-making bodies and bureaucracies, the allocative bodies and the quality assurance bodies. At the same time, key decisions are taken through the invisible colleges of academics, and some of these affect the allocation of resources. The two policy and decision-making systems have no formal connection with each other but affect, and generate energy between, each other. In our interviews we sometimes found evidence of convergence of views on policies and values between some of those most influential in the academic modes of policy making and the governments of the day. The two worlds of government regulation and invisible colleges connect through co-opted elites (see later) working through the allocative systems which are peopled by the co-opted elite. They retain strong representation by academics, who are, however, increasingly joined by non-academics.

According to one leading academic, the traditionally light touch in the UK meant that a series of the important reforms in areas which elsewhere might be regarded as the responsibility of central authorities were not imposed by the government or the UGC but, instead, had to come out of the institutions themselves. Since 1945, there had been major changes in admissions policy, mature students, the curriculum, teaching and assessment methods: '...enormous and genuine reforms within universities and they've had nothing to do with governments ... they are because institutions in this country have had the freedom to manage their own affairs. They've seen this is, perhaps, a better way of doing it – and the external examiner sees there's this change, vice-chancellors meeting and exchanging ... and if it's a good reform it spreads out' (mac.48).

A study of how and why current public policies for major change have emerged should take account of the political ideologies, processes and institutions through which issues emerge and conflicts are presented, negotiated and converted into policies, forms of institutional governance and academic and disciplinary practice and norms. In the main, our account demonstrates the potency of individual actors within government responding to major changes in the general policy context. This puts our account in descent from the account of issue emergence given by Premfors (1980) and away from the more ideologically determinist account of Salter and Tapper (1994).

In Chapter 6 we examined the role played by key ministers and bureaucratic actors in developing policy in relation to the changes in government machinery and the broader range of reforms. The role of Parliament in determining the nature of public policy in the UK is known to be weak; nevertheless, it has an influence that can be analysed before looking at the role of parties and interest groups.

The role of Parliament

Although new legislation has to pass through Parliament, strong party discipline ensures that in the UK most proposals emanating from the government are usually adopted. The amendments to the 1988 Education Reform Act, forced on the government by the House of Lords, were described in Chapter 6 and are regarded as exceptions to the general position and illustrate that higher education has a specially privileged position within the House of Lords, which is further discussed later in this chapter.

An examination of the impact on education policy, in general, of a range of parliamentary devices, conducted immediately prior to the start of our main period, revealed that:

> Parliamentary questions and debates do not closely relate to the
> development of the policies ... They do not anticipate policies and

provide no systematic critique of them. Select Committees reflect policy preoccupations more accurately and are more systematic in exposing the administration of policies. But none of these instruments gives Parliament substantive authority. (Kogan 1975, p.181)

Nevertheless, the detailed analysis undertaken to reach this conclusion reveals links with several of our themes developed elsewhere in this book. Thus, the assessment of Parliamentary Questions shows that of the 24 main educational topics about which there were questions in 1969, the third highest number of questions were on student unrest. This illustrates the importance of this factor, discussed in Chapter 3, in undermining support for universities. Even though select committees were seen as being of some importance, it was noted that in replying to the 1973 report from the Education and Arts Subcommittee of the Estimates Committee the DES virtually ignored the report's proposals which attacked the binary system and proposed joint machinery for the two sectors.

Salter and Tapper (1994) suggest that by the end of the 1970s 'parliamentary opinion on higher education as represented by the Select Committee on Education and Science and the Select Committee on Science and Technology was firmly dominated by the values of the economic ideology of education' (Salter and Tapper 1994, p.46). In 1976 the Select Committee on Science and Technology 'was quite clear that underlying its concern with university science were the beliefs that scientific endeavour "should contribute to the social and economic welfare of the community"' (p.45). As we noted in Chapter 6, they also referred to the Committee's criticism of the DES for 'its far too passive' attitude towards the question of what Tapper and Salter called the manpower ideology. A criticism, they suggest, 'the DES will almost certainly welcome since it validates any further intervention in higher education it may be contemplating' (Tapper and Salter 1978, pp.172–173).

Salter and Tapper's suggestion that select committee pressure increased from 1979 fits with the points made in our previous chapters about the increased attention given to the UGC by the Public Accounts Committee and the newly formed Education, Science and Arts Committee chaired by Christopher Price. Although Salter and Tapper trace the long-term interest that the Public Accounts Committee had had in encouraging the UGC to be more accountable, the intensity of this pressure increased as various weaknesses were revealed in the UGC's response to the 1981 cuts and the consequent redundancy scheme, and finally over Cardiff. The climate created by their enquiries and reports helped provide a justification for the government's various moves to strengthen accountability mechanisms. In the early 1980s the Labour MP chairing the Public Accounts Committee questioned the chairman of the Social Science Research Council over its funding of abstruse research: 'He asked how a study of changes in the kinship system and the allocation of sex roles in a modern Polish village was relevant to the national needs of the United Kingdom' (Thomas 1985, p.1). Such attacks reflected a climate of some hostility towards social science research. Parliament played a role in the early 1980s in encouraging the Social Science Research Council, and its successor, the ESRC, to develop policies to improve the completion rates of social science PhDs. Thus, the report into the ESRC's completion rate records:

> Public debate was however launched again in 1979, when the Comptroller and Auditor General reported on poor social science completion rates ... This led to an appearance of the chairman of council before the Public Accounts Committee and an urgent review of postgraduate training. (Winfield 1987)

The inquiry by the Education Committee into the organisation of public sector higher education in the early 1980s helped to focus the attention of ministers and officials on this issue: 'Through most of 1980, the need for ministers to respond to enquiries from, to present papers to, and to appear before the Select Committee effectively kept the range of issues warm in ministerial minds and thus contributed as much or more to the development of policy in this area as the substance of the committee's recommendations' (Jones 1983, p.7). Probably the most influential select committee was the House of Lords Science and Technology Committee. One of its reports resulted in a new strategy for Department of Health and NHS research. It reviewed and drew together many of the recommendations from its previous reports in its report undertaken as part the consultation exercise for the 1993 Science White Paper. If parliamentary committees played no decisive role in policy making, as do their US counterparts, some, nevertheless, contributed to the consideration of issues and the climate in which policies were formed.

The political parties

In theory, the parties play an important role in a system of represent-ative and responsible government by providing a link between the electorate and the policies pursued by the government. A key way in which this is achieved is through the commitments in the party manifestos presented to the electorate. These then become 'the battering ram of change' (Crossman 1972). For his seminar in the Leverhulme series, Crowther-Hunt, in examining the Labour Party manifestos for the February and October 1974 elections, and the Conservative manifesto for 1979, concluded, 'as far as higher education policy is concerned, recent manifestos have hardly been clarion calls to specific action' (Crowther-Hunt 1983, p.46).

In 1979 the Conservative manifesto merely referred to maintaining the excellence of British higher education and the need to increase the number of high-quality entrants to the engineering profession. The manifesto had earlier, however, promised a reduction in the proportion of the nation's income taken by the state. There was a lack of specific commitments on higher education in Labour's February 1974 manifesto and in October not much more than a general promise of educational opportunity and development of the Open University. As a result, Crowther-Hunt commented:

> No doubt this absence of clear party policy commitments in the sphere of higher education is one reason why in recent years the main policy initiatives seem to have come from departmental offi-cials. This was certainly what I found when I became Minister of State for Higher and Further Education after the election of Octo-ber 1974. To my surprise the Prime Minister gave me no general guidance about the government's higher education policy nor any indication of what he hoped I might achieve in the department when he offered me the job. Nor did the Secretary of State for Ed-ucation, Reg Prentice, when I reported to him during my first day at the Ministry. (Crowther-Hunt 1983, pp.47–48)

In 1997 both the Conservative and Labour parties seemed happy to let higher education policy be kicked into touch and announced they would await the findings of the Dearing Report.

We have already noted how major policy shifts during the 1980s and 1990s did not result from a change of government, or from an explicit change of party policy, but from changes in minister – particularly the appointments of Keith Joseph, Kenneth Baker and Kenneth Clarke. Even a major change initiated immediately after the 1992 election (the creation of the OST) had not been in the

Conservative manifesto. The proposal to incorporate the poly-technics was contained in the Conservative 1987 manifesto, but, Baker records in his autobiography, the decision was reached when he gained Mrs Thatcher's approval at a meeting on 25 February 1987 (the meeting at Number 10 with two polytechnic directors came later that day) (Baker 1993). Even this decision, therefore, does not suggest the drive for policy change was coming from within the party. That manifesto also stated the approach to science policy that Mrs Thatcher was then supporting: '...resources need to be better targeted. The task of government is to support basic research and to contribute where business cannot realistically be expected to carry all the risks' (Conservative Central Office 1987, p.41).

The party did, perhaps, play some role in stopping two policy initiatives: over public sector higher education and student grants. As we have seen, in January 1981 there was a leak, in the *Times Higher Education Supplement*, of proposals to introduce formula funding and a national body with minority local authority membership for public sector higher education. The local authorities 'succeeded in creating an alliance with the Conservative Party's National Advisory Committee on Education which effectively fragmented the policy dynamic and ended the DES's chances of getting its radical new scheme adopted in the near future' (Salter and Tapper 1994, p.140). In 1984 the Autumn Statement from the Chancellor of the Exchequer, Nigel Lawson, contained an agreement that the Chief Secretary to the Treasury had made with Keith Joseph to increase the science budget, but abolish the minimum maintenance grant, and introduce a means-tested contribution to tuition fees for better-off parents. There was an immediate row and Joseph was 'given a roasting' (Lawson 1992, p.309) by the Conservative backbench Education Committee. Lawson claimed that it was the parents between the poor and the rich who would be hit: 'They were the people who comprised the bulk of the Party activists in the constituencies and, in particular, the local Party officers. It soon became clear that we would not get the changes through the House of Commons, and that a tactical retreat was inevitable' (Lawson 1992, p.309).

These two issues involved the party playing a negative role. In relation to schools policy, there were major disputes between those who wished to use centralising methods to raise standards and those who wanted to introduce market mechanisms such as vouchers (Knight 1990). Although there were similar tensions over higher education policy (Salter and Tapper 1994, pp.30–45), the debate within the party does not seem to have been anything like as important. Much of the New Right thinking on higher education, as elsewhere, has been associated with think-tanks (see below). After describing the tensions between competing groups within both the Conservative and Labour parties, Salter and Tapper conclude: 'Despite their ideological differences, and adopting different routes, both parties have moved to embrace a version of the economic ideology of education' (1994, p.35). The policies of the parties seem, at most, to have formed the backdrop against which the leading politicians have formulated policy, and here the ideological disputes seem not fully to have been resolved. Thus, even Mrs Thatcher, in retrospect, admitted that some of the critics of her policy 'were genuinely concerned about the future autonomy and academic integrity of universities. I had to concede that these critics had a stronger case than I would have liked. It made me concerned that many distinguished academics thought that Thatcherism in education meant a philistine subordination of scholarship to the immediate requirements of vocational training. That was certainly no part of my kind of Thatcherism ... What those who have no real understanding of science are inclined to overlook is that in science – just as in the arts – the greatest achievements cannot be planned and predicted: they result from the unique creativity of a particular mind' (Thatcher 1993, pp.598–599 and 693).

Think-tanks and advisers

The right-wing think-tanks were generally thought to have been less important in relation to higher education policy (mac.110, 22) than in many other fields where they became increasingly important in the 1980s. However, one official (mac.6) thought they had become influential in relation to teacher education, which was certainly affected by individual right-wing members of the main advisory council. Various proposals were made by groups, including the Adam Smith Institute, Institute for Economic Affairs, and the Centre for Policy Studies for moves towards market mechanisms (Salter and Tapper 1994, p.34). Some in the think-tanks were the most vociferous opponents of the centralising aspects of the 1988 Act; the strong attacks by Kedourie (1988, 1989) were published by the Centre for Policy Studies and the Institute for Economic Affairs, respectively. The Minister for Higher Education at the time, Robert Jackson, faced severe criticism from such sources.

The Central Policy Review Staff (CPRS) in the Cabinet Office was known as the Think Tank and, unlike those discussed above, was an official government body. In producing its 1983 paper *Higher Education and Industry*, it faced 'an ideological division on the question of academic freedom versus industrial and economic relevance in higher education' (Blackstone and Plowden 1988, p.125). Shortly after, when the CPRS was abolished, one of the paper's authors was invited to advise the DES. 'As a consequence he was able to push some of the report's recommendations from within the department. The report was to some extent reflected in the [1985] Green Paper' (Blackstone and Plowden 1988, p.125).

The CPRS was merged into an enlarged Number 10 Policy Unit which, essentially, acted as a team of special advisers for the Prime Minister. Its head, Brian (now Lord) Griffiths, was particularly interested in education and was thought to have played a key role in the discussions about the 1988 Act (mac.28). The special advisers to ministers in the DES were not seen by some to be as influential on higher education as on schools policy (mac.21).

Media

The media impinge on the formation of opinion. Their coverage of student unrest was seen as exaggerated but was widely thought to have contributed to the loss of esteem in which universities were held. Thus, the former Vice-Chancellor of Essex noted: 'This is where the media were so often irresponsible – the view, for example, that LSE and Essex in the late 1960s were constantly in turmoil ... There were serious troubles in many institutions but they were grossly exaggerated. Teaching and research in British universities were rarely disrupted. In the 1950s and 1960s the mood of the public at large was for the expansion of higher education and for generous financial provision for that expansion. There was overwhelming support for Robbins. By 1970, thanks to unprecedented publicity for student militancy, that mood had evaporated' (mac.205).

The *THES* played a role in encouraging higher education to be looked at across the binary divide because of the way it covered higher education (mac.112). We noted above on the impact made by the leaking of one specific story, in the *THES*, about plans for public sector higher education. The various groups represented on the NAB were assiduous in using the press in general, and the *THES* in particular, to push their point of view, and this may have had some impact on ensuring that subsequent bodies were composed of individuals rather than interest group representatives (mac.111). The editor of the *THES* for many years, Peter Scott, was seen by some key actors as an influential figure (e.g. mac.201). In general, various interest groups attempted to influence the press (mac.32, 48, 216). The growth of higher education means that it is now seen as a more important issue for newspapers to cover, and some papers have played a role in raising questions about the quality of the provision in the current mass system.

II GROUPS THAT INFLUENCE HIGHER EDUCATION POLICY

The discussion below concentrates on the nature of the groups attempting to exert influence on public policy making. Generalisations about the role of interest groups in higher education policy making since 1975 are complicated by various factors. First, there were different patterns of consultation for universities and for public sector higher education. The membership of the Oakes Committee and the NAB resembled much more the traditional education policy pattern in that local authorities and unions were well represented. Second, ministers have varied in their apparent willingness to consult interest groups. Many interviewees suggest Gillian Shephard was more prepared to consult than her predecessors such as John Patten, Kenneth Clarke and Kenneth Baker. William Waldegrave was praised for his willingness to engage with a wide range of groups over science policy (mac.22, 42, 115). A minister from the 1970s, Crowther-Hunt, noting the criticism made in the OECD Report of 1975 (that too much of the DES's planning was undertaken in secret), suggested interest groups were insufficiently able – that is, not given the opportunity – to make their contributions 'to long term policy making while the departmental thinking was in its formative stage' (Crowther-Hunt 1983, p.49). Such comments probably would not have been made by ministers in the late 1980s and early 1990s. Third, the period when there was less consultation (late 1980s and early 1990s) might have coincided with a wider pattern across government departments (Jenkins 1996). Fourth, although, in general in public policy making, the governments since 1979 have consulted interest groups less than the previous governments, the actual amount of consultation with the CVCP has possibly increased because it was at such a low level in the traditional pattern. Fifth, there may have been, at least until Gillian Shephard's time, a qualitative change in the nature of whatever consultation did take place. In relation to the 1980s, one interviewee from the higher education system claimed, 'The DES doesn't understand what consultation is about and I once had to tell them so rather publicly ... "It's no good coming along with a finished product and asking if you've got any comments"' (mac.42). Sixth, one official suggested that because controls over universities had been relaxed the detailed negotiations with universities would not be appropriate.

The Committee of Vice-Chancellors and Principals (CVCP)

At the start of our period, Kogan had analysed the CVCP's position in national policy making as being 'essentially reactive and uncertain' (Kogan 1975, p.206). It was seen as being a legitimised interest group, though without a statutory relationship with the government, which 'because it is essentially a managerial body, is not able to challenge the government effectively even if it had collective policies' (Kogan 1975, p.208). Kogan also showed that in relation to the DES the CVCP 'tends to stand behind the UGC rather than go directly to the Secretary of State' (Kogan 1975, p.208). This might indicate, as we shall see later is argued by authors such as Tapper (1997), that the CVCP was not exactly a fully fledged interest group in the mid-1970s. Kogan, however, defined it as a sectional interest group and showed how on issues such as overseas students' fees it 'remonstrated openly with the government' (Kogan 1975, p.208).

Our current study indicates that although the CVCP was viewed as being effective in some of its activities and a reasonable level of consultation was usually maintained with ministers and officials, and some influence exerted as a result (mac.48), many respondents were critical of the CVCP's ability to make an impact as a lobbying interest group. Meetings of the CVCP were usually well attended by vice-chancellors, but its members were often seen as having difficulty in coming to a common line. Furthermore, given the importance of the autonomy of each institution, and the high status of each vice-chancellor, they would not necessarily adhere to any line adopted by the leadership. About half our interviewees commented on the effectiveness of the CVCP as an interest group. Only a few were strongly positive. Of the rest, one-third thought the CVCP had been effective at some periods or on some issues but not at other times, but two-thirds were dismissive of the overall effectiveness of the CVCP as an interest group. One interviewee commented that some of the leading interest groups – including the CVCP – played a comparatively small role. They would be consulted 'incessantly' but, on the whole, it was consultation not negotiation (mac.45).

The CVCP, however, played a bigger role as policy concern about higher education increased in the 1980s and the UGC was less able to act as the traditional champion of the universities. As we saw in Chapters 4 and 6, the CVCP attempted to keep issues such as the management of institutions and quality assessment in its own hands as far as possible, and with some success. It established the Jarratt and Reynolds Committees, and the Academic Audit Unit and successor bodies. (A more detailed account of its role in relation to quality is provided in Mary Henkel's forthcoming book.) It also worked with the UGC on various of these initiatives and on the introduction of performance indicators (Cave *et al*. 1997). The leadership of the CVCP saw these as useful ways of preventing the government from being even more directly involved in the running of universities. In organisational terms, the CVCP made various changes to increase its capacity to campaign on behalf of universities. Several interviewees referred to the effectiveness of the parliamentary campaigns organised for the CVCP by its official, Mary Morgan, especially over the 1988 Act and issues concerning academic freedom (mac.45). The CVCP did a lot to mobilise alliances of House of Lords academics. Again, as we saw in Chapter 6, the CVCP was seen as leading the campaign against elements of the 1988 Act, with the then chairman, Mark Richmond, playing a prominent role.

Despite further organisational development, the CVCP faced the additional problem in the 1990s that its membership greatly expanded with the ending of the binary line and, consequently, the interests of its members became even more diverse. Various groups sprang up within the CVCP – the Russell Group of large research universities, the '94 Group of smaller, non-medical school, research universities. Although there has been praise from those interviewed for successive chairs of the CVCP who oversaw the expansion and the emergence of a combined body, nevertheless, the CVCP remained unable to exercise any real sanctions over its members.

The Committee of Directors of Polytechnics (CDP)

The CDP was established in 1969/70 with the encouragement of the Secretary of State and DES officials but discouragement from the local authorities. Its position in the mid-1970s was that it did not have the full range of consultative relationships possessed by the CVCP but was clearly becoming more important as the polytechnics became stronger and their relationships with their parent local authorities and local authority associations not likely to become any easier (Kogan 1975, p.192).

We have already described the increasing influence and status of the CDP in the 1980s in relation to the incorporation of the polytechnics and the end of the binary line, which were its two principal triumphs. Although the CDP emerged as the one successful interest group, it had in its earlier days, at least, been regarded with some disdain by the vice-chancellors (mac.10). The CDP always had a small secretariat and, particularly when its office was funded through ILEA, the grant was small, and as a body it was dependent on the local authorities. This, together with the fact that there were vocal members of the CDP, such as Eric Robinson, who supported the link with the local authorities, meant that it would have been difficult for the CDP as a body to campaign for independence for polytechnics. As late as 1985, in its response to the Lindop Report (1985), the CDP was stating:

> Self-validation is a matter of academic concern. It should not, in the CDP's view, be regarded as leading to any weakening of the re-lationships with the maintaining authorities. (quoted in CDP 1986)

The CDP went over to being funded by institutional subscriptions from 1984/85. Even then, there was a difficulty getting that through some local authorities. Despite organisational development, some of the key meetings, such as that reported in Chapter 5 with Mrs Thatcher, involved a few individual directors rather than the CDP as a body.

Nevertheless, in general, the CDP felt that it was being consulted by ministers, officials and funding councils, even if they did not feel they had the same 'clubland access as universities – there was a good deal of paranoia, a second-class citizen, untouchable, think-speak around, but, certainly, we were able to talk to officials and we had meetings with ministers at appropriate levels on a regular or irregular basis. So consultation, insofar as it ever has a value, was always there.' This was more consultation than negotiation: 'Ministers would never regard themselves as seriously negotiating – it's a matter of consulting and then a judgement is made ... But on the whole ... up to those two measures [incorporation and unification], the feeling was that the inclination of policy was in the direction CDP wanted it to go' (mac.43).

Directors saw an overlap between their agenda and that of the government in providing expansion, industrially relevant courses and independence from local authorities. Rather than changing the government's agenda, the CDP 'facilitated it ... Government policy was assisted very greatly by the fact that CDP policy was the same and things coincided – universities were very cagey, they'd been, in a curious way, maintaining their autonomy too strongly' (mac.105). The CDP grew in acceptance in the 1980s. Bodies such as the British Council recognised the CDP on equal terms with the CVCP. The Overseas Development Agency insisted that the body that assisted Commonwealth universities in emerging countries had CDP representation. 'It was quite clear we were a new body to be reckoned with' (mac.105).

In the time before unification, they attempted to build up rapport with the CVCP, with varying success. 'We used to meet once a term and it depended who was chairman of CVCP whether we had a feeling of rapport and friendship or a certain coldness ... we tried to ensure, on both sides, that the agenda would be matters on which we were likely to find some accord' (mac.105). Once they had become universities, the former polytechnics continued to press their case and the majority of them created a group within the CVCP called the Coalition of Modern Universities. The Vice-Chancellor of Thames Valley University was reported by one interviewee as asking, in relation to research funding, 'If this is a level playing field on research funding, may we please change ends?'

The Royal Society and the British Academy

Fellows of the Royal Society and the British Academy are the most obvious representatives of the academic elite. Election to fellowship is highly selective; the British Academy, for example, elects about 14 or 15 fellows each year. Attempts to increase the fellowship were said to have been resisted by the late Sir Alfred Ayer on the grounds that they could not then exclude those whom they disliked (mac.216). The Royal Society elects, perhaps, three times that number. Election denotes an attained status within the academic fields and it follows that many of those elected are already contributing to academic decision making on the appointment to senior academic posts and the award of research grants.

Their role in national higher education science policy making is less certain. Both institutions are consulted from time to time, but the Royal Society seems to be consulted more and to carry more weight than the British Academy. Various interviewees referred to the importance of the individual characteristics of the President of the Royal Society in determining its impact at any given time. Limitations on the extent to which the Royal Society can express collective opinions derive both from its charter and from the diverse subject background of its members. According to one leading member involved in science policy, the Royal Society is most likely to swing into action only as a last resort when something appears to be going wrong in policy terms (mac.119). The Royal Society was seen, however, as one of the key bodies involved in the consultation over the 1993 White Paper from the OST (mac.42, 116). In the White Paper it is stated that in addition to studies specifically commissioned by OST, 'other studies and publications by, for example, both Select Committees, the Parliamentary Office of Science and Technology and the Royal Society were timely and valuable' (OST 1993, para. 1.12). The Royal Society has been thought to be particularly vocal in relation to policy on the careers for scientists. Meetings, held at the Royal Society, of the Foundation for Society and Technology were good opportunities for the wider academic elite to discuss science policy with political and industrial leaders (mac.116, 204).

It is, perhaps, the status they confer on, or, perhaps, reinforce in, individuals that ensures that many of the key posts in science and technology policy are held by members of the Royal Society. There is hardly, however, any similar correspondence between fellowship of the British Academy and chairs and chief executive posts in funding or research councils.

The British Academy has a role additional to that of acting as an honorific and learning society and an interest group. It administers postgraduate grants in the arts and humanities (although not in the social sciences which its fellowship covers). It has small sums available for sponsorship of minor research and publication grants. It has been ambivalent about the desirability of creating a humanities research council, as has recently been decided following a recommendation in the Dearing Report (1997). Some of its members feared that this would place their subject areas under the increasingly strong control of the Public Expenditure Survey and research allocation system (mac.214).

The Association of University Teachers (AUT)

In 1975 Kogan described the AUT as a 'trade union with no ultimate power ... it illustrates how the potency of education institutions and individuals reduces the effectiveness of collective bargaining' (1975, p.208). However, the AUT was seen as working easily with the DES and had meetings with the UGC, and the CVCP, and had frequent contacts with the press – especially the *THES*.

Throughout the period of reforms, the AUT was not seen as an influential body, and probably found it harder than before to make its voice heard, despite respect for the general secretary in certain ministerial and official quarters. Nevertheless, it has been involved in continuing consultations with bodies, including the education department, particularly over salary issues. It has published many reports which have contributed to policy debates.

National Association of Teachers in Further and Higher Education (NATFHE)

One of the forerunners of NATFHE was the Association of Teachers in Technical Institutions (ATTI), and 'the development of the polytechnics owes much to the ATTI's way of thinking' (Kogan 1975, p.187). Despite this initial impact, and its ability to represent the case with skill and force, Kogan suggested that the public sector higher education had its own powerful advocates within the system, and, therefore, in this field 'interest groups are less obvious in their impact than their counterparts in other areas ... the issues are regarded as more national and belonging to government than those in other areas ... The association has not had an easy time coping with a self-confident DES. And it now has competition from the directors of polytechnics as well as from other unions' (Kogan 1975, pp.186–187).

Nevertheless, under the more pluralistic arrangements for PSHE in the late 1970s and early 1980s, NATFHE had a voice on bodies such as the Oakes Committee and the NAB. Subsequently, it does not seem to have carried much weight in relation to higher education. One of the problems facing NATFHE has been the perception that the majority of its membership are in further education, and that this, rather than higher education, must therefore be its main focus of interest.

Local authorities

The importance attached to local authorities in the establishment of the polytechnics was described in Chapter 5. The power of the local authorities in the 1970s was demonstrated by their role on the Oakes working party and in the early 1980s by their domination of the NAB and their defeat of the original DES proposal for a national body for PSHE. As noted above, in the early 1980s representatives for local authorities were still influential in the Conservative Party and ministers such as Sir Keith Joseph and William Waldegrave believed in their importance (mac.106).

In higher education, as in education and the public services more generally, local authorities lost influence in the years of Conservative government. The 1988 Act removed their control over polytechnics and colleges and the 1992 Act made further education colleges independent of local authorities.

Industry/employers

Industry and employers increased their influence during the Thatcher era. More businessmen have been appointed to quangos, such as funding councils, and to governing bodies of institutions. Many polytechnics, and now an increasing number of old universities as well, developed strong links with local industries (mac.49, 115).

In terms of acting as a pressure group as distinct from the actions of individual industrialists, the position is more complicated. The CIHE has been listened to and well respected. However, industry has often found it difficult to express a common line in relation to higher education. Various interviewees thought that what ministers thought industry should want was often a more powerful influence than any views industry might have expressed. The mixed views about the role of the CBI in the debate on expansion were noted in Chapter 3.

The wider trade union movement

A major contrast with the position in Sweden is the virtual absence of any role in higher education policy formation for the wider union movement. Their voice does not come through any of the policy documents or media for the period. As noted by Becher and Kogan, 'major "corporatist" interests of labour and capital have been more significantly involved in the politics of higher education in Sweden than in France or the UK or the USA' (1992, p.58).

The National Union of Students (NUS)

The NUS became, according to Kogan (1975), a legitimised interest group in the late 1960s, particularly during the presidency of Jack Straw. In 1975 Kogan observed that the NUS has 'perhaps shown more development in role, structure and effectiveness than any other single interest group in the last ten years' (Kogan 1975, p.211). The late 1960s was the period when, as Minister for Higher Education, Shirley Williams was particularly keen to encourage consultation with groups such as the NUS.

In the 1980s the NUS was not seen as a body to be much consulted, but in the 1990s it has swung back more into favour within official thinking with the growing consumerist movement (mac.36).

The allocative bodies and research councils

The role of these bodies in policy making was discussed in Chapter 6, and our general conclusion, although this is a matter of some contention, was that the power formerly possessed by the UGC and the research councils to make policy decisions had been considerably reduced. The new funding councils are subject to instruction from ministers in a way that did not occur with the UGC. In relation to research councils, the 1993 White Paper made clear that there had been a centralisation of the research councils' activities and that this would be intensified with the creation of a Director-General. The intention was to build on the advances made in recent years by the Advisory Board for the Research Councils, 'to give more central co-ordination and strategic direction to the Councils' activities' (OST 1993, para. 3.24).

Clearly, however, these bodies influence the policy discussion of ministers and officials, and on many issues themselves retain the power to decide matters. For example, recently, both the MRC and the Biotechnology and Biological Sciences Research Council developed new strategies following the appointment of new chief executives, and the Foresight Initiative has been implemented in different ways by the various research councils (see Henkel *et al.* forthcoming). The heads of research councils formed a group, HORCs, to discuss matters of common interest. However, the exact status of these groups is unclear, as it was in 1975 when Kogan noted that 'the UGC is variously described by witnesses as both part of government and a universities' interest group' (Kogan 1975, p.200).

III RELATING THE THEORIES TO OUR EMPIRICAL DATA
The role of elites

As we saw in Chapter 2, the role of higher education elites in the UK was often analysed in terms of their relationship to the wider elites; the weakening of this relationship is seen as a factor in the reduced autonomy of universities.

We noted in Chapter 6 that analysis in terms of elites forms an important element in Tapper and Salter's account of the challenge to the traditional liberal university ideal presented by the rise of an economic ideology. They present the rise of the economic ideology in terms of a split between different parts of the elite. The notion of university autonomy was assumed rather than emphasised in the traditional university ideal:

> ... given the role of the university as the preserver of elite values and producer of elite people, conflict between one section of the elite (the government) and another section of the elite (the universities) was quite simply not a part of the traditional ideal model. Rather, the model assumed (and as late as 1968 Halsey argued was still the case), elite homogeneity based on elite consensus. The elite could be expected to look after its own. However, once a split between the universities and another section of the elite occurs then the idea of university autonomy becomes a critical part of their ideological defence and the frequency of its use a measurement of the extent of their insecurity. Part of the significance of Robbins, therefore, lies in the indications it gives of the beginnings of elite fragmentation. (Tapper and Salter 1978, p.150)

As one of 18 elite groups examined in their 1971 study, Wakeford and Wakeford (1974) included 'University Vice-Chancellors and Principals'. This group, which included heads of Oxbridge colleges, constituted over 10 per cent of the total number included as people 'in a position to be exercising considerable political and economic influence in Britain' (p.187). The Vice-Chancellors' group were more meritocratic than most, but 44 out of the 90 included in the survey were members of the Athenaeum Club – a figure far higher than for any other group. This led Wakeford and Wakeford to comment: '...we can only speculate whether membership of that institution enhances the chances of selection or merely follows as a concomitant of appointment' (p.191).

Our findings support the notion of a degree of elite fragmentation. As we have seen, some Conservative politicians showed less faith in higher education autonomy. Whilst Salter and Tapper (1994) saw civil servants as instigators of reform, one minister told us: 'Keith Joseph went in and was captured by the forces of elitism in the department', and was therefore likely to defend traditional higher education interests.

The theories of Wiener (1981) and Barnett (1986), concerning the influence of Oxbridge education on the 'decline of the industrial spirit', have received much attention, and, in reviewing the literature, Anderson notes that even though these theories have been criticised they have 'enjoyed great vogue in political and journalistic circles' (Anderson 1995, p.34). This might go some way to explaining the rather critical attitude adopted towards universities by politicians and the great change from the previous situation, in which central government policy making for the universities was traditionally conducted 'by like-minded members of the elite' (Halsey 1969, p.137) in the Treasury and the University Grants Committee, who shared a high level of trust. The close relationship between the UGC and the Treasury, and the impact this had on policy making for the universities, were discussed in previous chapters.

As far as elites or leadership groups are concerned, our main findings are that there is no single elite that can be assumed to operate within higher education. There are a range of groups, however, that can be considered, if not all as elites then as influencers of policy and opinion. Coterminosity between the groups is uneven; for example, the majority of Oxbridge heads of houses are not members of the academic elite, as defined above. Of those appointed vice-chancellor since 1960, only 14 per cent have been FRS and 5 per cent FBA (Smith *et al.* 1999). Individual members of the academic elite, particularly those eminent in science and technology, are part of the co-opted elite when they are appointed to research councils and allocative bodies, but the majority of co-optees are not members of the academic or institutional leadership elite.

A small number of individuals might figure in more than one group and some such individuals might make a major contribution. Names such as Brian Flowers, Fred Dainton, Peter Swinnerton-Dyer and David Phillips – and there are others – were mentioned by various interviewees as having been influential. Of the 16 members of the Advisory Council for Applied Research and Development in 1985, 5 were FRS and 5 Fellows of the Academy of Engineering (one being a member of both). Of the 24 members of the ABRC in 1983, 14 were FRS, 1 FBA, 1 Fellow of the Royal Society of Edinburgh, and 4 FEng (3 of whom were also FRS). Some of the scientific elite co-opted to these bodies worked in industry rather than academe, but the figures, nevertheless, illustrate how strongly members of the defined elite were represented on the top bodies advising on scientific policy. The ABRC showed continuity of type of membership: at the time of the controversial report *A Strategy for the Science Base* (1987), of its 23 members (excluding the two DES assessors) 12 were FRS, 1 FBA and there were 5 FEng (one of whom was also an FRS). It is claimed that, in practice, co-ordination of science policy in Britain tends to mean cross-membership of committees and 'the system probably only works because the people who sit on all these committees have so much in common' (Ince 1986, p.28). However, one observer believed that the initiative had passed away from that elite which was effectively longing for greater selectivity. 'All those groups that operated before 1992 evaporated. What we now have is a bureaucratic system that can't cope. People can't pull the levers any more' (mac.213).

Appointment to the co-opted elite was discussed earlier. Whilst for some, academic achievement was a factor, the ability to work in committees was also important. Increasingly, however, closeness to government thinking was a qualification. This makes it difficult to establish the original source of policy thinking. An analysis of the advice contained in the 1987 ABRC Report and government pronouncements in the 1987 Civil R&D White Paper led Edgerton and Hughes to conclude:

> The government is thus committed to a highly centralising and dirigiste science policy which is based on arguments which do not stand up to scrutiny, and which fly in the face of 'Austrian pre-scriptions' [see Chapter 2]. How is this ideological and policy contradiction to be explained? ... First, important and influential sections of the scientific community, and science policy experts, have argued for just such a policy. Secondly, this policy should be seen as part of a wider strategy to control the scientific commu-nity, and ... the wider academic community. (Edgerton and Hughes 1989, p.429)

A particular case of an academic elite group are members of the House of Lords who might be appointed either because of their academic eminence or because of their political allegiances. In addition, four academic peers have hereditary titles. Academic peers have been able to secure amendments to, and, in a few cases, defeat of, some government proposals. In particular, they were active in causing changes in the 1988 Act, with its implications for academic freedom, by collaborating with peers from all parties. This was also one of the few examples where the Committee of Vice-Chancellors was able to secure consensus among its members on a substantive issue of policy, to fend off attack on academic freedom, and their campaign on this was described earlier. Many peers, if not academics themselves, are university chancellors or chairs of council and they, as well as academic peers, can come out in force. In one debate, virtually all the speakers were highly critical of government resource policies and, to a lesser extent, the imposition of quality assurance measures (House of Lords 1996).

New elites have been created as a result of the expansion of higher education, the associated creation by government of bodies for resource allocation and quality assurance, and the incorporation into university status of formerly non-university institutions. In one significant case (leading to the demise of the binary system), one leadership group, the polytechnic directors, won the support of ministers and a corresponding elevation of institutional and individual statuses.

In the 1960s it was suggested that 'the scientific establishment had a strong effect on higher education policy' (Kogan 1975, p.203). Some claim that, at least on science policy, there remains an influence, but effected through small group interaction. One observer noted: 'In the absence of any systematic policy analysis at the heart of government or in the ABRC, what one was essentially engaged in was a face-to-face debate with a remarkably small number of people. There is not only an Establishment, but a very closely defined Scientific Establishment, and if one can obtain access to the venues where they come together then it is possible to argue and win the case. In this sense ... science policy making is dependent upon a small social network which supports its own subculture and with whom interaction needs constantly to be refreshed and renewed.'

In our period, however, with some significant exceptions, there are important limitations on the extent to which elites have influenced higher education policy making. One of these exceptions has been seen to be the influence exerted by the scientific elite on the decision to create OST (although at least one leading scientist and a member of the co-opted elite challenged the view that this attracted a consensus) and on the content of the subsequent White Paper. Individual access to policy makers is, to some extent, sustained partly because some politicians and bureaucrats have retained a respect for academic excellence and for the concept of academic autonomy. One academic respondent gave examples of the influence of the academic elites, which does not, however, add up to participating in the genesis of policy but rather its modification in practice:

When it comes to implementation, no doubt the politicking and ability of the elite to modify and ameliorate the impact in various ways are quite strong. The Royal Society has been pretty success- ful in protecting the science base. Oxbridge lobbying to protect the college fee, when everything else running towards standard formulaic models, has been very successful. As soon as elite groups saw the thrust of government philosophy was that the ex- pansion of higher education did not require, and certainly was not going to allow for, parallel amounts of money to be put into re- search in universities, they accepted ... selectivity and therefore worked hard to ensure that the system that came out protected ex- isting centres of research. (mac.16)

Similar views about the impact of academic elites come from another leading academic and political scientist: 'My impression is that they now wield very little influence, they've moved to the dignified part of the constitution. The way Royal Society and British Academy used to operate ... is that some deference would be paid by government to the views of the Presidents and other senior members of those two bodies, and so if they asked to see the minister or the junior minister or the permanent secretary it would be arranged for them to be able to make representations. They would have other opportunities to discuss informally their concerns with the real policy makers in higher education – it really was "a word in your ear, Minister" kind of stuff. I just don't believe that that system of influence and policy making operates any longer – the importance of connections and contacts and incumbency of high status office is much less important than it was ... There are still small, interlocking, self-recruiting groups who exercise academic power within the system – for example, they would influence the selection of professors and they are still exercising a bit of power through the RAE panels ... the old university sector is still disproportionately represented on the RAE panels. They will still exercise quite a lot of influence within the research councils, although not as much as they used to ... I'm not sure there are any elites in policy making in the higher education sector but if there are it's very much on the Robert Dahl polyarchy model – there are lots of elites that may have considerable influence in one area or subsector of policy, but they're competing with other elites who have influence in other areas of policy and different elites (if you want to call them that), or different interest groups, not only have a great deal more influence in some areas than others – but the arguments that they have wax and wane, so it's a kind of pluralist elite system' (mac.113).

The views expressed in this quotation are compatible with the earlier assessment of the limited role played by the two national academies in policy development. They also fit the contention that there are different and contending interests amongst the science community. We have also seen that SERC, led as it was by members of the academic elite, was sometimes resistant to the more dirigiste policies of concentration promoted by the ABRC.

The shift from an elite to a mass system of higher education probably caused a shift from an elite system of almost non-decision making and a move towards a more formal system. The question was raised as to how the traditional university function of elite cultural transmission could be applied to the vastly expanded university population (Tapper and Salter 1978, pp.158–159; see also Halsey 1992, pp.10–11). Certainly, the system has become more formalised and juridicised as a result of massification. This is also compatible with the view that the CVCP (Tapper 1997) and its Australian equivalent (Marshall 1995b) moved from being organisations whose composition made them elite bodies towards being more typical interest groups.

The role of interest groups

In examining the role of interest groups in higher education policy making, we start with the broad picture of how the role of such groups traditionally was viewed in the education department as a whole. Then we consider some general points about the role of interest groups in higher education since 1975, before returning to the theories and assessing how appropriate it would be to claim there has been a shift from a policy community towards an issue network, as had happened in rather similar circumstances in Australia.

Most respondents with a knowledge of how the DES operated before 1979 agreed with the picture described by Kogan (1975) of almost continuous consultation and negotiation with the main interest groups over schools policy; a depiction referred to in the original development of the policy community concept (Richardson and Jordan 1979). As we have seen, it was much less clear how far this notion could be applied to higher education before 1975 because until the 1980s, the 'old' universities did not use, possibly because they did not need to, their main body, the CVCP, or their more informal ways into government for sustained negotiation or bargaining throughout the period of expansion.

The UGC had great freedom, as did the 'old' universities, within a benignly administered policy framework, to meet their needs and make allocations. The UGC was seen as a buffer organisation between the universities and the government. How far it is appropriate to view such a body (and the relevant department and the funded universities between which it stood) as constituting a policy community is controversial and depends on how the UGC is defined. Nevertheless, Marshall (1995a) thought the term could appropriately be used to describe the traditional picture of the Australian buffer body before the reforms of the 1980s. However, the UGC members might be better seen as part of a co-opted elite, but Shattock (1994) suggests the UGC was the clearest example of Heclo and Wildavsky's (1974) depiction of British public administration as being 'the private government of public money'. And Dowding claims that in evolving this concept, Heclo and Wildavsky 'had used the idea of policy communities, suggesting that these develop around a shared framework of understandings' (Dowding 1995).

Unique importance attached to the notion of institutional autonomy of universities in the UK; until the 1980s it was not really seen as appropriate for the government to have many policies for the universities and certainly not in areas such as style and content of courses, standards and evaluation.

If, then, the term policy community could have been applied to the traditional world of the universities, it would not take the normal form of almost continuous consultation and negotiation, even though it would meet some of Rhodes and Marsh's (1992) other criteria such as limited membership and shared basic values. Marshall (1995a) applied these themes to Australian higher education and traced a move from a policy community up to the late 1980s, via a period of state domination under the Minister of Education, Dawkins, to an issue network in the 1990s. He earlier described how the Australian Committee of Vice-Chancellors had gone from an elite club with ties to the government, to a group that was powerless to stop a government determined to reform higher education and make it more responsive to the economy, to a group that had become more effective as an interest group (Marshall 1995b). In describing how powerful pressure groups had become, in general, in the UK, Hennessy refers to the failure of the universities to mount much of a campaign against the cuts in the early 1980s as 'an aberration which highlighted the norm' (Hennessy 1988, p.338).

Extensive pluralistic consultation processes have never been as strong in UK higher education, where the consensually accepted policies of expansion, a willingness by politicians not to interfere in academic matters, and the existence of buffer institutions, on which academic elites were strongly represented, made active negotiation largely unnecessary, except over the quinquennial grant. The key changes were often promoted by ministers. Although, as our earlier account showed, the interests were consulted in the 1970s, the comments we noted from Crowther-Hunt reinforce the view that the level of contact was insufficient to constitute a full policy community. The general picture that emerges is that less notice was taken of higher education interest groups in the post-1979 period. Several higher education ministers expressed this view. Rhodes Boyson agreed that his attitude would fit that of Mrs Thatcher's government in trying to take less notice of vested interest groups. Another minister believed that the Thatcher government decided to challenge some of the professional middle-class groups.

Another minister, Nigel Forman, did not agree that some groups were on the inside track and others excluded: 'Anybody who had a sensible view to put ... has been listened to ... The statutory consultees are always contacted by ministers because civil servants advise ministers to do so, but the people who volunteer views and information and experience are always free to do so.' Such consultation is taken seriously by ministers. On the other hand, and illustrating the complexities, he claimed that ministers would not be negotiating with groups and that 'there are many fewer veto groups in our political process than there were 20 years ago'. This fits nicely with Simon Jenkins's analysis that what Mrs Thatcher did 'was restore in Britain the concept of governability' (Jenkins 1996, p.5)

The change was graphically described by one interviewee, who contrasted Joseph's way of consulting the system with that of his successors:

> That was how Joseph believed you should work – he had all the new ideas but all his instincts and ways of working were old-fashioned ... Baker and Clarke, coming in almost simultaneously in Education and Health, believed that doing business in that way is what had slowed the government down and made it impossible to make progress, and that the device you had to copy was that of the blitzkrieg, and they both saw themselves as sort of Panzer Generals working out policy with no consultation – pretending after you'd propounded the policy that you were going to consult, but, in fact, working by fait accompli, meanwhile using the propa-

ganda machine of the Department to ensure that public opinion comes your way so that a total change took place. But it's very important to see that the change was very much more a change in how you did the business than in the debate. The debate was still relatively old hat but what changed was this decisiveness and that really does then build up momentum. In both cases, at the decisive moment, they used money – in HE, in the form of more bodies ... the whole system then swallowed that without, as would have happened in the old days, a long discussion. [The blitzkrieg style is now over] but it must have been very difficult for them to counter. (mac.46)

As part of higher education's exceptionalism, there is a debate on how far groups within higher education can be considered to be producer interest groups in the same way as in other fields. Thus, Forman claims: 'I don't believe we can really see the world of higher education, even after the reforms, as just another producer group – that's straining the language. It is a rather distinctive group of people with a distinctive ethos ... and traditions ... I would support them in clinging to those traditions because what makes British higher education ... among the best in the world is because we haven't lost sight of the original academic mission.'

A senior official referred to the relationship between those in government and the leaders of higher education institutions in the 1980s as 'patchy' (Bird 1994). Nevertheless, it must be recalled that there were occasions, such as the publication of Green and White Papers and the inquiries of parliamentary and other committees, when the major interest groups were invited to provide evidence, and, as discussed in Chapters 4 and 6, there was considerable debate over the details of quality policies even if the government determined the major policy line.

In considering how far we can apply policy network analysis, we have seen that our period began with a type of policy community that is unusual because of the particular nature of higher education's structures of influence. Even by 1975 there were the beginnings of greater interest group involvement. In the 1980s and early 1990s there were two somewhat contradictory moves. An increase in the sheer volume of higher education policy making generated more discussion. Yet there was less ministerial patience with academic autonomy and less concern to negotiate on key developments. These attitudes were particularly strong in the period of greatest policy change from the mid-1980s to the early 1990s. Latterly, particularly under the more conciliatory Gillian Shephard, there was more willingness to discuss with a wider range of interests in a pattern more resembling an issue network. This would resemble the pattern described for Australia by Marshall (1995a) and, as with Australia, partly reflects the wider range of interests involved in a mass higher education system.We have noted that Dowding (1995) questioned whether the terms 'policy community' and 'issue network' were not labels rather than useful explanations of reasons for change. Our findings for higher education indicate, as to some extent did Marshall's, that a crucial issue is the level of consultation that different ministers, and possibly whole governments, wish to pursue.

CONCLUSIONS

As we have seen, dual policy processes are at work in higher education, with many decisions taken through the invisible colleges of academics. Other decisions on public policy matters are made largely by ministers and officials. The influence of Parliament has not been great, although two of the most significant defeats suffered by the Conservative governments were over higher education policy: on aspects of the 1988 Act and Joseph's plans for student finance. Parliamentary select committees did generate some pressure for the DES and ministers to pursue more interventionist and instrumental policies. Generally, higher education policy has had a low salience within political parties, which has enhanced the ability of ministers to determine policy.

In terms of the policies that were pursued, a declared policy in favour of expansion was not the product of either sustained pressure from interest groups or from rationalistic planning, although there were elements of both in Baker's decision to adopt a more expansionist policy than his predecessor. Expansion led to greater control over the system and demands for efficiency, both of which were policies where pressure was also building from other sources, such as the wider moves to reform public services. Some policies were derived from the ideology of economic instrumentalism, e.g. attempts to modify the curriculum. But policy emergence in that field was impulsive, as is confirmed by accounts of the ministerial decisions to create the Enterprise Initiative. Some ministers such as Young and Joseph had strong ideological commitments.

In the past, higher education has not been an area of political salience. It is now more so, but the changes in the patterns of influence have as their starting point not an enlivening of the politics of higher education, but the greater assertion of central power which eschews any extension of the influence and voice of academics. Whilst this central authority is exercised by both ministers and civil servants, we give more emphasis to the former than do some other accounts. The classic academic elites remain in place and are able to create academic policies and make allocative judgements, but the larger issues of structure and resources are firmly in the hand of government. It exercises its power, in part, through co-option, and the co-opted elite are only, in part, coterminous with the academic elites and institutional leadership. There is thus no coherent policy network community and networks are fractionated, although we note evidence of some fairly intensive micropolitics at places where it has counted.

The main interest groups had hardly any place in the genesis of a range of policies, although, because much more policy was being instigated, the actual level of contact was quite high during the period of reform. Evidence of interest group or elite participation in policy making in the 1980s and 1990s, leading to recent reforms such as moves towards markets and managerialism, is difficult to find. A major exception is the politics of the ending of the binary system and the use of persuasive tactics by the polytechnics. But it was not a purposive policy in its origins. The DES had always hoped that the polytechnics would find their own separate identity. In campaigning for the abolition of the binary divide, the CDP was following a similar agenda to that of ministers.

The views of institutions on policy are mainly mediated through the CVCP or through individual membership of government-appointed bodies. There are no formalised mechanisms of consultation, let alone negotiation, of the kind to be found in the pre-1980s schools policy communities or, more latterly, in the National Advisory Body responsible for public sector policies and representing both the local authorities and the institutions. Nor is it clear that institutional views or those of academic staff go 'upwards' in such processes. The part played by the main honorific, professional and subject societies is known to be limited. There is always scope for leading members of the academic elite to have access to policy makers. Such individualistic contact, plus pressure from the House of Lords Science and Technology Committee, and the Royal Society, did contribute to the creation of the OST and the policies in the 1993 White Paper. The move that took the OST into the DTI demonstrated, however, that ministers might still move in a decisive way without consultation and, avowedly on behalf of industry in pursuit of an ideological belief, in making publicly funded research more fully meet the needs of the economy.

Our general conclusion is that whilst ideological predispositions might affect or dynamise an issue, or particular interest groups might affect an outcome, there is no clear and schematic place for either of them in an account of issue emergence and resolution. A major complication is that the ideological beliefs did not point consistently in one policy direction and ministerial and official interpretation of priorities and demands from the wider policy context fluctuated. The traditional picture was of an unusual type of policy community, of a system of decision making within a small elite, that for long periods was almost a system of non-decision making as the UGC was left largely alone. A climate was gradually building up in Parliament, parties and the media that some reform was required, and the voices demanding greater accountability and instumentalism were becoming stronger. This, combined with expansion, financial restraints, and changing beliefs about public institutions in general, created a background in which a series of reforms were largely imposed in an unsystematic way by ministers and officials. In this period, evidence of policy communities – never as strong as in other fields of public policy – and of corporatist exchanges virtually disappeared.

Towards the end of our period, however, there has been increased consultation with a wide range of groups, and the CVCP is more clearly playing a role in this as an interest group rather than an elite body. With more groups taking part in discussions, in a somewhat episodic manner, there has been some shift towards an issue network in which, in Rhodes and Marsh's terms, there are fluctuations in contacts, access and levels of agreement and unequal powers among the groups. Despite these moves, policy making in higher education largely retains its dual processes and idiosyncratic nature.

Chapter 9

Reflections and Some Emerging Conclusions

In this volume we have shown how the 'reforms' attempted in higher education in England from the mid-1970s until the advent of the Labour government in 1997 involved changes in the objectives, government and the styles of higher education policy. In doing so, we have set the background for a companion work which analyses the impact of the reforms on academic values and working and 'epistemic identities' (Henkel forthcoming). Here, we bring together the main issues discussed and the conclusions reached in previous chapters, and identify key issues raised by our study.

What the book says

Chapter 2 considered the central theme of higher education and the role of the state. We noted how, within the wide spectrum of British institutions, universities held a particular place. This spectrum can be placed alongside a spectrum of normative accounts of state actions, values and purposes. We located UK universities as being at the free and chartered end of the spectrum of public institutions, but shifting into a position partly determined by a particular form of radical conservative theory. This contained many ambivalences, both devolutionary and centralist, and pursuing some policies such as selectivity and funding with considerable determination whilst looking for market patterns of behaviour which would be aimed to free up institutions. The attempts to roll back the frontiers of the state forced central policies and patterns of behaviour on the intermediary bodies, the institutions and, ultimately, on individual academics. We noted how theories of the state had developed subsets in the form of New Public Management and the precepts associated with the Evaluative State.

In Chapter 2 and the later empirical chapters, we described how, from a set of largely independent enterprises allowed by the state to pursue their own values and activities, by the 1990s the universities had become increasingly subject to central policies. By the 1990s, their position within Clark's triangle had shifted from the corner of professional academic control towards those of the state and the market. Universities had become unequivocally public institutions, and part of the public policy frame. Much still remained within the control of academics – the setting of standards whereby new entrants to staff and student body were judged, the award of prized academic positions and grants and other statuses – but all within a more urgent policy frame not set by themselves. At the same time, the polytechnics were growing in both political appeal and in their ability to offer competition to what the universities could offer, particularly to a wide range of students.

Chapters 2 and 8 take up political science theories of policy making and policy systems relevant to our themes. We examine the policy process, and the ways in which particular groups have exercised influence. We hold up for critique existing depictions of elites in Britain and consider the role of the policy communities and corporatist arrangements in policy making and implementation.

We noted the enduring power of a normative political theory idiosyncratic to higher education which was, however, under test from more social and managerial assumptions about higher education's functions and policies. At the same time, a strong degree of exceptionalism and assumptions of autonomy persisted. The theories developed for higher education can be assessed against the typifications of changes in the way in which the state operates. On the basis of these analyses, we can confirm what in fact happened to British universities as government became more interventionary, more persuasive about the benefits of market behaviour and more inclined to managerial than to professional control. The extent to which New Public Management and the Evaluative State held sway could then be assessed.

We concluded that powerful contexts, of demography, economic and social change affecting higher education policies, interacted unsystematically with the multiple ideologies and the proclivities of powerful actors, particularly ministers and some key members of the co-opted elites.

Chapter 3 contains a fuller account of these contexts within which policy changed and, in particular, the great expansion of higher education which constituted both the context and consequence of policy change and the context of further 'reforms'. Expansion policies had become an international commonplace reflecting changing social expectations and the assumed demands of a knowledge-based economy.

The universities shifted from state-subsidised independence to increased dependence on, and deference to, state policies, and the system began to respond to newly sharpened instrumentalism and selectivity, particularly in research grading and funding, which had excellence as its leading criterion. Institutions were invited to respond to the needs and demands of the markets constituted by students and research sponsors, described by the Secretary of State in 1989 as 'a movement towards mass higher education accompanied by greater institutional differentiation and diversification in a market-led and multi-funded setting' (Baker 1989). They meant they were now more clearly seen as part of a mixed economy in which funding depended not only on esteemed public policy attributes (high research ratings and good student recruitment in the right areas) but also on their entrepreneurial capacities. The extent to which traditional academic values and ways of working would actually change under these prescriptions was the question we set ourselves for our total project.

In contrast to some other moves, the shift towards markets, to the extent that it was implemented, could be seen as a move on the spectrum away from the state control/collectivist position. However, to a large extent, the deficiency principle – under which the state provided those resources that institutions could not find for themselves – remained in place; no institution under present arrangements could manage without state funding.

The enabling or facilitatory role of the state (Neave and Van Vught 1991) had given way to more interventionary stances. From 1967, when the balances between different kinds of students were determined by the UGC for the first time, until the present, there was a succession of changes. Their impact was often to increase power at the centre. Objectives-setting by the central authorities came alongside the academic norms and modes of self-governance of the academy. In the 1980s higher education was juridicised. There were attempts to influence, though not prescribe, the curriculum and modes of delivery through such projects as the Enterprise Initiative (Chapter 4). But complex and somewhat contradictory ideologies were at play and the predispositions of individual ministers were also behind policy shifts.

Yet whilst the policy changes were radical and had deep effects on the work of academics and their institutions, there were also policy continuities. Economic instrumentalism had never been absent from higher education's agenda, at least from 1945 onwards. Quality assurance, under peer control, had been taken for granted. It now became explicit, and public, and under increasing state surveillance. The hierarchy of esteem and the differential resources which came with it had always been present, but became steeper and public, and reputations, hitherto almost a matter of private peer group knowledge, became explicit.

Policy making followed no rational model. Policies were created largely on the hoof and were, as we have said, the product of a complex interplay of context, ideologies, ministers and bureaucracies (Chapters 3 and 4). The selectivity policies emanated from micro-political action within small elite groups, but were not subject to the operation of clear policy communities and the public deliberation that might go with their interaction.

The ending of the binary system (Chapter 5) showed the UK following the logic of development that seems to apply to other systems. It was a major case study in the post-1970s politics of higher education. Central government responded to those interests whose objectives coincided with theirs. The issue was decided by the interaction of quite closed interests and politics. The moves against local authority control were connected, too, with changing assumptions about public institutions. Now there was a theory of institutions free to compete with each other but working within far tighter funding and demands for accountability, as largely expressed through quality assurance.

The 'old' universities lost the protection accorded to those whose standards were accepted without challenge. Some reshuffling of the order of esteem, particularly at the point of previous overlap, could be expected.

Changes in policy led to changes in governmental structures and the policy making and planning processes in which they engaged (Chapter 6). The institutional arrangements for greater control were the replacement of the University Grants Committee by the funding councils, able to demand the submission of mission statements and other planning declarations and planning and financial data, controls over student numbers in more specified categories, and the research assessment exercises and teaching quality assessments. Research councils were required to submit their priorities for scrutiny under the Public Expenditure Survey procedures. As we write, the Quality Assurance Agency, which has taken over the functions of the CVCP-run Higher Education Quality Council and the Quality Assessment Committee of the HEFCE, is entering the fields of curriculum coverage and external examining. The funding and research councils came under lay chairmanships. There were stronger lay influences in, and greater scrutiny by, Parliament. These changes display the new vulnerability to policy of the higher education enterprise at large and the increasing accountability which seems to challenge traditional autonomy. The size and cost of the whole system and its greater political importance had given higher education a new vulnerability in the polity, with no apparent constituency to support it. The defenders of university autonomy had been of the elite and their influence, and the small size of the whole activity had kept it off the wider political agenda.

Chapter 7 concerns the impact of changes in the state on institutional government. We consider how institutions position themselves in the polity, and attempt to conceptualise their changing role and identity. The perception that universities have become more managerial but that, 'paradoxically, most universities are still struggling ... to be collegial in their values but are forced in their practices to be increasingly managerial' (mac.42) raises the issue of whether the essentials of higher education work are consistent with managerialist values. The Jarratt Report (1985) was the ultimate expression of the managerial theory of higher education government, in which power was explicitly to move from the academics at the base to the managers at the centre of the institution. Within the managerial and the entrepreneurial university remain powerful counter-forces which still place more credence on individual discretion than on management power.

In Chapter 8 we analyse the influences exerted on policy by groups external to government. We relate existing and developing theories of elites and interest groups to our empirical data. For the most part, we find no comprehensive structure of external influence which effectively conditioned, restrained or advanced government policies.

Discussion
Explanations of change

We can offer no clearly schematic picture of how policies emerged and ideologies were sponsored. Intentions were forged partly by belief systems, partly by the power of circumstances, and partly by opportunistic reactions to what might not have been planned or even rationally contemplated. Our own preference is to take note of the power of intention and ideology, but, dissenting from others in the field, not to assume it to be always the driving force of change.

Many changes derived from within the higher education system as institutions responded to the growth of knowledge and of student numbers from 1945 onwards. Such changes as the prolific growth of taught masters' courses and the opening up of university governance to junior staff and students were not directed from outside.

But internal developments took place within increasingly strong external frameworks. Economic duress, resulting from the oil crisis of the 1970s, imposed increasing resource restrictions, at the same time as social expectations and economic demands led to the 'massification' of the system. Student demand was also driven by youth unemployment. These interacted with the ideologies of the post-1979 government, advanced by determined individual politicians, to cause change. When the Conservatives came to power in 1979, the economic ideology was embraced together with a more interventionist stance, which seemed necessary if higher education was going to be pushed more into serving the economy; yet this clashed with the classic liberal notions the government espoused of rolling back the frontiers of the state and encouraging a market system.

Despite the fact that most commentators believe there has been a shift towards control by the state, some, including those at the centre of the reforms, do not share the view that autonomy has been reduced but claim that 'the state is seeking, within certain constraints, to maintain and even increase the autonomy enjoyed by higher education institutions in most aspects of their work while endeavouring to make them more responsive and accountable to their market, in which the state is, itself, a major customer' (Tight 1992, p.1389).

Existing theory does not fully meet the case of higher education. Nor do the earlier descriptions of elite connection stand as appropriate for what is now observable. There are connections between the academic elites and those co-opted to policy making. There are also connections between institutional leadership and policy makers and the academic elites. But they do not constitute a traditional policy community. Connections are more often personal and ephemeral rather than systematic. The processes of national policy making operate at one level. At the same time, the academic system makes its own judgements on who will get what by way of reputation, which is itself a cashable commodity. These two universes interact not by direct connection so much as separate systems producing fields of force between them.

The processes and institutions through which issues emerged were not structurated, largely because higher education had no need to develop a fully formed policy community for the articulation of its interests before the 1980s. But policies, however inchoate and episodic their formation, were converted into new machinery, and new forms of institutional governance (Chapter 7).

Witness evidence, whilst supporting the notion that the economy became a salient element of policy, does not point to explicit intentions and a coherent philosophy of government. Our evidence is rather that the restrictions on autonomy derived from Treasury-demanded reductions in expenditure in 1981, and from the exigencies created by the unplanned expansion of the system. The preconditions for the directly interventionist policies emerged first from Sir Keith Joseph's individual and political preferences. Joseph and Baker, perhaps more than anybody, exemplify the role played by individual ministers. These, from our evidence, were often the more important driver of policies than any bureaucratic centralisation impulse or any systematic reading of economic and social demands.

We can thus find no simple explanation of the changes. Our theoretical position will be seen to be that of eclecticism. We eschew general hypotheses but look to political and other social theory to illuminate and help us to classify the experiences undergone by higher education in the UK between 1975 and 1997. In doing so, we have brought theorising about higher education governance into the mainstream of normative theory about the nature of the state.

In terms of Clark's triangle, the shift towards the state and the market meant a move away from the corner of professional academic control. In Britain it is widely assumed that there has been a victory of the political and administrative laity over the academic professionals. One description of the dynamics of change in education (Wirt 1981) notes how in public institutions the professionals gain dominance at a time when new provision is being set up, client needs identified and codified, and systems established. Within, perhaps, a generation, the distribution of power and resources embodied in those dispositions come up for challenge and the laity asserts itself. This cycle of dominance sustains itself until procedures and new expertise set in. In academic history, there have been such cycles of dominance, although in some systems there has been a stand-off when the dominant state allows power to the guild of professors, whilst retaining central control.

From this position of academic dominance, concerns orthogonal to academic interests emerged – on the pursuit of the market, on quality assurance, on internationalisation, on institutional planning to encompass research, and, more recently, on ways of prescribing better modes of teaching. These concerns entailed assumptions about the nature of leadership and control that were often far distant from the theories underlying the traditional professional-academic models. Whether they will spring back into place can be only the subject of surmise.

Exceptionalism, continuity and change

Higher education, increasingly, became a subset of larger public policies and systems but was idiosyncratic in the way in which it had been allowed to develop. Government did, indeed, aim to shift the dependence on government funding to different forms of market earnings, and to impose various forms of accountability, the most important of which concerned the insistence on quality assurance. Higher education participated in many of the policy shifts imposed generally on public institutions. To some extent, the universities were being treated to some of the prescriptions, particularly on funding practices, that had always been applied to other services, and the treatment felt correspondingly more unfavourable. Cumulative cuts in resources allowed for each higher education student place meant standards of provision, such as staffing ratios, were drastically reduced. Yet (Chapter 3) in important respects, higher education was able to exempt itself from some of the cutbacks that were felt elsewhere, and its gross expenditure increased dramatically.

Whilst the policy changes discussed above were substantial and had considerable impacts, not all of them derived from the purposive action of policy makers in the 1980s, but originated from factors present before that time. Some examples of continuity follow:

- Although structures changed, the nature of much of the most powerful parts of the enterprise endured; the elite group of universities were always elite, and they were joined by a small group of 1960s universities. In the UK there was virtually no merging of former polytechnics and colleges with the original universities, but in the 1990s some reshuffling of the hierarchy of esteem at the middle of the newly consolidated list had begun. Whilst all institutions were affected by the changes in the policy context, massification hardly affected the workings of the elite parts, even if also subject to expansion, which remained alongside the majority of less-protected 'old' universities and a now stronger 'new' university system whose traditions could be found in their early antecedents in non-university higher education.

- The demand that universities set themselves up to act in the market required them to act in a contra-academic manner, by seeking pecuniary gains rather than pursuing the truth disinterestedly, and taking as much time and care in doing so as is necessary. But market behaviour is not far different from the competitiveness which has always informed academics. The sale of expertise reinforces the power of academics at the base of the system. Competitiveness has always been part of the process by which individuals acquire reputations and the benefits that flow from them. The difference is that individuals can now make money, and departments become more independent of their universities as a result. Academics moving into market operations have, however, to develop different networks and expertise for working in them.

- Quality assurance has proved to be the most potent of the change agents. But whilst quality audit and teaching assessment sponsor more relativistic notions, such as fitness for purpose, research selectivity reinforces traditional excellences. One senior academic (mac.221) said that research assessment was not far different from what had always happened, although the publication of gradings and the funding changed the context and tone of evaluative procedures, and has had a substantial impact on institutional culture. The institutions take a strong interest, and the invisible colleges are more explicitly incorporated into the state through the working of the RAE.

- Nor was managerialism absent earlier. It took several forms. The public sector institutions were always less collegial in their internal governance than the universities. But also some well-esteemed 'old' university departments were led in strongly managerial fashion. Now, however, almost all universities have structured themselves for a more detailed planning and managerial role vis-à-vis departments and research centres.

Even Oxford and Cambridge have full-time vice-chancellors now.

Thus, the developments associated with New Public Management, the Evaluative State and the moves to markets, ambiguous and unclear as they often were, invited universities to reconcile two policy drives. The first was towards more effective and accountable management. The second was the drive towards more freedom of action, at institutional level. On this dimension, their capacity to succeed in markets was affected by their performance in statutory evaluations (particularly the RAE). They finished up as a part of a state service whilst remaining as independent institutions.

A principal force for continuity was the presence of particular groups in particular roles. As Trevor-Roper (1992, pp.xii–xiv), writing of the cataclysmic revolutions of mid-seventeenth century Britain, warns us:

> ... History has its continuities as well as its breaches; continuities contained within the experience of generations. Those who exercise power and determine policy are generally men whose minds are informed by events 20 or 30 years before: thus the lessons of one crisis may be applied, or misapplied, in another, 20 or 30 years later ... Apparently dramatic changes may as well have resulted from an accumulation of continuities ... To understand the politics of the past we must recapture the memories and experiences of a generation.

A prime source of continuity was that, for some generations, the ablest have secured admission to elite universities; over the last 20 years they have admitted almost wholly on merit. Particularly at Oxford and Cambridge, excellent teaching is provided, as are good facilities for graduate training; for example, the number of Oxbridge college research fellowships is about equal to the number of post-doctoral fellowships provided for the whole system by public funds (Becher, Henkel and Kogan 1994). This builds up enduring academic cadres, sharing similar approaches to academic values, work and statuses. The academics deriving from the more elite centres occupied the key academic, institutional and system leadership jobs, even if they no longer had a monopoly of them (Halsey 1992). Between 1960 and 1996, over one-third of UK vice-chancellors had attended Oxbridge (Smith *et al.* 1999). Not only were there 'institutional sagas' (Clark 1983) but, in a sense, the whole system had a saga by which it lived. The traditional academic ideals persisted in both research aspirations and teaching practices.

Universities' positions in the system were conditioned not only by current differential flows of revenue, but also by the fixed capital, in buildings and equipment, and financial resources, that they have inherited. This was true not only of the sciences and technologies, but also of the humanities and social sciences where the location of the major libraries strongly affects research potential. Any attempt to seriously reorientate the nature of the academic enterprise would have to contend with these historic distributions.

There are, however, some conditions that must be placed against this account. First, some institutions – for example, two of the technological universities – succeeded in rising within the hierarchy of esteem. Whilst 60 per cent of research funds go to 12 universities, in social sciences the money given by the Economic and Social Research Council goes largely to a small number of institutions. Nevertheless 'there is a long tail of institutions receiving money' (mac.212). Overall, institutional success in the competitive race for total levels of research funding was conditioned, in part, by discipline formations.

Resistances to change reside in what has been called essentialism. Many academics attempted to defend what they regard as the core academic values of the disinterested search for truth and particular forms of power and professional relationships from the social demands created by government and other sponsors. We have noted how academic identities are formed in both undergraduate and postgraduate experiences. They retain a belief in essential procedures for the creation of knowledge, and these, to some extent, carry over into the transmission of knowledge, though not so powerfully (Henkel forthcoming).

Those in leadership positions in the former public sector did not come mainly from those elites and need not carry with them the same assumptions about what constitutes academic worth. But although they now carried countervailing weight in funding and quality councils, they have hardly penetrated the peer groups upon whose judgements allocations by research and funding councils depend. There was thus a dialectic at work between traditional academic values and those stemming from concepts of public utility. None of them was new. Their confrontations, and the taking of sides by government, were. Continuity was embodied, as Trevor-Roper would predict, in the values promulgated and the powers exercised in traditions that far antedate the heroic ministers of the Thatcher era. Even without detailed biographical analysis, we can see how not a few of the tendencies that came to the fore in the 1980s were already in the mouths and minds of those both within and outside academe.

'Organic' evolution or imposed change?

To what extent were the changes the result of the 'organic' evolution of systems of higher education? If elites can be inferred to act as a source of continuity, they had to come to terms with the dynamic of the system as it responded, sometimes unwillingly and almost unknowingly, to external pressures. Intentionality, individual consciousness and free will are always present, but free individuals get used to what they regard as inevitable.

Thus, the propensity of higher education to expand was influenced by both the economic dynamic of demand for greater knowledge and skills, and the personal desires for access to better jobs and greater social mobility, all the consequences of rising standards of living and of expectations for better. We have seen how expansion hardly resulted from consistent planning, although, at times, politicians were, at least in part, responsible. Yet it is so universal a phenomenon that it all but acquires the status of a natural and inevitable force.

Expansion was further driven by an opportunistic use of student demand, and from the political weakness of institutions in the face of demands that they take more students on greatly reduced resources. In each case, expansion was blessed and legitimised once it was under way, and became a source of strength for previously less-recognised institutions. By the end of our period, government was resisting demands for an even higher level of recruitment; it had been surprised by the rapid success of the market approach to funding which encouraged institutions to recruit. In these respects, therefore, higher education has shown less an internal dynamic than a propensity to respond when it had to to external pressures. Left to themselves in the late 1950s, the universities would have been content to stay relatively still. The polytechnics responded with full vigour in the 1980s, partly when stimulated by the universities' reluctance to take in their previous levels of students on reduced funding, but much more as the decade went on as they sought the opportunity to build maturing institutions, and it has been argued that they have always believed in keeping the door open to those seeking opportunity.

The system responded to the power of the contextual factors (demography, the changing economic frames, the secular demands for better education and the ideologies of economic growth and equality of opportunity), all with origins outside higher education but fed by, and feeding, higher education. But then certain of the major trends seem likely to have resulted from virtually universal propensities to systemic development. Granted expansion, restratification in the UK has been part product of policy determination and of organic development; there is a natural propensity for systems, both to create their own new subject specialisations (Clark 1983) and to create or reformulate their own strata as the range of student recruitment and of research and teaching balances widens. This process was powerfully reinforced in the UK by policies. The implosion of the binary system seems to follow a trend manifest in other systems, which allows institutions to mature to a point where, for both academic and political or social reasons, they are admitted to independent status. It also must be associated with changing assumptions about what constitute the boundaries of university-provided research and teaching.

Contextual factors, such as economic, demographic and social, interacted with ideologies concerning the nature of the state to promote change, if in no systematic fashion. Massification led directly to changes in the functions and operational modes of higher education. The development of evaluation and accountability was the key factor in reducing the autonomy of academics and universities. The changes in the nature of the state, including NPM and the rise of the Evaluative State, and the formulation contained in Clark's triangle of co-ordination, are perhaps the most appropriate framework to use for considering these changes.

In observing radical changes, we believe it important not to exaggerate their effects, considerable though they were. Academic excellence still remained the leading and most prized criterion, against all the claims of competing ideology, as represented by the allocation of funds and the award of quality assurance grading through the research assessment exercise and the quality assurance systems. In other countries, expansion and the nationalisation of the universities had been accompanied by a deliberate equalisation in their statuses. The existing hierarchies of esteem, already so steep in the UK, were reinforced rather than reduced by these changes, although expansion and the implosion of the binary system certainly allowed for some readjustment, particularly in the middle of the pecking order, of statuses as between institutions. So far from enforcing single ideologies upon higher education, government, perhaps through avoidance of fundamental reappraisal, seem to be content to allow several ideologies, policies and practices to run in parallel with each other.

Links with our colleague volume

Our project was conceived to connect the issues of policy development and their impact on academics, and it was largely to give adequate space to both that we decided to produce two related volumes. A secure assessment of how changes in policy have affected the working and values of academics must be founded on the study of the nature of the policies and the values and practices assumed in them, as well as the values sets of those affected by, and effecting, policy change. It is clear from the analysis presented here that it is not possible to draw clear boundaries between those two groups of actors or, therefore, between macro and micro levels of policy.

The companion volume aims to pursue the analysis of the relationship between the two levels, building on the findings presented here, but drawing primarily on the perspectives of academics within their institutions, and using a different combination of theoretical frameworks. Both books are concerned, from different starting points, with shifts in the relationships between the state and higher education and between the discipline, the enterprise or institution and the individual academic. The analysis in the second volume centres upon the meanings of policy changes for academic identities. It assumes that individuals form and develop their identities through interaction with the communities in which they live and work. It takes disciplines and higher education institutions to be the key communities, and explores how this interaction has been informed and influenced by the policy process and outcomes of the period covered by the present book.

Glossary

ABRC	Advisory Board for the Research Councils
ACOST	Advisory Council on Science and Technology
AFE	Advanced Further Education
API	Age Participation Index
APR	Age Participation Rate
ATTI	Association of Teachers in Technical Institutions
AUT	Association of University Teachers
BBC	British Broadcasting Corporation
BTEC	Business and Technical Education Council
CAT	College of Advanced Technology
CBI	Confederation of British Industry
CDP	Committee of Directors of Polytechnics
CIHE	Council for Industry and Higher Education
CLEA	Committee of Local Education Authorities
CNAA	Council for National Academic Awards
CPRS	Central Policy Review Staff
CVCP	Committee of Vice-Chancellors and Principals
DEA	Department of Economic Affairs
DES	Department of Education and Science
DFE	Department for Education
DfEE	Department for Education and Employment
DTI	Department of Trade and Industry
EHE	Enterprise in Higher Education
EPSRC	Engineering and Physical Sciences Research Council
ESRC	Economic and Social Research Council
FBA	Fellow(s) of British Academy
FRS	Fellow(s) of Royal Society
GCSE	General Certificate of Secondary Education
HEFC	Higher Education Funding Council
HEFCE	Higher Education Funding Council for England
HEI	Higher Education Institution
HEQC	Higher Education Quality Council
HESA	Higher Education Statistics Agency
HMI	Her Majesty's Inspectorate
HND	Higher National Diploma

HORCs	Heads of Research Councils
ILEA	Inner London Education Authority
IMF	International Monetary Fund
IOD	Institute of Directors
IRC	Interdisciplinary Research Centre
LEA	Local Education Authority
LSE	London School of Economics
MASN	Maximum Aggregate Student Number
MRC	Medical Research Council
MSC	Manpower Services Commission
NAB	National Advisory Body
NATFHE	National Association of Teachers in Further and Higher Education
NHS	National Health Service
NPM	New Public Management
NUS	National Union of Students
NVQ	National Vocational Qualifications
OECD	Organisation for Economic Cooperation and Development
ONS	Office for National Statistics
ORT	Organisation for Rehabilitation through Training
OST	Office of Science and Technology
PCFC	Polytechnics and Colleges Funding Council
PIs	Performance Indicators
PPARC	Particle Physics and Astronomy Research Council
PRP	Performance Related Pay
PSHE	Public Sector Higher Education
RAE	Research Assessment Exercise
RTX	Research, Teaching and Mixed types of university
SCOP	Standing Conference of Principals
SERC	Science and Engineering Research Council
SRC	Science Research Council
SSEC	Secondary School Examinations Council
SSRC	Social Science Research Council
THES	*Times Higher Education Supplement*
TQA	Teaching Quality Assessment
TVEI	Technical and Vocational Education Initiative
UCCA	Universities Central Council for Admissions
UCL	University College London
UFC	Universities Funding Council
UGC	University Grants Committee
VC	Vice-Chancellor

Bibliography

[References to interviews are anonymised in the main text and identified by the suffix 'mac' and followed by the interview number.]

Advisory Board for the Research Councils (ABRC) (1987) *A Strategy for the Science Base*. London: HMSO.

Anderson, P. (1995) *Universities and Elites in Britain since 1800*. Cambridge: Cambridge University Press.

Archer, M.S. (1979) *The Social Origins of Educational Systems*. London: Sage.

Archer, M.S. (1981) Educational politics: a model for their analysis. In P. Broadfoot, C. Brock and W. Tulasiewicz (eds) *Politics and Educational Change*. London: Croom Helm.

Ashby, E. and Anderson, M. (1970) *The Rise of the Student Estate in Britain*. Cambridge, USA: Harvard University Press.

Ashby, E. and Anderson, M. (1974) *Portrait of Haldane at Work on Education*. London: Macmillan.

Association of University Teachers (AUT) (1996) *Professional Pay in Universities. The Problem and the Solution*. London: AUT.

Bachrach, E. and Baratz, M.S. (1963) Decisions and non decisions: an analytic framework. *American Political Science Review 57*, 641–651.

Baker, K. (1989) Higher education: the next 25 years. Speech at Conference, Lancaster University, January.

Baker, K. (1993) *The Turbulent Years. My Life in Politics*. London: Faber and Faber.

Baldridge, J.V. (1971) *Power and Conflict in the University*. New York: Wiley.

Barnett, C. (1986) *The Audit of War*. London: Macmillan.

Barnett, R., Parry, G., Cox, R., Loder, C. and Williams, G. (1994) *Assessment of the Quality of Higher Education. Report for HEFCE and HEFCW.* London: Centre for Higher Education Studies, Institute of Education, University of London.

Bauer, M. (1993) Changing contexts for quality assessment in higher education – the Swedish case. Paper presented at the conference on 'Changing Contexts for Quality Assessment', Amsterdam.

Bauer, M. and Henkel, M. (1997) Responses of academe to quality reforms in higher education – a comparative study of England and Sweden. *Tertiary Education and Management 3*, 2, 211–228.

Bauer, M., Marton, S., Askling, B. and Marton, F. (forthcoming) *Transforming Universities. Patterns of Governance, Structure and Learning in Swedish Higher Education at the Millennial Turn*. London: Jessica Kingsley Publishers.

Becher, T. (1989) *Academic Tribes and Territories: Intellectual Enquiry and the Culture of Disciplines*. Buckingham: The Society for Research into Higher Education and Open University Press.

Becher, T. (1993) Graduate education in Britain: the view from the ground. In B.R. Clark (ed) *The Research Foundations of Graduate Education*. Berkeley and Los Angeles: University of California Press.

Becher, T., Henkel, M. and Kogan, M. (1994) *Graduate Education in Britain*. London: Jessica Kingsley Publishers.

Becher, T. and Kogan, M. (1980) *Process and Structure in Higher Education* (1st edition). London: Heinemann.

Becher, T. and Kogan, M. (1992) *Process and Structure in Higher Education* (2nd edition). London: Heinemann.

Benn, R. and Fieldhouse, R. (1993) Government policies on university expansion and wider access, 1945–51 and 1985–91 compared. *Studies in Higher Education 18*, 3, 299–313.

Berdahl, R. (1977) *British Universities and the State* (2nd edition). New York: Arno Press.

Berdahl, R. (1990) Academic freedom, autonomy and accountability in British universities. *Studies in Higher Education 15*, 2, 169–180.

Bernstein, B. (1963) *Class, Codes and Control: Vol. 3. Towards a Theory of Educational Transmission*. London: Routledge, Kegan and Paul.

Bernstein, R. (1972) *Praxis and Action*. London: Duckworth.

Bethel, D. (1995) *The New Polytechnics and Their Directors: 1969–90*. Leicester: The Boar's Head Press.

Bird, R.A. (1994) Reflections on the British government and higher education. *Higher Education Quarterly 48*, 2, 73–85.

Birnbaum, R. (1989) *How Colleges Work. The Cybernetics of Academic Organization and Leadership*. San Francisco: Jossey-Bass.

Björklund, E. (1991) Swedish research on higher education in perspective. In M.A. Trow and T. Nybom (eds) *University and Society. Essays on the Social Role of Research and Higher Education*. London: Jessica Kingsley Publishers.

Björklund, S. (1993) *A Constitution for Disputation*. Stockholm: Council for Studies of Higher Education.

Blackstone, T. and Plowden, W. (1988) *Inside the Think Tank: Advising the Cabinet 1971–1983*. London: Heinemann.

Blau, P.M. (1964) *Exchange and Power in Social Life*. New York: John Wiley.

Blau, P.M. (1973) *The Organization of Academic Work*. New York: John Wiley.

Bleiklie, I. (1998) Justifying the Evaluative State: New Public Management ideals in higher education. *European Journal of Education 33*, 3, 299–316.

Bleiklie, I., Marton, S. and Hanney, S. (1995) *Policy Arenas, Networks and Higher Education Reform*. notat 9540. Bergen: LOS.

Booth, C. (1987) Central government and higher education planning 1965–1986. *Higher Education Quarterly 41*, 1, 57–72.

Boys, C.J., Brennan, J., Henkel, M., Kirkland, J., Kogan, M. and Youll, P. (1988) *Higher Education and the Preparation for Work*. London: Jessica Kingsley Publishers.

Brennan, J., Lyon, S., Schomburg, H. and Teichler, U. (1996) Employment and work of British and German graduates. In J. Brennan, M. Kogan and U. Teichler (eds) *Higher Education and Work*. London: Jessica Kingsley Publishers.

Brown, R. (1997) The new quality assurance arrangements in England and Wales. *Higher Education Quarterly 51*, 4, 270–285.

Burgess, T. and Pratt, J. (1974) *Polytechnics: A Report*. London: Pitman.

Carswell, J. (1985) *Government and the Universities in Britain*. Cambridge: Cambridge University Press.

Cavanagh, M., Marsh, D. and Smith, M. (1995) The relationship between policy networks at the sectoral and sub-sectoral levels: a response to Jordan, Maloney and McLaughlin. *Public Administration 73*, 527–629.

Cave, M., Hanney, S. and Kogan, M. (1991) *The Use of Performance Indicators in Higher Education. A Critical Analysis of Developing Practice* (2nd edition). London: Jessica Kingsley Publishers.

Cave, M., Hanney, S., Henkel, M. and Kogan, M. (1997) *The Use of Performance Indicators in Higher Education. The Challenge of the Quality Movement* (3rd edition). London: Jessica Kingsley Publishers.

Cawson, A. (1982) *Corporatism and Welfare*. London: Heinemann Educational Books.

Cawson, A. (1986) *Corporatism and Political Theory*. Oxford: Basil Blackwell.

Clark, B.R. (1970) *The Distinctive College* (1st edition). Chicago: Aldine Publishing Company.

Clark, B.R. (1983) *The Higher Education System: Academic Organization in Cross-National Perspective*. Berkeley: University of California Press.

Clark, B.R. (1984) The organizational conception. In B.R. Clark (ed) *Perspectives on Higher Education. Eight Disciplinary and Comparative Views*. Berkeley: University of California Press.

Clark, B.R. (1987) Conclusions. In B.R. Clark (ed) *The Academic Profession: National, Disciplinary, and Institutional Settings*. Berkeley: University of California Press.

Clark, B.R. (1991) The fragmentation of research, teaching and study: an explorative essay. In M.A. Trow and T. Nybom (eds) *University and Society. Essays on the Social Role of Research and Higher Education*. London: Jessica Kingsley Publishers.

Clark, B.R. (1992) *The Distinctive College* (2nd edition). New Brunswick, New Jersey: Transaction Publishers.

Clark, B.R. (1993) *The Research Foundations of Graduate Education*. Berkeley and Los Angeles: University of California Press.

Clark, B.R. (1998) *Creating Entrepreneurial Universities*. Oxford: Elsevier Science.

Clark, B.R. and Neave, G. (eds) (1992) *The International Encyclopedia of Higher Education*. Oxford: Pergamon Press.

Clarke, K. (1991) Higher education: a new framework. Letter to Chairman of PCFC. London: DES.

Coffield, F. and Vignoles, A. (1997) *Widening Participating in Higher Education by Ethnic Minorities, Women and Alternative Students*. Report 5, National Committee of Enquiry into Higher Education (Dearing Report). London: HMSO.

Cohen, M.D. and March, J.G. (1974) *Leadership and Ambiguity: The American College President*. New York: McGraw-Hill.

Cohen, M.D., March, J.G. and Olsen, J.P. (1972) A garbage can model of organisational choice. *Administrative Science Quarterly 17*, 1, 1–25.

Committee of Directors of Polytechnics (CDP) (1986) *Review of the Year: 1984–85*. London: CDP.

Committee of Vice-Chancellors and Principals (CVCP) (1946) *Note on University Policy and Finance*. London: CVCP.

Committee of Vice-Chancellors and Principals (CVCP) (1986) *The Future of the Universities*. London: CVCP.

Committee of Vice-Chancellors and Principals (CVCP) (1991) *CVCP Response to White Paper Higher Education: A New Framework*. Cm 1541. London: CVCP.

Committee of Vice-Chancellors and Principals (CVCP) (1994) *CVCP 11 Point Plan*. London: CVCP.

Committee of Vice-Chancellors and Principals, Committee of Directors of Polytechnics, Standing Conference of Principals (CVCP, CDP, SCOP) (1991) *Quality Assurance Arrangements for Higher Education*. London: CVCP.

Confederation of British Industry (CBI) (1986) *The Development of Higher Education into the 1990s – Cmnd 9524: The CBI Response*. London: CBI.

Confederation of British Industry (CBI) (1994) *Thinking Ahead. Ensuring the Expansion of Higher Education into the Twentieth Century*. London: CBI.

Conservative Central Office (1987) *The Next Moves Forward: The Conservative Manifesto 1987*. London: Conservative Central Office.

Council for Scientific Policy (1967) *Second Report on Science Policy*. Cmnd 3420. London: HMSO.

Crewe, I. (1974) Studying elites in Britain. In I. Crewe (ed) *British Sociology Yearbook Vol. 1, Elites in Western Democracy*. London: Croom Helm.

Croham Report (1987) *Review of the University Grants Committee*. Cm 81. London: HMSO.

Crosland, A. (1962) *The Conservative Enemy*. London: Cape.

Crosland, A. (1965) Speech on the binary system. Woolwich Polytechnic, 27 April 1965.

Crossman, R. (1972) *Inside View*. London: Jonathan Cape.

Crowther-Hunt, N. (1983) Policy making and accountability in higher education. (Speech made in 1975.) In M. Shattock (ed) *The Structure and Governance of Higher Education*. Leverhulme Programme of Study into the Future of Higher Education 9. Guildford: Society for Research into Higher Education.

Dahl, R.A. (1956) *A Preface to Democratic Theory*. Chicago: University of Chicago Press.

Dahl, R.A. (1961) *Who Governs? Democracy and Power in an American City*. New Haven: Yale University Press.

Dahllof, U. (1990) *Report of the IMHE Study Group on Evaluation in Higher Education*. Paris: OECD.

Dalton, I.G. (1987) Universities and science parks: a review of the issues. *International Journal of Institutional Management 11*, 3, 268–277.

Dasgupta, P. and David, P. (1994) Towards a new economics of science. *Research Policy 23*, 487–521.

Daugbjerg, C. (1998) Linking policy networks and environmental policies: nitrate policy making in Denmark and Sweden 1970–1995. *Public Administration 76*, 2, 275–294.

David, P. (1996) Science reorganised? Post-modern visions of research and the curse of success. Paper given at ESRC seminar on the regulation of science and technology, University of Warwick.

Davies, G. (1991) *UFC: Present and Future Policies*. Presentation to the residential meeting of the CVCP, Warwick.

Dearing Report (1997) The National Committee into Higher Education *Higher Education in the Learning Society*. London: HMSO.

Department of Economic Affairs (DEA) (1965) *The National Plan*. London: HMSO.

Department for Education (DFE) (1992) *Statistics Bulletin 18/92*. London: DFE.

Department for Education and Employment (DFE) (1993) *Higher Education Statistics*. London: HMSO.

Department of Education and Science (DES) (1966) (White Paper) *A Plan for Polytechnics and Other Colleges*. Cmnd 3006. London: HMSO.

Department of Education and Science (DES) (1978) (Brown Paper) *Higher Education into the 1990s*. London: HMSO.

Department of Education and Science (DES) (1981) (Consultative Paper) *Higher Education in England outside the Universities: Policy, Funding and Management*. London: HMSO.

Department of Education and Science (DES) (1985) (Green Paper) *The Development of Higher Education into the 1990s*. Cmnd 9524. London: HMSO.

Department of Education and Science (DES) (with Welsh Office, Scottish Office and Northern Ireland Office) (1987) (White Paper) *Higher Education: Meeting the Challenge*. Cm 114. London: HMSO.

Department of Education and Science (DES) (for Secretaries of State for Education and Science, and for Scotland, Northern Ireland and Wales) (1991) (White Paper) *Higher Education. A New Framework*. Cm 1541. London: HMSO.

De Weert, E. (1992) Responsiveness of higher education to labour market demands. In J. Brennan, M. Kogan and U. Teichler (eds) *Higher Education and Work*. London: Jessica Kingsley Publishers.

Dill, D.D. (1998) Evaluating the 'Evaluative State': implications for research in higher education. *European Journal of Education 33*, 3, 361–377.

Dill, D.D. and Helm, K.P. (1988) Faculty participation in strategic policy making. In J.C. Smart (ed) *Higher Education: Handbook of Theory and Research*. Vol. 4. New York: Agathon.

Douglas, J.W.B. (1964) *Home and School*. London: Macgibbon and Kee.

Dowding, K. (1995) Model or metaphor? A critical review of the policy network approach. *Political Studies XLIII*, 136–158.

Dunleavy, P. and O'Leary, B. (1987) *Theories of the State: The Politics of Liberal Democracy*. Basingstoke: Macmillan.

Eccles, D. (1960) Speech in House of Commons on Crowther Report. *Hansard*. 1 March 1960.

Eckstein, H. (1960) *Pressure Group Politics: A Case of the British Political Association*. London: Allen and Unwin.

Edgerton, D. and Hughes, K. (1989) The poverty of science: a critical analysis of scientific and industrial policy under Mrs Thatcher. *Public Administration 67*, 4, 419–433.

El-Khawas, E. (1998) Strong state action but limited results: perspectives on university resistance. *European Journal of Education 33*, 3, 317–330.

Elzinga, A. (1985) Research, bureaucracy and the drift of epistemic criteria. In B. Wittrock and A. Elzinga (eds) *The University Research System, the Public Policies of the Homes of Scientists*. Stockholm: Almqvist and Wicksell.

Etzioni-Halevy, E. (1985) *The Knowledge Elite and the Failure of Prophecy*. London: Allen and Unwin.

Farrington, D.J. (1994) *The Law of Higher Education*. London: Butterworth.

Flather, P. (1987) 'Pulling through': conspiracies, counterplots and how the SSRC escaped the axe in 1982. In M. Bulmer (ed) *Social Science Research and Government*. Cambridge: Cambridge University Press.

Floud, J., Halsey, A.H. and Martin, F.M. (1956) *Social Class and Educational Opportunity*. London: Heinemann.

Flowers, B. (1970) Science in Universities. Public Lecture delivered at Nottingham University, 6 March.

Forth, E. (1996) Report in *THES*, 9 February.

Frazer, M. (1997) Report on the modalities of external evaluation of higher education in Europe: 1995–1997. *Higher Education in Europe XXII*, 3, 349–401.

Frederiks, M., Westerheijden, D. and Weusthof, P. (1994) Stakeholders in quality. In L. Goedegebuure and F.A. Van Vught (eds) *Comparative Policy Studies in Higher Education*. Utrecht: Lemma.

Fulton, O. (1995) Unpublished paper given at conference held at Villa Vignoni, September 1995 on Carnegie Study of Academic Professions.

Fulton, O. and Elwood, S. (1989) *Admission to Higher Education. Policy and Practice*. A Report to the Training Agency. Sheffield: Training Agency.

Geertz, C. (1964) Ideology as a cultural system. In D. Apter (ed) *Ideology and Discontent*. New York: Free Press.

Gibbons, M., Limoges, C., Newotny, H., Schwartzman, S., Scott, P. and Trow, M. (1994) *The New Production of Knowledge. The Dynamics of Science and Research in Contemporary Societies*. London: Sage Publications.

Giddens, A. (1979) *Central Problems in Social Theory*. London: Macmillan.

Godin, B. (1998) Writing performative history: the new Atlantis? *Social Studies of Science 28/23*, 465–483.

Goedegebuure, L., Kaiser, F., Maassen, P.A.M., Meek, L., Van Vught, F. and De Weert, E. (1993) *Higher Education Policy. An International Comparative Perspective*. Oxford: Pergamon Press.

Goedegebuure, L. and Van Vught, F.A. (1996) Comparative higher education studies: the perspective from the policy studies. *Higher Education 32*, 4, 371–394.

Gornitzka, A., Kyvik, S. and Larsen, I.M. (1998) The bureaucratisation of universities. *Minerva 36*, 21–47.

Grant, W. (ed) (1985) *The Political Economy of Corporatism*. New York: St. Martin's.

Gumport, P. and Sporn, B. (1998) Institutional adaptation: demands for management reform and university administration. In J. Smart (ed) *Higher Education: Handbook of Theory and Research. Volume XIV.* New York: Agathon.

Haas, P. (1992) Introduction: epistemic communities and international policy coordination. *International Organisation 46*, 1–36.

Hague, D. (1991) *Beyond Universities: A New Republic of the Intellect*. Hobart Paper 115. London: Institute of Economic Affairs.

Halsey, A.H. (1969) The universities and the state. *Universities Quarterly 23*, 2, 128–148.

Halsey, A.H. (1992) *Decline of Donnish Domination: The British Academic Professions in the Twentieth Century*. Oxford: Clarendon Press.

Halsey, A.H. and Trow, M. (1971) *The British Academics*. London: Faber and Faber.

Harman, K.M. (1990) Culture and conflict in academic organization. *Journal of Educational Administration 27*, 3, 30–54.

Heclo, H. and Wildavsky, A. (1974) *The Private Government of Public Money: Community and Policy inside British Politics*. London: Macmillan.

Henkel, M. (1991) *Government, Evaluation and Change*. London: Jessica Kingsley Publishers.

Henkel, M. (1995) Higher education reform and academic values. Paper presented to the Workshop on 'The Politics of Education', Joint Sessions of Workshops of the European Consortium for Political Research, Bordeaux, 27 April–2 May.

Henkel, M. (1997a) Academic values and the university as corporate enterprise. *Higher Education Quarterly 51*, 2, 134–143.

Henkel, M. (1997b) Teaching quality assessments: public accountability and academic autonomy in higher education. *Evaluation 3*, 1, 9–24.

Henkel, M. (1998) Evaluation in higher education: conceptual and epistemological foundations. *European Journal of Education 33*, 3, 285–298.

Henkel, M. (forthcoming) *Academic Identities and Policy Change in Higher Education*. London: Jessica Kingsley Publishers.

Henkel, M., Hanney, S., Vaux, J. and Von Walden Laing, D. (forthcoming) *Academic Responses to the UK Foresight Initiative. Research Report*. Uxbridge: CEPPP, Brunel University.

Henkel, M. and Kogan, M. (1996) The impact of policy changes on the academic profession. Paper given at Annual Conference of Society for Research into Higher Education, Cardiff.

Henkel, M. and Kogan, M. (1998) Policy changes and the academic profession in England. *European Review 6*, 4, 505–523.

Hennessy, P. (1988) *Whitehall*. London: Secker and Warburg.

Higher Education Funding Council for England (HEFCE) (1993) *HEFCE Assessment of the Quality of Education. Circular 3/93*. Bristol: HEFCE.

Higher Education Funding Council for England (HEFCE) (1995) *Developing Quality Assurance in Partnership with the Institutions of Higher Education*. Bristol: HEFCE.

Higher Education Funding Council for England (HEFCE) and Higher Education Funding Council for Wales (HEFCW) (1994) *The Quality Assessment Method from April 1995*. Circular 39/94. Bristol: HEFCE.

Hoggett, P. (1991) A new management in the public sector? *Policy and Politics 19*, 4, 243–256.

Holland, G. (1995) A marriage is arranged. *Times Higher Education Supplement*. 14 July.

Hölttä, S. (1995) *Towards the Self-Regulative University*. University of Joensuu: University of Joensuu Publications in Social Science.

Houghton Report (1974) *Report of Committee on Teachers' Salaries*. London: HMSO.

House of Lords (1996) *Parliamentary Debates*. Official Report 'University Funding'. Col. 300–385.

Ince, M. (1986) *The Politics of British Science*. Brighton: Wheatsheaf Books.

Jackson, R. (1989) Government and universities. *CRE-Action 89*, 4, 69–76.

Jarratt Report (1985) Committee of Vice-Chancellors and Principals *Report of the Steering Committee for Efficiency Studies in Universities*. London: CVCP.

Jenkins, A. (1995) The research assessment exercise, funding and teaching quality. *Quality Assurance in Education 3*, 2, 4–12.

Jenkins, S. (1996) *Accountable to None: The Tory Nationalisation of Britain*. London: Penguin.

Jones, Sandra (1995) Managing curriculum development: a case study of Enterprise in Higher Education. In J. Brennan, M. Kogan and U. Teichler (eds) *Higher Education and Work*. London: Jessica Kingsley Publishers.

Jones, Stephen (1983) *From Oakes via GMP to NAB: Reflections on a Capped Pool*. Paper presented at a seminar on the operation of NAB. Mimeo.

Jordan, G. and Schubert, K. (1992) A preliminary ordering of policy network labels. *European Journal of Political Research 21*, 7–27.

Joss, R. and Kogan, M. (1995) *Advancing Quality. Total Quality Management in the National Health Service*. Buckingham: Open University Press.

Karlsson, C. (1996) The academic and administrative interface in Scandinavian universities. *Higher Education Management 8*, 2, 29–35.

Kavanagh, D. (1987) *Thatcherism and British Politics: The End of Consensus?* Oxford: Oxford University Press.

Kedourie, E. (1988) *Diamonds into Glass: The Government and the Universities*. London: Centre for Policy Studies.

Kedourie, E. (1989) *Perestroika in the Universities*. Choice in Welfare Series No. 1. London: Institute of Economic Affairs.

Keep, E. and Mayhew, K. (1996) Economic demand for higher education – a sound foundation for further expansion? *Higher Education Quarterly 50*, 2, 89–109.

Knight, C. (1990) *The Making of Tory Education Policy in Post-War Britain 1950–1986*. Basingstoke: Falmer Press.

Kogan, M. (1969) Audit, control and freedom. *Higher Education Review 1*, 2, 16–27.

Kogan, M. (1975) *Educational Policy Making. A Study of Interest Groups and Parliament*. London: Allen and Unwin.

Kogan, M. (1984) The political view. In B.R. Clark (ed) *Perspectives on Higher Education. Eight Disciplinary and Comparative Views*. Berkeley: University of California Press.

Kogan, M. (1987) The DES and Whitehall. *Higher Education Quarterly 41*, 3, 225–240.

Kogan, M. (1988) *Education Accountability* (2nd edition). London: Hutchinson.

Kogan, M. (1989) Managerialism in higher education. In D. Lawton (ed) *The Education Reform Act: Choice and Control*. London: Hodder and Stoughton.

Kogan, M. (1992) Political science. In B.R. Clark and G. Neave (eds) *The International Encyclopedia of Higher Education*. Oxford: Pergamon Press.

Kogan, M. (1996) Academic and administrative interface. Paper given at IMHE Seminar on Staffing and Institutional Infrastructures, Budapest, August.

Kogan, M. (1999) The academic–administrative interface. In M. Henkel and B. Little (eds) *Changing Relationships between Higher Education and the State*. London: Jessica Kingsley Publishers.

Kogan, M., Bauer, M., Bleiklie, I. and Henkel, M. (forthcoming) *Transforming Higher Education: A Comparative Study*. London: Jessica Kingsley Publishers.

Kogan, M. and Henkel, M. (1983) *Government and Research*. London: Heinemann Educational Books.

Kogan, M. and Kogan, D. (1983) *The Attack on Higher Education*. London: Kogan Page Publishers.

Lawson, N. (1992) *The View From No 11: Memoirs of a Tory Radical*. London: Bantam Press.

Lindop Report (1985) *The Report of the Committee of Inquiry into the Academic Validation of Degree Courses in Public Sector Higher Education*. Cmd 9501. London: HMSO.

Lockwood, G. (1996) Continuity and transition in university management: the role of the professional administrative service. *Higher Education Management 8*, 2, 41–51.

Lowi, T. (1972) Four systems of policy, politics and choice. *Public Administration 32*, 4, 298–310.

Maassen, P.A.M. (1996) *Governmental Steering and the Academic Culture. The Intangibility of the Human Factor in Dutch and German Universities*. Utrecht: De Tijdstroom.

Maassen, P.A.M. and Van Vught, F.A. (1988) An intriguing Janus-head: the two faces of the new government strategy for higher education in the Netherlands. *European Journal of Education 23*, 1/2, 65–76.

Mackay, L., Scott, P. and Smith, D. (1995) Restructured and differentiated? Institutional responses to the changing environment of UK higher education. *Higher Education Management 7*, 2, 193–205.

Manpower Services Commission (MSC) (1987) *Enterprise in Higher Education. Guidance for Applicants, December 1987*. London: HMSO.

Marquand, D. (1988) *The Unprincipled Society*. London: Jonathan Cape.

Marshall, N. (1995a) Policy communities, issue networks and the formulation of Australian higher education policy. *Higher Education 30*, 273–293.

Marshall, N. (1995b) The Australian Vice-Chancellors' Committee: from gentleman's club to political lobby. *Higher Education Quarterly 49*, 1, 37–57.

Marton, F., Howell, D. and Entwistle, N. (eds) (1984) *The Experience of Learning*. Edinburgh: Scottish Academic Press.

Marton, S., Hanney, S. and Kogan, M. (1995) Interest groups and elites in higher education policy making: the cases of England and Sweden. Paper presented at the European Consortium of Political Research, Bordeaux, 27 April to 2 May.

McPherson, A. and Raab, C.D. (1988) *Governing Education. A Sociology of Policy since 1945*. Edinburgh: Edinburgh University Press.

McVicar, M. (1989) *The National Advisory Body Planning Exercise 1984/5: An Analysis of Educational Policy Making and Implementation*. Doctoral dissertation, Institute of Education, University of London.

Merrison, A. (1982) *Report of a Joint Working Party on the Support of University Scientific Research* ('Merrison Report'). Cmnd 8567. London: HMSO.

Merton, R.K. (1973) *The Sociology of Science*. Chicago: Chicago University Press.

Metcalfe, L. and Richards, S. (1990) *Improving Public Management* (2nd edition). London: Sage.

Middlehurst, R. (1993) *Leading Academics*. Buckingham: Society for Research into Higher Education and Open University Press.

Mill, J.S. (1962) On liberty. In M. Warnock (ed) *Utilitarianism*. London: Collins.

Ministry of Education (1956) *Technical Education*. Cmnd 9703. London: HMSO.

Moodie, G.C. (1983) Buffer, coupling and broker: reflections on 60 years of the UGC. *Higher Education 12*, 331–347.

Moore, P.G. (1987) University financing, 1979–86. *Higher Education Quarterly 41*, 1, 25–42.

Mulkay, M.J. (1977) Sociology of the scientific research community. In I. Spiegel-Rosing and D. de Solla Price (eds) *Science, Technology and Society*. London/Beverley Hills: Sage Publications.

National Academies Policy Advisory Group (1996) *Research Capability of the University System*. London: NAPAG.

National Advisory Body (NAB) (1984) *A Strategy for Higher Education into the Late 1980s and Beyond*. London: HMSO.

National Advisory Body (NAB) (1987) *Management for a Purpose: The Report of the Good Management Practice Group*. London: NAB.

Neave, G. (1985) Higher education in a period of consolidation: 1975–1985. *European Journal of Education 20*, 2/3, 109–124.

Neave, G. (1986) On shifting sands. *European Journal of Education 20*, 2/3.

Neave, G. (1988) On the cultivation of quality, efficiency and enterprise: an overview of recent trends in higher education in Western Europe, 1986–1988. *European Journal of Education 23*, 1/2, 7–23.

Neave, G. (1998) The Evaluative State reconsidered. *European Journal of Education 33*, 3, 265–284.

Neave, G. and Rhodes, G. (1987) The academic estate in Western Europe. In B.R. Clark (ed) *The Academic Profession: National, Disciplinary and Institutional Settings*. Berkeley: University of California Press.

Neave, G. and Van Vught, F.A. (1991) *Prometheus Bound. The Changing Relationship between Government and Higher Education in Western Europe*. Oxford: Pergamon Press.

Neave, G. and Van Vught, F.A. (1994) *Government and Higher Education Relationships across Three Continents*. Oxford: Pergamon Press.

Nettle, J.P. (1965) Consensus or elite domination: the case of business. *Political Studies 13*, 1, 22–44.

Niblett, W.R. (1952) The development of British universities since 1945. In *The Yearbook of Education*. London: Evans Institute of Education.

Nozick, R. (1974) *Anarchy, State and Utopia*. New York: Basic Books.

Oakes Report (1978) *Report of the Working Group on the Management of Higher Education in the Maintained Sector*. Cmnd 7130. London: HMSO.

Office of National Statistics (1987) *Annual Abstract of Statistics.* London: HMSO.

Office of Science and Technology (OST) (1993) (White Paper) *Realising Our Potential – A Strategy for Science, Engineering and Technology.* Command 2250. London: HMSO.

Office of Science and Technology (OST) (1997) *The Quality of the UK Science Base.* London: Department of Trade and Industry.

Oxford University Gazette (1986) Green Paper on the development of higher education into the 1990s. 27 February.

Ozga, J. (1987) Studying education policy through the lives of the policy-makers: an attempt to close the macro–micro gap. In S. Walker and L. Barton (eds) *Changing Policies, Changing Teachers.* Buckingham: Open University Press.

Page, E.C. (1995) Comparative public administration in Britain. *Public Administration* 73, 1, 123–141.

Part, A. (1990) *The Making of a Mandarin.* London: André Deutsch.

Patten, J. (1994) *Secretary of State's Speech to HEFCE Conference.* 12 April.

Pearson, R. (1985) The demands of the labour market. In D. Jaques and J. Richardson (eds) *The Future for Higher Education.* Windsor: SRHE and NFER-Nelson.

Polanyi, M. (1962) The republic of science: its political and economic theory. *Minerva* 1, 1, 54–73.

Pollitt, C. (1993) *Managerialism and the Public Services. The Anglo-American Experience* (2nd edition). Oxford: Basil Blackwell.

Pollitt, C. (1995) Justification by works or by faith? Evaluating the New Public Management. *Evaluation 1,* 2, 133–154.

Pollitt, C., Hanney, S., Packwood, T., Rothwell, S. and Roberts, S. (1997) *Trajectories and Options: An International Perspective on the Implementation of Finnish Public Management Reforms.* Helsinki: Ministry of Finance.

Polytechnics and Colleges Funding Council (PCFC) (1990) *Recurrent Funding and Equipment Allocations for 1990/91.* London: PCFC.

Premfors, R. (1980) *The Politics of Higher Education in a Comparative Perspective: France, Sweden, United Kingdom.* Studies in Politics 15. Stockholm: University of Stockholm.

Raab, C.D. (1992) Taking networks seriously: education policy in Britain. *European Journal of Political Research 21,* 69–90.

Raab, C.D. (1994) Theorising the governance of education. *British Journal of Educational Studies XXXXII,* 1, 6–22.

Ranson, S. (1980) Changing relations between centre and locality in education. *Local Government Studies 6,* 6, 3–24.

Reynolds Report (1986) *Academic Standards in Universities.* London: Committee of Vice-Chancellors and Principals.

Rhodes, G. (1992) Organisation theory. In B.R. Clark and G. Neave (eds) (1992) *The International Encyclopedia of Higher Education.* Oxford: Pergamon Press.

Rhodes, R.A.W. (1981) *Control and Power in Central Government–Local Government Relations.* Aldershot: Gower.

Rhodes, R.A.W. and Marsh, D. (1992) New directions in the study of policy networks. *European Journal of Political Research 21,* 181–205.

Richardson, G. and Fielden, J. (1997) *Measuring the Grip of the State: The Relationship between Governments and Universities in Selected Commonwealth Countries*. London: Commonwealth Higher Education Management Service.

Richardson, J. and Jordan, G. (1979) *Governing under Pressure*. Oxford: Martin Robertson.

Robbins Report (1963) *Higher Education*. Report of the Committee appointed by the Prime Minister under the Chairmanship of Lord Robbins, 1961–63. Cmnd 2154. London: HMSO.

Robertson, D. and Hillman, J. (1997) *Widening Participation in Higher Education for Students from Lower Socio-Economic Groups and Students with Disabilities*. Report 6, National Committee of Enquiry into Higher Education (Dearing Report). London: HMSO.

Robinson, E. (1968) *The New Polytechnics*. London: Cornmarket.

Roizen, J. and Jepson, M. (1985) *Degrees for Jobs. Employers' Expectations of Higher Education*. Windsor: SRHE and NFER-Nelson.

Rothschild Report (1971) *A Framework for Government Research and Development*. Cmnd 4814. London: HMSO.

Royal Society (1997) *Memorandum for an Incoming Government*. London: Royal Society.

Salter, B. and Tapper, T. (1981) *Education, Politics and the State*. London: Grant McIntyre.

Salter, B. and Tapper, T. (1994) *The State and Higher Education*. London: Woburn Press.

Sanchez-Ferter, L. (1997) From bureaucratic centralism to self regulation: the reform of higher education in Spain. *West European Politics 20*, 3, 164–184.

Sartori, G. (1970) Concept misinformation in comparative politics. *American Political Science Review 64*, 1033–1053.

Saward, M. (1992) *Co-Optive Politics and State Legitimacy*. Aldershot: Dartmouth.

Schumpeter, J. (1956) *Capitalism, Socialism and Democracy*. New York: Harper and Row.

Science and Engineering Research Council (SERC)(1989) *Corporate Plan, 1989*. London: SERC.

Science and Engineering Research Council (SERC) (1990) *Bulletin*. Number 5. London: SERC.

Science Research Council (SRC) (1970) *Selectivity and Concentration in the Support of Research*. London: SRC.

Science Research Council (SRC) (1977) *The Support of Research and Postgraduate Training in Polytechnics*. London: SRC.

Scott, P. (1995) *The Meaning of Mass Higher Education*. Buckingham, UK and Philadelphia, USA: Society for Research into Higher Education and Open University Press.

Scruton, R. (1980) *The Meaning of Conservatism*. London: Macmillan.

Secondary School Examinations Council (SSEC) (1963) *Report of the English Language Examining Committee*. London: HMSO.

Segal, Quince and Partners (1985) *The Cambridge Phenomenon: The Growth of High Technology Industry in a University Town*. Cambridge: Segal, Quince and Partners.

Select Committee on Science and Technology (SCST) (1976) *Third Report of the Select Committee on Science and Technology.* London: HMSO.

Selznick, P. (1966) *TVA and the Grass Roots: A Study in the Sociology of Formal Organisations.* New York: Harper and Row.

Shattock, M. (1989) Higher education and the research councils. *Minerva 27*, 2–3.

Shattock, M. (1994) *The UGC and the Management of British Universities.* Buckingham, UK and Philadelphia, USA: Society for Research into Higher Education and Open University Press.

Shattock, M. (ed) (1996) *The Creation of a University System.* Oxford: Blackwell.

Shattock, M. and Berdahl, R.D. (1984) The British University Grants Committee 1919–1983: changing relationships with government and the universities. *Higher Education 13*, 2, 471–499.

Silver, H. (1990) *A Higher Education.* Basingstoke: Falmer Press.

Sizer, J. (1988) *Institutional Responses to Financial Reductions within the University Sector.* Final Report. London: DES.

Smith, D., Bargh, C., Bocock, J. and Scott, P. (1999) New leaders at the top?: the educational and career paths of UK university vice-chancellors 1960–1996. *Higher Education Management 11*, 2, 113–135.

Stewart, W.A.C. (1989) *Higher Education in Postwar Britain.* London: Macmillan.

Sutherland, S. (1989) *The Teaching Function. Quality Assurance* (The Sutherland Report) (VC/89/160a). London: CVCP.

Tapper, T. (1997) Who will speak for the universities? The Committee of Vice-Chancellors and Principals in the age of mass higher education. *Higher Education Quarterly 51*, 2, 113–133.

Tapper, T. and Salter, B. (1978) *Education and the Political Order.* London: Macmillan Education.

Tapper, T. and Salter, B. (1995) The changing idea of university autonomy. *Studies in Higher Education 20*, 1, 59–71.

Taylor, W. (1987) *Universities under Scrutiny.* Paris: OECD.

Teichler, U. (1988) *Changing Patterns of the Higher Education System: The Experience of Three Decades.* London: Jessica Kingsley Publishers.

Templeman, G. (1975). Interview referred to in Chapter 10, Note 14 of M. Kogan (1975) *Educational Policy Making. A Study of Interest Groups and Parliament.* London: Allen and Unwin.

Thatcher, M. (1993) *The Downing Street Years.* London: HarperCollins.

Thomas, P. (1985) *The Aims and Outcomes of Social Policy Research.* London: Croom Helm.

Tight, M. (1992) Institutional autonomy. In B.R. Clark and G. Neave (eds) *The International Encyclopedia of Higher Education.* Oxford: Pergamon Press.

Trevor-Roper, H. (1992) *Counter Reformation to Glorious Revolution.* London: Secker and Warburgh.

Trist, E. (1972) Types of output mix of research organisations and their complementarity. In A.B. Cherns, R. Sinclair and W. Jenkins (eds) *Social Science and Government. Policies and Problems.* London: Tavistock Publications.

Trow, M. (1970) Reflections on the transition from mass to universal higher education. *Daedalus 99*, 1–42.

Trow, M. (1984) The analysis of status. In B.R. Clark (ed) *Perspectives on Higher Education. Eight Disciplinary and Comparative Views*. Berkeley: University of California Press.

Trow, M. (1991) Introduction. In M. Trow and T. Nybom (eds) *University and Society – Essays on the Social Role of Research and Higher Education*. London: Jessica Kingsley Publishers.

Trow, M. (1993) *Managerialism and the Academic Profession; the Case of England*. Studies of Higher Education 1993:4. Stockholm: The Council for Studies of Higher Education.

University Grants Committee (UGC) (1948) *University Development 1935–1947*. London: HMSO.

University Grants Committee (UGC) (1953) *University Development 1947–1952*. Cmnd 8875. London: HMSO.

University Grants Committee (UGC) (1958) *University Development 1952–1957*. Cmd 534. London: HMSO.

University Grants Committee (UGC) (1968) *University Development 1962–1967*. Cmd 3820. London: HMSO.

University Grants Committee (UGC) (1977) *Annual Survey 1975–76*. Cmnd 6758. London: HMSO.

University Grants Committee (UGC) (1983) *UGC Report 1982–83, Appendix F: Development of a Strategy for Higher Education (Letter from Sir Keith Joseph to Sir Edward Parkes)*. London: UGC.

University Grants Committee (UGC) (1984) *A Strategy for Higher Education into the 1990s. The UGC's Advice*. London: HMSO.

University Grants Committee (UGC) (1985) *Planning for the Late 1980s: The Resource Allocation Process*. Circular letter from Chairman of UGC to Universities 22/85. London: UGC.

University Grants Committee (UGC) (1986) *Planning for the Late 1980s: Recurrent Grant for 1986/7*. Circular letter 4/86. London: HMSO.

University Grants Committee (UGC) (1987) *Monitoring Research Selectivity*. Circular letter 9/87. London: UGC.

University Grants Committee/National Advisory Body (UGC/NAB) 1984 Statement (1984) *A Strategy for Higher Education into the 1990s: The University Grant Committee's Advice*. London: HMSO.

Van den Daele, W., Krahn, W. and Weingart, P. (1977) The political direction of scientific development. In E. Mendelsohn, P. Weingart and R. Whitley (eds) *The Social Production of Scientific Knowledge*. Vol. 1. Dordrecht, Holland and Boston, USA: D. Reidel, Boston Publishing Company.

Van Vught, F.A. (1985) Negative incentive steering in a policy network. *Higher Education 14*, 193–216.

Van Vught, F.A. (1989) (ed) *Governmental Strategies and Innovation in Higher Education*. London: Jessica Kingsley Publishers.

Vincent, A. (1992) Conceptions of the state. In M. Hawkesworth and M. Kogan (eds) *Encyclopedia of Government and Politics*. Vol.2. London: Routledge.

Wakeford, F. and Wakeford, J. (1974) Universities and the study of elites. In P. Stanworth and A. Giddens (eds) *Elites and Power in British Society*. Cambridge: Cambridge University Press.

Waldegrave, W. (1994) Operation of the research councils. Letter to the Chairman of EPSRC. Annex A of: *Priorities for the Science Base: Government Response to the Second Report of the House of Lords Select Committee on Science and Technology, 1993–1994*. Cm 2636. London: HMSO.

Walker, D. (1989) Quoting 'Minutes of a cabinet committee, 1958'. *Times Higher Education Supplement*, 6.1.89.

Weaver Report (1970) *A Teaching Council for England and Wales*. London: HMSO.

Wiener, M. (1981) *English Culture and the Decline of the Industrial Spirit 1850–1980*. Cambridge: Cambridge University Press.

Williams, G. (1984) The economic aspect. In B.R. Clark (ed) *Perspectives on Higher Education. Eight Disciplinary and Comparative Views*. Berkeley: University of California Press.

Williams, G. (1990) Higher education. In M. Flude and M. Hammer (eds) *The Education Reform Act – 1988*. London: Falmer Press.

Williams, G. (1992) *Changing Patterns of Finance in Higher Education*. Buckingham, UK and Philadelphia, USA: Society for Research into Higher Education and Open University Press.

Williams, P. (ed) (1981) *The Overseas Student Question: Studies for a Policy*. London: Heinemann.

Winfield, G. (1987) *The Social Science PhD. The ESRC Inquiry on Submission Rates*. (Winfield Report). London: ESRC.

Wirt, F. (1981) Professionalism and political conflict: a developmental model. *Journal of Public Policy 1*, 1, 61–93.

Woodward, J. (1965) *Industrial Theory and Practice*. Oxford: Oxford University Press.

Wright, M. (1988) Policy community, policy networks, and comparative industrial policies. *Political Studies XXXVI*, 2, 4, 593–612.

Young, H. (1989) *One of Us*. London: Macmillan.

Ziman, J. (1995) *Prometheus Bound*. Cambridge: Cambridge University Press.

Subject Index

Author Index